TWENTY MILES FROM YESTERDAY

THE SAGA OF ANTHONY BOWEN

By

Thomas B. Hargrave, Jr.

ISBN: 1-4107-0718-0 (e-book)
ISBN: 1-4107-0719-9 (Paperback)

This book is printed on acid free paper.

1stBooks – rev. 07/07/03

ACKNOWLEDGMENTS

While serving as President of the YMCA of Metropolitan Washington, the Board of Directors granted me a sabbatical to begin writing the Washington Association's 135-year history.

During the period of my research, I met ninety-five year old Arminius M. Haynes, the grandson of Anthony Bowen. I knew that Anthony Bowen founded the first YMCA for free African Americans in our nation's capital in 1853, one year after the establishment of the YMCA of Washington. After arriving in Washington with his young family in 1836, he became one of Washington's outstanding African American leaders during the turbulent years 1850-1871. From Arminius' oral narrative, I became intrigued with his stories about his grandfather, who was born a slave in Prince Georges County Maryland in 1809. When Anthony was twenty-one, he purchased his freedom from his master for the sum of 425 dollars.

Following the publication of my history, I told Arminius that at some future date I would write a novel about Anthony Bowen's quest for freedom. After I retired in 1992, I began work on the novel four years later. Based in part on the oral narrative of Arminius Haynes, *Twenty Miles from Yesterday: The Saga of Anthony Bowen* is the inspiring story of Anthony Bowen's early life as a slave.

I am grateful for friends and family who helped me with their editing, comments and suggestions, and my graphic artist Leslie M. Rollins.

My wife, Meredith, my mother-in-law, Ellen Moore, daughter, Anna, Hope Maridin, Norman and Winfred Williams, and Dr. Marlene Kelly for taking time to proofread my manuscript. Special thanks to my sister, Yolande Adelson, artist Kenneth Higgins and friends, Kathleen Shahan, Vanessa Dixon and Kirk Perrow for their editing and valuable suggestions.

I cherish the memory of the late Arminius M. Haynes for sharing his oral history with me.

Thomas B. Hargrave, Jr.

DEDICATION

For Angie Reese Hawkins, President
YMCA of Metropolitan Washington

And the
Youth and Families of
YMCA Anthony Bowen

CHAPTER 1

The First Bells of Freedom:

Ruth Bowen stood at the open kitchen window fanning herself with a hand towel while watching a hazy morning sky. She covered her eyes when a sudden gust of wind blew dust in her face. The first days of June 1822, had been excessively hot, and for three weeks not a drop of rain had fallen on the parched fields of the Bradley Manor plantation. She overheard her master, William Bradley, saying to his wife that all of Prince Georges County, Maryland would turn into a dust bowl if it did not rain soon. She wiped a cinder from her eye and reminded herself to water the vegetable patch behind her cabin. The crowing of roosters in the distance reminded her of the task that lay ahead. She hurried to the wood box, removed a hand ax and stroked its edges a dozen times on her whetstone, then tested its sharpness with her finger.

Ruth's twelve-year-old son, Anthony, sat outside on the steps, whittling a block of wood with a short knife. She motioned for him to come to the table for a breakfast of grits and cornbread, covered with thick black molasses. She smiled when he wiped the sweat from his chestnut colored face, then draped a wet cloth over his head while eating. On hot days there was no relief from the stifling heat, made worse by a cast iron stove and the stone fireplace with built-in brick ovens on each side of it.

Ruth tapped Anthony on his head as she walked toward the back door. "Don't you be going no where, you hear? You gotta clean my chickens that I'm bring back. You know what needs doing. Master William and Miz Mary Alice got important guests coming out here from Washington City and we got lots to do. They will be here tomorrow noon."

Ruth hurried to the chicken yard, her sandals crushing parched grass that only weeks before had been lush and green. The heavy air, with its pungent smell of manure, filled her nostrils when she entered the fenced-in yard armed with a stick. The feathers on the head of the rooster rose as it started in her direction. It quickly retreated when she poked the stick into its feathered chest. Satisfied the bird would keep its distance, she went beside the chicken shed and picked up a crate containing four hens she had been fattening all week. Ruth took the squawking chickens outside the enclosed yard, placed each on a stump and chopped off its neck. The hundred hens in the yard squawked nervously at the sight of headless chickens flopping in the dust. The rooster charged at the wooden fence and paced back and forth.

1

"Your day coming soon, Big Red," Ruth said, while bending over and placing the chicken heads into her pouch. "You gonna be baking in my oven for supper this very next Saturday." Just as she placed the last head in her pouch, something in the dry weeds glinted in the sun, causing her to squint momentarily. Using the toe of her shoe, she kicked it over and was surprised to see a silver buckle with the face of a bull on its broad surface. Beside it were the severed heads of two chickens covered with ants. After looking in all directions, she picked up the buckle and ran her finger over its raised surface.

"This is real silver," she whispered. Taking the chicken heads by their combs, she shook them vigorously to remove the ants. By the torn skin, she felt certain the intruder had simply twisted the necks off.

"Somebody been out here stealing Master William's chickens," she muttered under her breath while placing the buckle in the pocket of her apron. After gathering up the headless chickens by their feet, she noticed heavy boot prints in the dirt near the dirt path. "Ain't none of our folks got shoes like that." After looking anxiously in all directions, she hurried the fifty yards back to the Manor kitchen.

Anthony had already filled the wooden tub with boiling water from the black kettle hanging in the fireplace. Ruth rushed through the door, dipped the chickens into the scalding water several times, then placed them in another tub. She wiped the perspiration from her face on the back of her apron before throwing it into the hamper.

"Don't you sit there like a bump on a log. Put what you doing away and get ready to pull the feathers off these chickens. Be careful, that hot water's gonna loosens up the feathers. Wait 'til they cool off some. Clean them real good, cause I can't have no burnt feathers on my roast chickens, you hear?" Ruth hastily primed the handle of the indoor pump until cool water flowed. Taking a bar of lye soap, she washed her hands briskly.

"Who's coming for dinner, Mama?"

"I'll tell you all about it later. I gotta go tell Master Bradley about some ugly goings on out in the chicken yard."

"What kind of goings on?"

"Never you mind. Just clean those chickens," Ruth said. After drying her hands, she rushed out of the kitchen through the dining room, across the hallway and paused at the library door. When she saw it closed, she knew her master was conducting business. She knocked anyway. When it opened, she stared into the suntanned face of William Bradley. His broad, six-foot frame filled the doorway.

"I hate to bother you, Master William, but I need to tell you something important."

William removed his cigar and motioned for her to enter. She paused momentarily when she saw the overseer, Joseph Hanks, seated next to her master's desk. William took his seat and closed his oversized inventory book.

"What's so important that it can't wait, Ruth?"

"Master William, somebody been stealing chickens. I find two chickens' heads over by the fence outside the chicken yard," she said, reaching in her pouch and holding up a chicken head by its comb.

Joseph Hanks sat up and shouted, "I knew it. Mr. Bradley, I told you we been missing chickens. The count is down by seven this week. Ain't no fox stealing that many chickens. Its gotta be one of our niggers."

William Bradley swiveled his chair and faced his overseer. The chill of his steel blue eyes caused Joseph's shoulders to droop momentarily. No words were needed to let the overseer know that William Bradley did not tolerate the use of the despised word 'nigger' in his presence.

"Sir, I didn't mean no disrespect," he sputtered, glancing in Ruth's direction.

"I got more to tell you," Ruth said, pretending to ignore the exchange that took place.

"What is it?" William said, still irritated by his overseer's crude remark.

"I found this here belt buckle near those chicken heads," she said, placing it on the desk. "And I seen where somebody left his shoe mark in the dirt, and it sure don't look like no shoes our folks wear."

William examined the buckle, then tossed it to the overseer. "She's right. This does not belong to anyone here."

"This is a mighty fancy buckle," Joseph said, running his thumb over its surface. "The thief must have stole it."

"Thank you for reporting this, Ruth. You may go now," William said, rising and escorting her to the door.

Ruth took a deep breath, then hurried to the kitchen. The overseer's remarks had angered her. "I'm sorry I saw the day Master William hired that ugly man. It's just like him to go saying our folks stealing chickens," she grumbled, taking some consolation that her master had stared him down in her presence.

Anthony rolled up his sleeves and began the distasteful job of removing the feathers. The scalding water made the work easier. Worst of all, he hated gutting the chickens and removing the entrails, which were thrown in a bucket. He saved the hearts, livers, gizzards, heads and feet. The livers and gizzards were tossed in Ruth's giblet skillet. He accepted Ruth's reason for saving the chicken's head, neck and feet, even though they contained mostly

3

skin and bones. She had told him it was a sin to waste any good thing the Lord provided and the head, feet and chicken necks would be soup for them. Every time he cut off the beak and removed the chicken's eyes he felt sad. He stared at the chicken's severed head as he took the knife and prepared to remove its eyes.

"I remember you when you were just a biddy. Sorry I gotta do this to you."

Ruth entered the kitchen from the dining room. Anthony knew from her frown that it was not the time to ask questions. After cleaning the chickens, he placed them in a pan and took it to the pantry where shelves were lined with jars of green beans, tomatoes, squash and corn, all preserved the previous fall. Opening a small trap door located in the center of the floor, he carefully placed the pan on a pile of cold damp sawdust. During the previous winter he had helped the adult slaves chop blocks of ice from the river and stack them in the pit. Layers of sawdust that served as insulation during warm weather were placed over the ice. He had learned early that cold winters in Maryland meant ice was available for household needs well into the summer months. Mild winters often meant an empty ice pit, unless an ice wagon from the mountains of Pennsylvania happened to come by.

"Mama, you said you gonna tell me who's coming to visit," Anthony inquired after seeing her natural buoyant smile returning.

"Well now, Master Bradley's cousin, Senator Gerald Calvert and his wife from Savannah are staying here for a few days. They are bringing a preacher and his wife from up in Boston. Now that's something for sure. It's been many a year since folks from up north come here."

"How long they gonna stay?"

"Two, maybe three days. Aunt Hattie heard Master William tell Miz Mary Alice that Senator Calvert done hired a colored coachman to drive them out here from Washington City. She says that coachman is a free man," she whispered.

"Free?" Anthony blurted out. "How he gets to be free?"

"Not so loud, son. You wanna wake up the dead?" Ruth said, looking over her shoulder. "I don't know. I 'speck you have to ask him when he gets here."

"Free," Anthony whispered under his breath. He knew his mother and his grandparents had always been slaves on the Bradley plantation and that their master had sold his father when Anthony was only four. The very thought that there were free blacks in Washington City excited him. What would it be like to be free? He carelessly took the iron thongs and turned the log in the fireplace. A spark exploded and landed on his hand.

"Ouch, I burned myself."

4

"Son, I done told you more than once to put on your work gloves when you go poking in that fire. You gotta keep you mind on what you doing. Here, put your hand in this cool water. You be careful 'cause you gotta help Uncle Jim serve the guests tomorrow night. Mrs. Mary Alice got Hattie making a new suit for you, and she bought you your first pair of dress shoes."

"I get to dress up like Uncle Jim?" Anthony asked, while Ruth inspected his hand.

"You sure do. My little man is gonna look so fine in that new suit. You gonna look like a little gentleman," she said proudly.

Anthony knew "Uncle" Jim Bradley, the head butler, was not related to him or any of the other slaves at the plantation. It was a title conferred on him by their master. In addition to being the valet to William Bradley, Uncle Jim supervised all the personnel who worked in the Manor house. Every Monday morning he summoned the house workers to review the week's work. They included Ruth Bowen, age twenty-seven, head cook; Sarah Learner, twenty, assistant cook; Hattie Johnson, forty-one, seamstress; her two daughters, Betty, eighteen, and Cathy, seventeen, chambermaids; and Anthony who did chores throughout the house and in the flower garden.

After Anthony finished mopping the floor, Ruth gave him permission to leave. "After you finish playing, clean our cabin, then draw a bucket of water and wash yourself from head to toe. Use some of that lye soap. I can't have you smelling up those new clothes you gonna wear, come Sunday."

Anthony ran to the barn, hoping to find several of the field boys. Out of curiosity, he stopped to watch four field hands repair a wagon. When the men took their break, he walked over and sat beside them.

Kenneth Anderson, a heavyset black man in his sixties, passed out ears of boiled corn.

"A fellow over at the Anderson farm told me a good one the other day. Ya'll wanna hear it?" Kenneth said. When heads nodded, he grinned. "Seems this old Massa had a young bull he planned to take to market. One night a mountain lion come out of the hills, killed the bull and ate it up. When Massa come the next morning, all he find left was skin and bones. He got his gun and his hound dogs, and off he go ah' hunting for that cat. They finds him sitting on a rock, howling at the moon about how good that bull taste. Massa shot that cat stone dead, skinned him and hung his head over his fireplace. Now they say, if you full of bull, you better keep yo'-big-trap-shut," Kenneth said, laughing the loudest at his own tale.

Anthony tapped Kenneth's shoulder. "My mama say a colored man coming here Sunday, and he's free." The men ignored him as they continued eating. "I ain't never met no free colored man before."

Kenneth stared at Anthony and mumbled with his mouth full. "House boy, all I got to say, if he free, like that old mountain lion, he best keep his black trap shut. If slave catchers gets they hands on him, they will sell that nigger's ass in a hot minute." The raucous laughter that followed puzzled Anthony.

"Listen boy. Don't be coming around here with no freedom talk. We's don't want to hear about what ain't never gonna be. Now you git," Kenneth said irritably, waving him away. Their dismissal did not bother Anthony. He was growing up with the sons of field hands and they had toughened him. After walking a short distance he saw several of his friends racing across the field.

"Willie, Joe, wait up for me," Anthony shouted. By the time he caught up with them their numbers had grown to five.

"We going over in the woods to play fo' it get dark. You wanna come? Willie asked.

"Yeah, but I got tell you something. My mama say a colored man that's free gonna be coming here tomorrow."

"Where you hear that?" Joe asked sarcastically. "Massa Bradley don't allow free niggers to come out here."

"It true. Mama say Aunt Hattie heard it from Master Bradley himself."

"Stop yo' lying before it's too dark to play," Willie said. "We gonna play hide and seek." With nods and smiles they raced to the edge of a thick grove of trees.

All agreed a stump would serve as home base with Willie as the first hunter. "Ya'll go hide. If I finds ya', and I runs to the base fo' you do, you dead meat. When I close my eyes and start singing the bull frog song, go hid yo'self. Soon as I finish singing, I's come looking for ya'."

Willie covered his eyes and sang, "Bull frog jump to the bottom of the well. He thought fo' sho he jumped in hell. Bullfrog jumped in the frying pan, and now he's swimming in the promise land. Ready or not, here I came."

Joe teamed with Anthony and both ran to the trees. They pushed aside the undergrowth searching for a suitable hiding place.

"Watch yo'self. This place got lots of thorns," Joe whispered, trying to avoid the blackberry bushes.

"You smell something cooking?" Anthony whispered.

Joe paused and sniffed the air. "Yeah. Smells like chicken, and I see smoke over yonder."

Both moved cautiously in the direction of the smoke. After stepping over a fallen log, they found themselves in a clearing. Beside the smoldering ashes in a rock pit, lay a pile of chicken bones.

"We best be getting out of here," Joe whispered, flinching when they heard a twig snap behind them. Both turned and stared into a bearded face with bulging blue eyes. The bushy-hair vagrant's mouth hung open, revealing rotten tobacco stained teeth. He held a tangled net in his left hand.

"Don't you niggers move," the vagabond shouted, his matted brown hair rose above his head like an angry rooster. He grunted while tossing a wide net high over them. It fell harmlessly to the ground as Anthony and Joe darted in different directions. Both ran through the underbrush screaming, unmindful of the briars that tore their exposed arms and faces. When they reached the clearing, the other boys were already out of their hiding places. None needed an explanation as they raced toward the slave compound.

Big George Jackson, the plantation's black field boss ran to meet them. Anthony and Joe shouted simultaneously. He knew something unusual had happened when he saw the scratches on their faces.

"Quiet down, "Big George shouted. "Joe, what you boys' been up too?"

"We seen the devil over in them woods. He had red eyes and sharp ugly teeth," Joe wailed.

"He tried to catch us with a net, but we got away," Anthony shouted.

"That must be the varmint that been stealing Massa Bradley's chickens. You boys best go home. I gotta report this to Capt'n Hanks right away."

Still trembling, Anthony hurried to the slave compound and entered the one-room cabin where he lived with his mother. He remembered Ruth telling him to bathe after cleaning the cabin. After a short rest, he finally felt calm enough to work. He took a cloth and dusted the nightstand, the two straight back chairs, the handcrafted rocking chair and the four-foot long shelf across the top of the fireplace. Satisfied with the dusting, he removed the dead flowers from the cracked blue vase that sat in the center of their table. The vase had once occupied a prominent place in the Bradley Manor parlor. Ruth had retrieved it after it was accidentally chipped and discarded. During the summer she filled it with wild daisies and black-eyed Susans, her favorite flowers.

Anthony often wondered why his mother refused to move into one of the nicer brick cottages reserved for the house servants. They would not have had to walk the two hundred yards to the Manor kitchen and back twice a day. The several times he had asked, she would just sit and reflect, then tears would fill her eyes. She told him she would explain it to him when he was older.

Anthony took a bucket to the rain barrel that sat under the cabin eaves. After filling it, he returned and poured the rainwater into the wash basin. While preparing to wash himself, he saw mosquito larvae swimming in the water.

"You little wiggle tails ain't gonna like this soap," Anthony said. The cold water was refreshing as he washed himself and picked the last painful thorn embedded in his arm. Tired from the long days work, he threw himself on his bed. By concentrating on the coming visit of the freeman he put the encounter with the stranger out of his mind.

"If I get free like him, I'll never clean the feathers off another chicken as long as I live." He yawned, turned over on his side. "That's unless I gets to eat him."

CHAPTER 2

Moab Jackson's carriage made its final approach to the Bradley Manor plantation. The morning skyline, with its apron of mixed red and yellow clouds, caused the woodlands to take on a shimmering rustic hue. On impulse, the black coachman decided to rest at a scenic point at the crest of a hill. After stopping the carriage, he called to his four passengers to step out to stretch their legs.

"Folks, you gonna like what you sees. The good Lord done painted his morning the colors of Indian corn," Moab said, pointing to the sky and landscape.

Senator Gerald Calvert, a middle-aged man with a waistline the size of a watermelon, was impressed. Until that moment it had never dawned on him that blacks would take special notice of such a spectacular sight. Calvert had rented Moab's carriage when he heard from fellow senators that the freedman had a reputation for getting his passengers to their destination on time. Moab had assured him he would reach the Bradley Manor plantation by noon, Sunday. After stretching their legs, the passengers climbed back inside. Three men on horseback rode up and motioned for Moab to remain where he was. He knew they were lawmen by their badges.

The Senator leaned out the window and shouted, "Moab, what's holding you up? Is anything wrong?"

"These here lawmen wants to talk, sir."

The lead rider lowered his head and looked in the carriage window. "Where you folks headed?"

"We are on the way to the Bradley Manor plantation. I'm Senator Calvert from Savannah, Georgia, and I'm traveling with my wife and two family members. Why were we stopped?"

"I'm sorry to hold ya'll up, Senator. We are hunting for a varmint name Nehemiah Jones. He's been passing himself off as a bounty hunter. The lying thief is part of a gang that's been stealing slaves in these parts. There is a hundred-dollar reward on his head, dead or alive. If we catch him, we plan to string him up."

"I ain't seen nothing on this road all day, mister," Moab said.

The rider stared at Moab. "I was speaking to the Senator, not you, nigger." He turned to Calvert, "If your darky spots a white man with bushy brown hair and long beard, instruct him to keep moving. He shot one of my boys a spell ago. Do you have protection on your person?"

"Never leave without it," Senator Calvert said, removing a pearl-handled pistol from his handbag. "I hope you catch him soon."

When the men rode off, Moab leaned over and shouted, "Don't ya'll worry none. I ain't never loss no paying passengers yet."

It seemed to Anthony only minutes had passed since he went to sleep. When he heard the plantation bell ringing in the distance, he pulled the thin cover over his head and refused to move.

"Getting up time, Anthony. The day needs doing, and I know you gonna make it a good day," Ruth said, pulling the cover from his head.

Anthony sat up and rubbed his eyes. Suddenly remembering it was the day the guests would be arriving, he dressed and ran to the community well. After waiting his turn to draw water, he splashed it on his face and washed his hands. When he returned to the cabin with an arm full of firewood, Ruth gave him a plate of grits and fried fatback, the skin from slaughtered hogs reserved for slaves. After breakfast, they hurried toward one of the brick cottages located close to the Manor house. Ruth knocked on Sarah Learner's door.

"I's almost ready," Sarah shouted. She turned and kissed her two sons, ages four and six. "I see you boys later. Thomas, don't you take your brother in them woods. Stay close by, you hear?" She turned to Ruth and whispered, "I sho' hope they finds that varmint that scared the boys yesterday."

When they entered the Bradley Manor kitchen, Sarah took one look at the iron rack beside the fireplace, then pointed Anthony toward the woodpile located in the back yard.

"Wood getting low, Anthony. Don't do like old Sam and go splitting yo' big toe down the middle with that ax." Anthony grinned and headed out the door. He loved Sarah almost as much as his mother. Her jovial disposition made her a joy to be around.

Ruth and Sarah spent the next hour baking bread and pies. The chickens that Anthony had cleaned and stored in the ice bin were now roasting in the oven.

"Girl, I can't wait to see that man that be bringing Master Bradley's friends out here. I wonder what he looks like?" Sarah whispered.

"You about as bad as Anthony. You married. You ain't 'spose to be thinking about no man but your husband."

"Sister, ain't nothing wrong with thinking. It's the doing that gets you in trouble." Both women cut the conversation short when Anthony entered with an armload of logs. As the heat in the kitchen grew warmer, Ruth sat by the open window shelling peas and singing quietly to herself, "By and by, I'm gonna lay down this heavy load."

It was almost noon when Ruth took Anthony to the back porch where they sat in the shade together eating thick slices of bread spread with apple butter.

"Mama, Reverend Harris said he's gonna preach this Sunday about Moses and Pharaoh. Uncle Jim read me the story. You think the Lord would ever send a plague here, like what happened in the land of Egypt, especially if white folks don't set us free some day?"

"Child, you must be getting freedom fever." She paused and reflected on the year typhoid fever struck Bradley Manor. "Some years back a plague come on all us here, but it killed white and colored folks alike. Even Master Bradley's little son died, and for awhile I thought I might lose you," Ruth said, reflectively. She kissed Anthony's cheek and returned to the kitchen to inspect the heat in the brick ovens. Here she cooked her chickens and mouth-watering corn pone, specialties for which the Bradley's table was famous countrywide. For the remainder of the morning, the women chatted as they busied themselves hanging the pots, pans and skillets along the hooks on the ten-foot iron rods held by wires hanging from the ceiling.

At high noon the bell at the entrance gate began ringing, signaling the arrival of guests. Sarah had just placed a bucket of potatoes in front of Anthony. In his excitement, he ran out the back door, knocking over the bucket and sending water, peelings and potatoes across the floor.

"Sakes alive. Anthony, come back here, you hear me," Ruth shouted.

"He done gone fo' sure," Sarah said, shaking her head as she picked up the potatoes.

Anthony raced around the side of the house as the bell continued to toll. Although he had heard it many times, never had it sounded so sharp and clear. He had waited anxiously for the guests to arrive, and although he heard his mother calling, he just had to be in the front yard to see that coachman. Rolling up the long driveway was the splendid carriage pulled by two horses, their shiny coats glistening in the sunlight like new copper pennies. Five hounds that had the freedom of the plantation chased behind it. Anthony watched in awe-struck silence as the carriage, driver, and guests approached in front of the big house. There he was, the handsome black coachman seated high on the carriage, dressed in a black coat, white britches and a high black hat.

"Anthony, help Uncle Jim with the luggage," William Bradley shouted. Anthony flinched when he saw William standing on the front portico leaning on one of the six columns that graced the entrance of Bradley Manor. His wife, Mary Alice, had said his muscular, six-foot frame reminded her of the Biblical figure Samson pictured in the family Bible.

11

William turned to the front door and shouted, "Mary Alice, Gerald and his family are here." When the carriage rolled to a stop, he strode down the marble steps onto the circular gravel driveway, followed by the butler, Uncle Jim. The first to emerge from the carriage was Senator Calvert, followed by his wife, Sue Ellen. Her wrinkled face, coated with thick powder, made her look much older than her forty-five years. Her silk dress and three petticoats were ill suited for warm weather travel. William shook Calvert's hand and slapped his back. A tall young man wearing a black suit with a white clerical collar stepped out and assisted his wife down the carriage's two steps. The young woman wore a light brown cotton dress. The family paused to admire Bradley Manor's stately Colonial architecture.

"Cousin Bill, you're a sight for sore eyes. Let me introduce you to these kin folk of mine from Boston," Gerald Calvert said. William approached the young man and shook his hand. The minister grimaced from the strength of William's grip.

"This is Reverend Samuel Cox, my sister's youngest boy and his lovely wife, Betty." Calvert said. William looked surprised. Although they were second cousins, William had never heard one word about Calvert's youngest sister, Margaret, having a son. Very strange.

"Welcome to Bradley Manor. I hope that your trip from Washington City was not too tiring," William said.

"Bill Bradley, my husband knows I hate carriage trips and the twenty miles it took to get here was no exception," Sue Ellen complained.

"Well, come inside and rest yourself. We have delightful refreshments ready for you," William said, pausing to light a cigar. "I only wish the weather had been more cooperative."

"Mrs. Cox and I enjoyed the ride. This is truly beautiful country," Reverend Cox said.

"I can't wait to see Bradley Manor. Sue Ellen has told us all about it, especially your beautiful flower gardens, Mary Alice," Betty Cox said.

"You've come at the right time, my dear. The roses are in full bloom," Mary Alice said with pride.

William turned to Samuel Cox. "While our newspapers give scant reports of what is going on up there in Boston, I do want to hear what you folks are thinking these days," William said.

"I'm afraid we can't tell you much. When I finished the seminary five years ago, Mrs. Cox and I went to Egypt where I studied and worked," Samuel replied.

William took Gerald by the arm and walked toward the Manor house, followed by the others. "Gerald, I've been following the developments involving the Antelope, that ship that was intercepted off the Florida coast by our Treasury cutter. Are there any new developments?" William asked.

"Yes, and it's very complicated. The Portuguese and Spanish governments have both entered the case. A number of the Africans on board were registered to their nations. But get us inside out of this heat."

Reverend Cox turned to Gerald Calvert. "I have not heard about this case, uncle."

"You are aware that in 1808 Congress made it a crime to import slaves into this country. The captain of the Antelope was attempting to smuggle more than two hundred Africans into Maryland. All were chained in the hole of the ship under deplorable conditions. Seven were dead and others died days after they were taken from the ship. The matter is now before the federal courts," Gerald said, taking a glass of water from the tray offered by Anthony.

As William escorted his guests into the house, he noticed Anthony gawking at the coachman. "Don't just stand there, boy. Show the driver where we keep the horses and carriages." William opened the front door leading into a spacious hallway that extended the length of the house.

Samuel Cox entered and paused by the marble busts of George Washington, Caesar, and Alexander the Great that sat on pedestals near the front entrance.

"Welcome to Bradley Manor," William said. The guests followed William into the oak-paneled living room and took their seats.

Betty Cox rose and made her way around the room viewing the oil paintings of country scenes and villages. She paused to run her fingers along the elaborate gold material on the couch and chairs that highlighted the furniture's hand carved olive wood.

Mary Alice escorted her into the dining room where Betty admired the room's wallpaper, with its large hunting scene, showing hounds and hunters on horseback pursuing a fox through a pristine forest. The oak table in the center of the room was large enough to seat twenty guests, and the cabinet displayed porcelain, all decorated with a delicate yellow rose pattern.

"Let us join the men for tea. There will be ample time to tour Bradley Manor during your stay," Mary Alice said.

Moab tapped Anthony on his shoulder. "Little fellow, how you at handling horses? This pair can be mean at times."

"I'm good. Horses like me. I can ride any horse you've got, and I know how to groom them," Anthony replied with pride. "My name's Anthony Bowen. What's yours?"

The coachman grinned. "Moab, Moab Jackson. We're gonna be here a couple of days. You'll get your chance to show me yo' stuff with these horses," he said, handing the reins to Anthony.

"Moab! That's a funny name. Why your folks name you Moab?" Anthony asked, climbing beside Moab on the seat of the carriage.

"It's a name my pappy give me. He say it come from the Bible."

"Is it true you're free?"

"Free as the wind is free." There was a special pride in the coachman's reply.

Anthony saw his mother approaching. "So here you are. Boy, you get back to my kitchen and finish your chores." He could see she was trying hard to control her temper in front of the stranger.

"Master Bradley told me to take these horses and carriage to the barn. This the free man, Mama. His name is Moab Jackson. Moab's a Bible name."

The coachman bowed. "Howdy, I's mighty pleased to meet you. You got a fine boy here."

"Well, he be a lot finer when he gets his work done," she said, pausing to study the coachman's smiling face. "I guess you must be hungry after such a long trip?"

"Yes ma'am. I could sho' use some home cooking."

Ruth found his rough bronze skin, prominent cheekbones and hawk-bridged nose attractive. He reminded her of her husband who had been sold seven years ago.

"My name is Ruth. That's also a Bible name," she said proudly. "Anthony, when you get through putting those horses in the stable, bring him to my kitchen."

Moab watched as the afternoon sunlight highlighted the richness of her unblemished complexion. When she started toward the Manor house, Moab whispered to Anthony, "Excuse me boy, but you sho' got one pretty mama."

After feeding and grooming the horses, Moab followed Anthony to the Manor kitchen, entering through the back door. Ruth directed Anthony to the bucket of potatoes then handed Moab a three-legged stool.

"Sit yourself right over here," she said, pointing at the table. Moab took his seat beside Anthony who busied himself peeling potatoes.

"Now Anthony, keep working and let him eat in peace," Ruth said. "You way behind with peeling my potatoes."

"He don't bother me none. I like chillun, 'specially boys," Moab said, eyeing the black-eyed peas and corn bread Ruth placed in front of him.

Moab stood up when three women entered the kitchen. The younger girl, with the peach-skinned complexion, was holding a white baby with

14

curly blond hair. The smiling stout woman extended her hand. "Howdy, I'm Hattie Johnson and these my daughters, Betty and Cathy, and this here is my precious little grand baby," she said proudly. "My girls just had to meet you. All the folks at the Manor knows you here and wants to meet you."

Moab shook Hattie's hand. "I's glad to meet all of you folks. You sho' got some pretty daughters, Mrs. Hattie," he said, glancing at the child.

Betty and Cathy giggled as Ruth pushed them toward the door. "Ya'll get to see him later. Clear out of my kitchen 'cause we got lots of work to do. Hattie, you stay 'cause I wants you to taste this soup." Taking a soupspoon, she dipped it into the pot and handed it to her. Hattie smiled after tasting it.

"This soup's coming along real fine. It just needs a pinch more garlic, few more carrots and red pepper," Hattie said, pulling a stool beside Moab. "Anthony move your little butt over."

"You the first colored man I've ever met that's free. How did you get free?" Anthony asked.

"Well, that be a long story. To make it short, I bought myself," Moab said, his dark face beaming with pride.

"What do you mean, you bought yourself?" Anthony asked, looking puzzled.

"It be like this. I was once a slave like ya'll. My owner was an old widow woman who says she was a Christian. One day I up and tells her I wants my freedom. After a bit of thinking, she say she give me my freedom if I work for her during the day, and hire myself out at night for pay. She say if I earns two hundred and fifty dollars and give it to her, she free me just before she die." Moab's words were muffled as he ate and spoke at the same time.

"Two hundred and fifty dollars. That's more money than I ever hear tell of. How long it take you to get yourself that much money?" Hattie asked.

"I works at night for fifteen years. Fifteen long years. Sometime making a couple of pennies here, a nickel there, but I wants my freedom so bad I never gives up on my dream. Sometime I say to the Lord, 'It don't look like I ever gonna get no two hundred and fifty dollars.' The Lord say back to me in a dream, 'Just keep on working, Moab.' That's just what I did. Now when I give her the two hundred and fifty dollars she says I be free the day she die. Well, the Lord took his good time about it. She up and lived another three years, but when she died she kept her word and I was a free man," Moab said proudly.

"I've prayed so long for freedom," Ruth said, wiping tears from her cheek. "But God don't seem to hear nothing I say. I want Anthony to be free

15

some day. They sold my husband when he was a little boy, and all my prayers that he will return some day ain't been answered.

Anthony rose from his stool and hugged Ruth. "We gonna be free one day, Mama. Don't cry."

"Ain't that sweet. That great day surely coming, boy," Moab said, flashing a toothy grin. "But you gotta keep hope alive and you gotta have a plan."

"What you mean, a plan?" Anthony inquired.

"Listen up, boy. First, you gotta wants freedom so bad you can taste it. You gotta breathe it. The good Lord ain't gonna send down no angels to set you free. You gotta set your mind on freedom and plan for freedom," he said, scooping the last of the black-eye peas from his plate. "You gotta let the good Lord help you think about freedom and 'do for freedom. That's what I mean about having a plan."

The passion in his voice reminded Ruth of their preacher. For a few moments there was silence in the kitchen. Ruth looked up at the ceiling and spoke in a strong determined voice. "You know, Moab Jackson, I think the spirit of the Lord be in this place. Last Sunday our preacher says he gonna preach this very evening 'bout how Moses got freedom for his people. Now here you come with all your freedom talk."

"The Lord works in mighty strange ways. Never forget that. I worked for fifteen years to be free. After I had worked twelve of them fifteen years, I almost gave up hope. Then, one Sunday I went to church. Must confess I don't go much, but that Sunday I was sitting there when the preacher told us the story about Jacob and Rachel that's in the Bible."

"Jacob and Rachel?" Anthony asked.

"Miss Ruth, before I tells him that part, could I have a little more of them black-eyed peas?

"You sure can, but save some room for some of my apple pie," Ruth said proudly, scooping peas on his plate.

"Sit closer to me boy, but keep on peeling those potatoes." Moab leaned forward and looked in his eyes. "Now it says in the Bible that back in olden times, this boy Jacob be in love with a gal named Rachel. This Rachel had a no-good pappy named Laban. Now Laban had two daughters. The oldest daughter was named Leah. She had pretty eyes, but she was one homely looking gal. In other words, the gal was just really ugly." He paused until everyone stopped laughing. "Like I say, that boy was in love with her younger sister, Rachel, who was good looking. I mean that gal was so fine it would make a tadpole wanna kiss a catfish in its mouth." Again he paused as Ruth and Hattie broke into another fit of laughter. Anthony stared at him, wide-eyed, wanting to hear the freedom part.

"Moab, you so silly," Ruth said, laughing.

"Now, Pappy Laban was a sneaky rascal. He made Jacob work for seven years; seven long years, for Rachel. Guess what? On his wedding night, Jacob was in this dark tent just a'waitin for his Rachel. There he was, all excited and he couldn't wait to get his hands on her," Moab said, rubbing his hands excitedly. "That night the pappy sent Leah into that tent. He must have told her to keep her mouth shut and don't say nothing, 'cause, come first light, Jacob found out it was Leah. There he was, in bed with his arms wrapped around that ugly looking gal."

"You hush your mouth!" Ruth said, indignantly.

"Jacob jumped up like bed bugs bit him and he ran to Laban and cried, 'What you done to me?'"

"I never hear tell of no mess like that in the Bible," Ruth said, throwing up her hands in disgust.

Moab laughed, "Laban say in his country the oldest daughters' gotta be married first. Guess what? Poor Jacob had to work another seven years so he could have Rachel. And he did it, that boy did it."

"So he ended up married to both Rachel and Leah?" Anthony asked.

"That's right. Back then you could do such. So I say to myself, if that boy love that gal so much he would work fourteen years fo' her, then I surely love freedom as much. So I kept on working as long as it took and I got my freedom."

Ruth raised her arms and shouted, "Praise the Lord." Regaining her composure, she asked, "You a church man?"

"Well I believes in the Lord, but, like I say, I ain't set feet in a church for some time."

"We having our Sunday evening church under that big oak tree out yonder. You care to join us?" Ruth asked, smiling.

"I just as soon not. Got lots to do to get my horses and carriage fit for the trip home." Moab could see she was disappointed, but the long trip from Washington was about as much sitting as his rear-end could stand for one day.

Looking up from the worktable, Anthony was surprised to see Jim Bradley standing inside the kitchen door. Everyone had been so engrossed with Moab's story they did not hear him enter. When Moab realized Jim had been listening, he frowned and lowered his head.

"Anthony, it's time for us to set the table for the master's guests," Jim said sternly.

Anthony followed Jim into the dining room. He could see that Jim was not pleased when he overheard Moab talking about how he acquired his freedom. He wanted Anthony's full attention during the dinner to be served that evening. Talk about freedom was the last thing Anthony needed to hear.

Joseph Hanks sat in his small office that extended off the cow barn. He reached into his desk and removed a bottle of rye whiskey, filled a cup and took several swallows. He usually reserved his drinking for Saturday nights but William Bradley had kept him busy this Saturday going over the inventory books. He could not afford to be drunk Monday with guests visiting, so he decided to have no more than one drink. While filling his cup, he heard a knock at the door.

"God damn it, who is it?" The irritation in his voice was followed by a moment's silence.

"It's me, Capt'n Hanks. I gots something to tell you," Big George said finally.

Hanks opened the door. "It better be good."

"That Senator that just come here this afternoon told Massa Bradley a killer's loose in these parts, and there be a hundred-dollar reward on his head, dead or alive. He been going around saying he's a bounty hunter, but he steals colored folks and sells them down south. Massa Bradley told me to come tell you to be on the look out for him. I be thinking that he might be that fellow that tried to catch Anthony and Joe over in the woods last night, and he might be the one that been stealing Master Bradley's chickens."

"You say there is a hundred-dollar reward on his head?"

"Yes sir. One hundred dollars dead or alive. That's a heap lot of money."

"Any of our folk missing?"

"Not that I knows of, sir."

Joseph placed the whiskey bottle aside, then went to the wall and removed a pistol. "Do a head count of our niggers, then meet me behind the barn after dark. We're going hunting."

CHAPTER 3

The bell signaling the slaves to Sunday service rang at four o' clock in the afternoon. Ruth and Sarah put their pans aside and rushed into the dressing room to change into their Sunday dresses. Ruth opened the window and called, "Anthony, I know you heard that bell. Go wash your face. You can finish chopping wood when we get back. We leaving right now."

After priming the outdoor pump and slashing water on his face, Anthony raced to catch up with Ruth and Sarah. They walked to the spreading oak where outdoor services were held, weather permitting. Both women brought blankets and spread them on the ground in the shade of the tree. Ruth was grateful for the mild breeze that filtered the air, clearing out the stench from the nearby hog yard. Families from the compound soon filled the area; some bringing with them homemade stools.

Anthony spied his friends, Willie and Joe, stepping over outstretched arms and legs to reach him. "Can Anthony sit with us?" Joe asked.

"No, 'cause when you boys get together you get to acting up. This the Lord's hour and Anthony's gonna sit quietly beside me and hear the word. Now if you want to be with him, sit yourself down right here so I can keep an eye on you," Ruth said.

Anthony grinned when they squeezed beside him. He wished, however, that Ruth had chosen a spot not so close to the platform because when Reverend Harris started preaching, the shouting from the women folks seated up front sometimes hurt his ears.

By the time the service started, the black multitude of one hundred and sixty men, women and children were present and seated. Deacon John Cook announced that Sister Barbara Ann would sing the opening song. The young woman made her way to the platform. Her strong alto voice rippled through the late afternoon air, *"Go down Moses - way down in Egyptland - Tell old Pharaoh to let my people go."* Clapping, humming and shouting sounded as the congregation joined in the song.

Reverend Thomas Moses Harris, the slave preacher, stepped to the front of the portable platform and gripped the sides of the wooden crate that served as his lectern. He was one of several field slaves on the plantation who had been taught to read and write. The Bible was the only book he was permitted to read to his congregation. He smiled and cleared his throat.

"Now I want every eye shut and every head bowed low and repeat after me. 'The Lord is my shepherd,'" he shouted. The congregation began repeating the words of the Lord's prayer, as was the custom among slaves who were illiterate. His intelligent black face broke into an infectious smile at the conclusion of the prayer. Although Ruth could not read or write, she had memorized many Biblical passages by this oral tradition. By this method, her command of the English language was quite good, for a slave.

A hush fell over the congregation as they waited in anticipation for the sermon to begin. "Today I'm gonna preach about the Hebrew people who were once slaves down in Egyptland. You remember what I told you last Sunday. How Pharaoh ran Moses out of Egypt after Moses killed this Egyptian that was whipping on one of his folks. Moses had to flee to a land called Midian. He met the Priest of Midian who gave him a job, tending sheep. After that, he married a young girl named Zipporah. One day Moses went looking for a sheep that got lost on the mountainside, and when he climbed up there he saw a burning bush, but nothing be happening to the bush. All right now," he shouted as scattered 'amens' rose from the 'amen corner,' that special section near the pulpit reserved for elderly slaves.

Reverend Harris stepped to the left side of the podium and lifted the Bible over his head. "And when Moses came closer, he heard a loud voice calling out of that burning bush, saying, 'Come closer boy, 'cause you are standing on holy ground.'" Leaning over the podium, he shook his finger at the ground as his voice thundered. "Did ya'll hear me? I said, Moses was standing on *holy ground.*" He took a deep breath as the 'amens' and 'hallelujahs' from the multitude grew louder. "Well, Moses turned pale as a sheet after a good Saturday scrubbing and he turned and started running down the mountain. But the Lord grabbed him by his shirt tail and pulled him back to that burning bush," Preacher said, reaching out and pretending to pull the imaginary Moses back to the laughter of the congregation.

"Moses stood in front of that burning bush, trembling and shaking. He wasn't cold, he just scared. Then the Lord called out to Moses from the fire and told him to throw his walking stick on the ground. When he did, it turned into a big, black, coach-whip snake. You know the kind."

"Yea, I killed one just the other day," an elderly man shouted out.

"Moses looked at the snake and the snake looked at Moses. Then Moses jumped back." The preacher enacted the scene by jumping back, but lost his balance and fell off the platform, tripped over a root extending from the tree and fell to the ground. The congregation roared with laughter. Anthony, Willie, and Joe sat giggling and pointing at Reverend Harris when they felt sharp slaps to the backs of their heads. Turning, they looked at Ruth's scowling face.

Preacher Harris climbed back on the platform, laughing at himself. "Guess the devil must be pulling one of his tricks on me, 'cause he don't want me to preach this sermon. I'm gonna preach it 'cause the Lord put it in my heart this morning to tell this congregation how he sent Moses to free the Hebrew children from the land of bondage." As he spoke, the rhythm of his rich baritone voice held the congregation's attention as the story seemed to take on a life of its own.

"Where was I? Oh yes. Then the Lord say, 'Moses, pick up that snake by its tail.' Poor old Moses cried out, 'You know I'm scared of snakes, Lord'."

"Lord knows that's truth," Sarah shouted, fanning herself. "I hate snakes."

Preacher Harris pointed to the ground. "*Moses,* pick up that snake like I tells you. Well, Moses got to shaking and cried out, 'Yes, Lord.' When he reached down and grabbed that snake's tail, right off it turned back into a walking stick." He wiped his forehead and waited for the laughter to subside. "Then the Lord says to Moses, 'Now you know I am the Lord your God, and I ain't gonna let nothing harm you. I want you to go down to Egyptland and tell old Pharaoh to let my people go.' Now Moses was scared that if Pharaoh got his hands on him he would kill him, but he did what the Lord say. When he got down in Egyptland, he says to old Pharaoh that the Lord wants him to set the Hebrew children free. Pharaoh laughed in his face and say, 'Who you, coming back here after all these years. I just may make a slave out of you.' You see, that Pharaoh was one hardhearted man and he refused to free the Hebrew children. Now I'm gonna tell you what the Lord did next."

Some older folks nodded and shouted, "Preach brother. Tell us all about it."

"First, the Lord sent plagues upon Pharaoh's land. We all know about plagues, like when that fever killed folks some years back. First, lots of frogs came out of the Red Sea. Thousands and thousands of frogs jumping in the streets, in the houses, in the wells. There were so many frogs you couldn't walk without stepping on them," he shouted.

Anthony smiled and whispered, "Frog legs taste good, Mama. Maybe that's the reason Pharaoh didn't let the people go free."

"Hush your mouth," Ruth whispered, giggling.

Preacher Harris cleared his throat. "Next time, the Lord sent a plague of lice. Nasty lice crawling on all the people and animals, making the hair on their heads and under their arms itch." Uncontrolled laughter erupted when he scratched under his armpits and buttocks. "But Pharaoh still would not free the Hebrew children. Well, the Lord got real mad. That's when he sent the angel of *death.*" The word "death" echoed off the nearby barn like a clap of thunder as the congregation grew quiet. Drawing his coat around himself, he spoke in a low voice with fear shining from his glistening black face. "One cold morning old Pharaoh heard his wife screaming that their first born son was dead." The preacher paused, knowing he had their full attention. His strained voice grew louder, "Pharaoh learned that not only his son but all the first born sons of every Egyptian family had been slain during the night." His eyes now took on the aura of an avenging angel as the hypnotic sermon cast its frightening spell.

All present were now participants in the ancient tale. Women screamed as others shouted their 'amens.' Preacher Harris raised his hand and in a deep voice said reassuringly, "Not one of the Hebrew children was touched by the angel of death. Nothing happened 'cause that angel told them to sprinkle the blood of the lamb over their cabin doors. When old death came that night, he passed by the Hebrew children. Let the congregation say *Amen*," he shouted.

The amens that followed were amens of reprieve. Those who heard his message now envisioned themselves among God's chosen people, safe from the terrible vengeance of the Lord that spread throughout Egypt. The screams gave way to shouts as several women stood up, threw up their arms, and danced around the multitude. Reverend Harris tiptoed around the wooden platform, then raised his hands for order.

"Well, old Pharaoh finally let the Hebrew children go. Next morning that fool changed his mind and sent his army to bring them back into slavery. But God stretched out his mighty hand and drowned Pharaoh's army in the Red Sea and his children were free. Great God almighty, they were free at last."

The high drama resulted in a spiritual orgasm that was felt by many. Some cried, others fell on the ground and shook, a few older folks spoke remembered African words, while others danced.

Ruth refused to be caught up in the emotional tidal wave. The message evoked thoughts of freedom. She whispered a prayer, asking God to allow her to see the day when Anthony would be free. As the preacher raised his hand for order, Sister Harriet Mason was called to the platform to sing, and all the congregation joined in: "*O' Mary don't you weep, don't you mourn, Pharaoh's army got drowned, O' Mary don't you weep.*" The sky suddenly turned dark, followed by a lightning bolt and sharp claps of thunder.

Preacher Harris shouted, "Folks, looks like the Lord's gonna give us some rain, so this the closing prayer. Thank you Jesus, Amen. Folks, take cover in the barn until this storm blows over."

Ruth took Anthony by the hand and followed the congregation into the barn. Anthony whispered, "Mama, do you think the Lord will ever hear our prayers and help us get free?"

"Son, all that time Preacher Harris was preaching, I had my mind set on freedom. I pray all the time that you and me will be free one day, and we find your father. But sometimes I think the good Lord's too busy with all the sinners in the world and he ain't got time for us just yet," Ruth said, holding on to her hat. "Soon as this here rain lets up, we gotta hurry to the kitchen." Ruth regretted that Moab Jackson had not been present to hear the sermon.

Moab sat on a stool watching the blacksmith, Joe Learner, hammer out a horseshoe. His powerful black muscles flexed as he shaped and molded the red-hot metal. Holding the metal with iron tongs, he lowered it into a bucket of cold water. The hissing sound startled one of Moab's horses, causing it to kick the side of its stall.

"You spooked him. He thinks he hears a rattlesnake. One bit him on his leg when he was just a colt, and he almost died. He sho' don't like that sound," Moab said, walking to the stall where he calmed the horse.

Joe removed the horseshoe and held it up. "Well, freeman, how you like this one?" Joe asked. Moab nodded his approval. "You best let me take a look at all your horseshoes fo' you gets back on that road."

"You do just that. Man, you sho knows your stuff. I ain't never seen nobody make no horseshoe that quick. Where you learn your trade?"

Joe picked up a rag and wiped the perspiration from his upper body and face. "Over at the Samuel Espy farm in Virginia. That's where I was born. After them British fellows burned down Washington City a few years back, Master Bradley bought me from old man Espy. That be after he learnt I could do this kind of work and lay brick. He paid a pretty penny fo' me," Joe said, proudly.

"How you like it here?"

"This a nice place to be for a slave. It ain't no heaven, but if you lived part of your life in hell, it sure is a heap lot better. The Espy place was a black man's hell fo' sure. Don't misunderstand me. We got folks here that get the devil in them now and then, but they behave themselves most of the time. That's 'cause Massa Bradley, his wife and his sister, Miss Roberta, they the best Christian folks you ever did meet. Massa Bradley don't take kind when folks mess up, be they white or black. Long as you follow his law, you do just fine. Just don't cross him. If you do, you in a heap of trouble. His wife, Miz. Mary Alice, she one nice lady, and her daughter, Louise, is just like her for the world. Miss Louise is married and lives over in Virginia, somewhere. Their son, Henry, he away in college. Got nothing to say about him."

"Tell me about the house niggers here."

"Careful how you talk about house folks. My Sarah be one of them," Joe warned. Moab relaxed when he sensed no hostility in Joe's reply.

"Don't mean no disrespect, but I don't trust house niggers."

"I understands what you say. The house folks here ain't like the house folks over at the Espy place. Over there, if you wipe your ass the wrong way, they go running and telling the Massa. Couple of them related to him or some of his kin, one way or the other. I know for a fact, he makes babies by his black women."

"What about that high yella fellow they call Uncle Jim?"

"Uncle Jim? Well, the old folks say he related to Massa Bradley. They be half blood brothers, but it stops there. He's a slave like us but he got lots of book learning. They tells me that way back yonder, Massa Bradley's old pappy took up with a colored gal after his wife died. She must have put something good on him, 'cause he never looked at another white woman after that. She be the one that's Uncle Jim 's mama. She died ten years back. But he ain't no white man's nigger, that's for sure. You never hear tell of Jim running and telling Massa Bradley nothing, that be unless some fool gets to stealing or beating on his woman. Them two things Master Bradley don't cotton with, and Jim don't either. You beat on yo' woman you gets yo' black ass whipped fo' sure."

"What about Miss Hattie's gals. I seen the cute one hanging out clothes. That white baby she be carrying, is it hers?"

"It's hers."

"Some white man must have got in her honey pot?"

"I don't talk about folks behind they back." Joe paused as he picked up a tin cup and sipped some water.

"I 'spect that. But it don't take much to know his pappy ain't likely colored. That's the very reason there are so many high yellow niggers walking around Washington City today. White men bedding down our women," Moab said bitterly. "Tell me about Ruth."

"Ruth? She's one fine sister. I never knowed her husband, but folk say he was one of the best brick layers in this state. He went with the Massa to help fight them Brit folks during the last war, but when they come home this place was near ruin."

"That's about the same time I got my freedom. Washington City was still being rebuilt when I come there."

"With all them buildings burned down, Massa Bradley sold Ruth's husband to save this place. They tell me when Ruth found out, she almost died. She ain't taken no new husband. Almost every single man, and a few married ones, done tried to make her, but they all give up."

"She ain't met the right man," Moab replied, boastfully.

"Man, if you got eyes for her, you wasting your time. Now Maggie Jones, over in the quarters, she been dying to meet you. That gal will show you a good time. They say she makes a blind man see stars."

24

"Thank you just the same, but I got my mind on Miss Ruth," Moab said, smacking his lips. "How long you been married?"

Joe smiled and said, "Going on seven years."

"Your woman come here with you?"

"No. She born right here on this plantation twenty years ago. Both her mama and papa come from Africa. Sarah ain't got no white blood in her," he said proudly. The barn door opened and the sound of heavy footsteps interrupted their laughter.

"You got time to be laughing and talking with this nigger?"

Moab saw a heavyset white man stepping out of the shadows. As he approached, Moab looked into the jaundiced, bloodshot eyes of Joseph Hanks. The scowl on his pockmarked face deepened as Joe and Moab rose from the bench to face him.

"Capt'n Hanks, I done finished all the work you give me, sir," Joe replied, bowing twice. Moab took a quick glance at Joe's terrified face.

Hanks walked closer to Moab and stood inches from his face. "Nigger, you be careful while you here. I'll be watching your black ass. You hear me?" he drawled.

"I hears you, sir," Moab replied, standing erect and staring into his adversary's eyes. He watched as Joseph Hanks turned and staggered from the barn.

CHAPTER 4

Butler Jim Bradley stood in front of his mirror inspecting his dinner jacket. It pleased him that Hattie had made changes so that it fit perfectly on his broad shoulders. As he looked at himself, he reflected on a comment he had overheard during the last dinner party. An intoxicated white woman pointed at him and whispered that, if his olive skin was white, he could pass for a member of the Bradley family. In truth, his father was James Oliver Bradley, the former patriarch of Bradley Manor, and his mother, Barbara Hill, was James Oliver's favorite slave. She became his mistress after his wife died. James Oliver had built a special cottage for his slave son and taught him to read and write. His tastefully decorated room included a bed, writing table, dresser, mirror, two chairs and a well-worn rug that covered the entire floor. These were discarded, but still serviceable items that once had furnished the former master's bedroom.

Upon arriving at his station, Jim straightened his bow tie, opened the pocket doors to the parlor and announced, "Dinner is served."

William Bradley put out his cigar, rose and escorted Senator Calvert and Reverend Cox to the dining room. Mary Alice, Betty and Sue Ellen had already entered from the living room.

For the special occasion, Mary Alice wore her favorite white satin gown, trimmed elaborately with pink lace, complimented by a sixteen-inch pearl string. Her matching satin turban was crowned with ostrich plumes. Sue Ellen, still looking ashen from the trip, wore a full-length blue flowered dress with a blue silk sash. Mary Alice so wanted to tell her that twisting her graying hair into childish curls did nothing to enhance her face, but instead she offered only a disingenuous smile. Betty Cox wore a simple ankle-length white dress with no frills. Her smooth facial skin required no makeup.

"I regret my sister, Roberta, will not be dining with us this evening. She is not well," William announced affably. Mary Alice nudged him, hoping he would not discuss Roberta's health problems. Roberta was William's fifty-year-old spinster sister. She had been experiencing mood swings for the past six months and at the last minute sent word that she would not be coming down for dinner.

"Give them any damn excuse you want," Roberta had shouted through her locked bedroom door.

William nodded for Jim and Anthony to bring the first course. Both left their assigned stations by the door and proceeded to the kitchen. Ruth handed them trays containing walnut salad. Jim's slight frown was the only outward sign of his nervousness. Turning to Anthony, he whispered, "Now don't forget what I've taught you. Close your ear to all you hear."

As Anthony carefully placed the salad plates before the guests, William asked, "I want to know more about this nephew of yours, Gerald. I thought you had told us about all your kinfolk?" William said, nodding patronizingly in Samuel's direction.

"I thought we had. Samuel is my sister Margaret's youngest boy. He's one of seven children. Guess we lost track. His departed mother, rest her soul, married a fellow from up in Maine. It near broke pa's heart. Sam was born in Savannah, but his father took Margaret and Sam to Boston when he was a baby." Pointing his fork at Betty Cox, he spoke with his mouth full, "Sam's lovely wife here was born and bred in Boston, but we don't hold that against her," Calvert said, chuckling as Betty blushed.

"Are you folks Methodist?" Mary Alice asked.

"No. We're Unitarians," Betty replied.

There was a moment's pause. William placed his fork on his plate. "I've read about the free thinking Unitarians. Some folks say your beliefs are heresy, but let us not talk about religion at my table," William said, taking a sip of wine.

"Good," Mary Alice interjected. She turned and motioned for Jim to bring the second course, an appetizer that consisted of braised bits of smoked rabbit garnished with olives and tomatoes.

"Gerald, yesterday we spoke of that ship, the Antelope, that was seized off the coast of Florida. What's the government's position regarding this matter?" William asked.

"It's shaping up as the first test of the 1808 law banning the importation of slaves. We all knew the embargo laws were going to be impossible to enforce. If you recall, additional penalties were added to the law in 1820." Gerald turned to Reverend Cox. "The provision states that crews of ships importing slaves to our shores will be treated as pirates. I knew when they passed that law it would not stop smugglers from shipping slaves into Savannah, Charleston and other southern ports. President Monroe knows this, and the capture of that ship has become the first important test case for his administration. We will just have to wait and see how strongly he and his Secretary of State, John Quincy Adams, supports it. There is also a question of who has rights to the property. The cargo has an estimated value of seventy-five thousand dollars," Gerald replied.

"By property, I take it you are referring to the Africans?" Reverend Cox asked.

"Of course," Gerald replied, pausing to sip his wine. "Under the 1820 provision, Africans found on ships and smuggled into our ports directly from Africa will be freed unless it can be proven they are slave property. The Spanish government registered the ship, although it was built in New England. Both Spain and Portugal have filed claims for some of the slaves. It seems that sixty-three were registered as Spanish slaves, and one hundred and forty-two were Portuguese property, each valued at $300."

Betty Cox went scarlet as she rose from her seat, "Please excuse me for a moment."

Mary Alice followed her to the door and whispered, "If you need to go to the Necessity House, would you like me to go with you?"

"That won't be necessary. I'm feeling a little overheated. I'll return shortly," Betty said as she walked into the hallway and took several deep breaths. The discussion had sickened her. She composed herself then returned to the table. William rose and pulled back her chair. No one noticed her hands trembling as she adjusted the napkin on her lap.

William turned to Anthony. "Anthony, you may be excused after you bring Uncle Jim two more bottles of white wine." Betty watched as Anthony quickly left through the kitchen door. "I think it best the boy not be around for this conversation. Now, what were you about to say, Gerald."

"Lawyers from the American Colonization Society have involved themselves on behalf of the Africans. The society has succeeded in establishing a homeland in Africa for free blacks in this country who wish to return to their native land. I believe those that returned have named the place Liberia."

"I've read a little about the Colonization Society. Who's heading it?" William asked.

"The lead attorney is the Washington lawyer, Francis Scott Key. He is one of its founders."

Betty Cox muttered under her breath, "Good for him."

"Francis Scott Key," William said reflectively. "I met him at the battle of Bladensburg during the late war with England. He gained the release of my friend, Dr. Beanes, who was taken prisoner by the British."

"Isn't he the young man who wrote that lovely poem we now sing with the title, 'The Star Spangled Banner?'" Betty Cox interjected.

"Key wrote the words, but the tune is from the English drinking song, 'To Anacreon in Heaven,'" Mary Alice replied, proud that she had finally gotten a word into the conversation.

"Uncle Gerald, what is your position on the embargo laws?" Samuel asked.

"I believe the law is a clear invasion of state's rights. Cousin Bill will speak for himself."

"I support it. We can't keep importing blacks forever. Some counties in the deep south have more slaves than whites. If we don't stop importing them, within a generation whites will be in the minority throughout the south," William said, turning to face Samuel. "Reverend, having been born in the south and reared in the north, what are your views on slavery."

Samuel hesitated, pondering his response. He had been looking forward to restful, tension-free days and did not want to offend his host. "I prefer to reference the opinions of that Virginia neighbor of yours, Thomas Jefferson, our third President. He wrote in 1814 that the Republic's failure to eradicate slavery is a moral reproach on our nation and a source of moral and political reprobation. I tend to agree with Mr. Jefferson."

William stared at his nephew. "I know Jefferson. He's one of the biggest slave owners in Virginia and a free thinker," William said, his voice elevated.

Betty blushed. She glanced at the butler and saw him swatting at an insect as though totally oblivious to their conversation. What must he be thinking?

"Now Mr. Bradley, you promised not to bring up the subject of religion. You know it upsets you," Mary Alice whispered. She only called her husband by his last name when she sensed he was losing his temper.

"I only said Jefferson's a free thinker," he retorted loudly. "The man's an atheist."

"Bill, I suggest we change the subject," Gerald said quietly. "Samuel, tell us about your work in Egypt," Gerald said. A relieved Samuel nodded.

During the momentary lull Jim, with quiet dignity, announced, "The main course will now be served."

"Tell us about it after we eat. I want you to enjoy yourselves," William said, hoping to set a more festive tone.

Anthony went to the kitchen pantry, removed two bottles of wine from the ice cellar and placed them on a tray. Returning to the dining room, he handed them to Jim, then hurried from the room into the hallway, up the stairs and into the sewing room that was located directly above the dining room. He found Aunt Hattie sitting by an open grate situated above the fireplace in the dining room below. Anthony knew this was the way she kept all the house folks informed about the important events taking place at Bradley Manor. She cautioned Anthony to be quiet if he wanted to listen in on the conversations below.

"Aunt Hattie, Master William made me leave just when their talk was getting interesting" Anthony whispered.

"When white folk gets to talking about us, they think it best a little fellow like you not hears it," Aunt Hattie whispered. "Come here and lay down and put your ear to this grate. You can hear every word they say."

"This wine is from our very own vineyard," William said, boastfully. "In fact, this plantation is self-sufficient. Our people have been trained as the best brick layers, carpenters, well-diggers, fishermen and farmers on earth. In 1798, my father sent some of our boys to help build our Capitol in Washington City."

Samuel felt relaxed after Jim poured him a third glass of wine. "I read in a Boston magazine that skilled slaves were leased by their masters to build our Capitol. How were they compensated?"

William placed his fork beside his plate and stared at Samuel. "They were compensated the same way I compensate all my people. Here at Bradley Manor every soul is well clothed, fed, and housed. All receive the best medical care available. And I require that they are baptized in the Christian faith," William said, pausing to sip his wine. "I have seen the working conditions of the poor laboring classes in the North that are flocking to our shores. The poor wretches would envy what we provide our people. Are the working conditions of the poor in Boston of equal concern to you, Reverend?" William asked, pointedly.

"The wretched of the earth, be they black, white or red, are my concern, uncle," Samuel responded, quietly.

"Would anyone like to have more wine?" Mary Alice interrupted, fanning herself profusely.

Jim moved forward and quickly refilled the wineglasses, then went to the kitchen and returned with dishes of vanilla ice cream mixed with strawberries. The dessert seemed to relieve the renewed tension.

"Where were you stationed in Egypt?" William asked.

"I was at the University of Cairo. After I finished the seminary at Princeton, a Presbyterian medical missionary urged me to apply for a fellowship to study there."

"Now where exactly is Egypt? I never was good in geography," Mary Alice said, smiling.

"It's in the northeast corner of Africa."

"Africa? Somehow I've never associated Egypt with Africa," William interrupted.

"That's where it is, uncle. Egypt is a marvelous blend of both Middle East and African cultures."

"African cultures? What possible influence could primitive African cultures have on Egypt?" Gerald asked.

30

Samuel smiled, knowing this was his opportunity to enlighten his host. "The African influence in Egypt and in East Africa is considerable. We in the West are ignorant of the fact that the first civilizations that developed in the Nile valley were of African origin. We know nothing of the kingdoms of Kush, Nubia and Ethiopia. These African kingdoms flourished when Europeans lived in caves."

"You aren't suggesting that blacks back then were civilized, are you?" Gerald asked.

"Indeed many were. Ethiopia is mentioned in the Bible. While we were visiting Memphis, the Frenchman Jean François Champolion discovered the tomb of the great Pharaoh Amenhotep III. He wrote to his colleagues in Paris that 'the Negro type predominates among the figures of the king.' His features, carved in giant statues, look more Negroid than many of your people," Samuel said, nodding discreetly in Jim's direction. "Champolion spoke at the university months after his discovery, and gave me a small statue of that Pharaoh. I will be glad to show it to you." From the cold stare on Calvert's face, Samuel half expected to be cut off in the middle of his statement.

"Maybe we should bring this conversation to an end," Calvert stated.

"Gerald Calvert, where are your manners. Let the young man have his say," admonished Mary Alice.

After a brief pause, Samuel decided to open a risky line of questioning. His Unitarian temper was up and there was no stopping him.

"Is it true that here in the South any person with one drop of Negroid blood is classified as colored?"

"Of course it's true. No self respecting southerner would ask such a question."

"Then by that definition the largest percentage of people in the lower Nile valley of Egypt are what you would call mulattoes. In the upper Nile, the Egyptian people are more Negroid," Cox said.

Gerald Calvert lowered his voice and spoke slightly above a whisper, "Samuel, blacks are an inferior race that has made no contribution to civilization. God put them on earth to serve the white race. You know your Bible. The good book speaks against race mixing, doesn't it?"

Samuel's throat felt extremely dry. "There is a story in the Old Testament's Book of Numbers that sheds some light on the subject. It states that Moses married an Ethiopian woman. Ethiopians are primarily a Negroid people. The Bible tells us that the anger of the Lord was kindled, not against Moses, but against his sister and brother, Miriam and Aaron, who spoke out against the marriage."

Gerald coughed violently, sending a spray of wine across the table. Mary Alice closed her eyes and shuddered. "Are you certain Ethiopians were black in those days?" Mary Alice whispered.

"As sure as a leopard has spots."

William rose from his seat. "This may be a good point to retire to our respective rooms. Gentlemen, will join me in the library. We will let you ladies enjoy the parlor."

"Thank you for *letting* us ladies enjoy the parlor," Mary Alice said, sweetly.

While walking toward the library, Gerald placed his hand on William's shoulder and whispered, "If that nephew of mine had spoken such nonsense at my table, I would have had him horse whipped."

"Cousin Gerald, I think he had one drink too many," William replied, slapping his back.

Jim opened the door to the library. Samuel excused himself, went to his room and returned with a small package.

After William passed out cigars, Jim served small glasses of after-dinner liqueurs. William was pleased with the dinner, despite the outrageous comments by Samuel. He smiled when Samuel accepted the drink. "I see Unitarian preachers drink on occasions such as this. We Methodists don't allow our preachers to drink, but I'm sure some do," William said, motioning for Jim to refill his glass from an ornate decanter.

"Jesus' critics accused him of being a glutton and a drunkard," Samuel said, reaching beside his chair and placing a package on his lap. He unwrapped and placed on the table a small wooden statue. "What I have here is a replica of a much larger statue. It's the likeness of one of Egypt's greatest builders, the Pharaoh Amenhotep III. This black Pharaoh ruled the most powerful kingdom on earth thirteen hundred years before the birth of Christ. We in the West refuse to believe what our eyes have seen."

William and Gerald leaned forward and studied the statue's features. "Well I'll be damned. Without that head dress, that could be any one of my people," William whispered under his breath. After reflecting for a few moments, he went to the library shelf and removed an encyclopedia.

"Young man, I want you to know I am well read," William said, turning the pages to a section entitled *The History of Egypt.* "Reverend, it says right here that the Egyptians are a dark-skinned people who belong to the white race. Here is the picture of Queen Nefertiti. She is as white as the driven snow, and that proves my point," William said, thumping the page and grinning with satisfaction.

Reverend Cox calmly took the book and read silently for several moments. "It says here that Nefertiti was one of the wives of the Pharaoh

Akhenaton. He was the son of this Pharaoh, Amenhotep III," Samuel said, pointing to the statue. Akhenaton was also the world's first monotheist."

"Are you telling us the woman depicted in this picture was married to a black?" Gerald protested.

"Yes, Uncle. Some Egyptian historians are convinced she was one of his foreign wives."

Throughout the exchange, Jim had managed to maintain his composure. Despite himself, he smiled just as William looked in his direction.

"What the hell are you grinning about? Do you find all this amusing?" William shouted, highly agitated.

Unnerved by the outburst, Jim dropped the tray containing the decanter that was one of the family treasures. He reached out and managed to recover the precious bottle in mid air. Not a drop of the rare liqueur spilled.

Joseph and Big George sat in the shadows of the chicken coop. The night sky was partly cloudy and a quarter moon gave them only occasional light. Joseph nervously fingered the trigger of his pistol to ease the tension. Big George, armed with an ax handle, whispered, "Capt'n Hanks, you 'speck that fellow gonna come here tonight after he knowed them boys done seen him?"

"Hell, I don't know," he said impatiently, biting off a plug of tobacco. "If he gets a hankering for more chicken, he will. I sure as hell ain't gonna wait all night. You keep watch while I go in them woods and flush him out."

"You going in them woods by yo'self, Capt'n?"

"You god-damn right I am," Joseph replied, thinking of the reward. "He don't scare me one bit."

"What you want me to do if he come running out of them woods?"

"Keep your eyes on what direction he goes 'til I get back. Don't lay a hand on him, you hear? That's a white man out there, boy. Now stay close to me." Big George understood all too clearly.

When they reached the thicket of trees, Joseph motioned for Big George to hide himself. Pushing his way into the brush, he cursed under his breath as thorns from a blackberry bush tore at his arms. He paused and listened to a whimpering sound. Cautiously, he kept moving until he reached a clearing. He saw a young black girl tied to a tree with a rag stuffed in her mouth. As he moved closer, the girl's eyes widened in terror. He heard a sound, like the snapping of twigs. Just as he turned, a club brushed the side of his skull, causing his gun to discharge prematurely. Joseph found himself pinned to the ground with a strong hand gripping his throat. Dazed, he managed to hold on to his pistol as the assailant struggled to take it from him. The pistol discharged a second time as the struggle continued. Joseph heard a thump, like the sound of a watermelon being dropped. His attacker loosened his grip and crumpled to the ground beside him. Gasping for breath, Joseph looked into the face of Big George who stood poised over him, holding an ax handle.

"I hears the shot and I comes running, Capt'n. I never lay a hand on him, like you say," Big George said, dropping the ax handle and holding up both hands. Joseph staggered to his feet and rubbed the lump on the side of his head. Big George untied the girl who had lost consciousness during the struggle. "This here's Pete's gal, Diane. He must have caught her over by the well. Looks like he done her in real bad."

"Don't say one word about what happened here tonight. You hear?" Joseph whispered.

"I hears you, Capt'n."

Joseph stood over the man who was regaining consciousness. He noticed a rope held the two ends of the intruder's belt together. Reaching into his pocket he dangled the buckle before him.

"Who you steal this off, you son-of-a-bitch?" Joseph said, placing the barrel of the pistol to the man's temple. The vagrant stared at Joseph, but remained silent.

"You gonna take him to the sheriff?" Big George asked.

"Take that gal to her cabin, then go hitch the wagon and bring it back here," Joseph said. When Big George turned to leave, Joseph kicked his assailant in his face.

Big George lifted the girl and had carried her only a short distance when he heard a shot. "Well, that reward was fo' him, dead or alive. Guess Capt'n wanted to bring him in dead." Big George said. He hurried his pace from the woods.

CHAPTER 5

The grandfather clock in the dining room chimed eleven times. Ruth and her five-member crew busily finished cleaning the kitchen. While Betty and Cathy scrubbed the floor, Sarah hung the remaining copper pots and pans on a rack in the pantry. Hattie stored the leftovers from the dinner in jars that would be taken to the field hands the next day. Every scrap of food from the master's table, including the fat left on William's steak bones, was highly prized by the workers. A welcomed night breeze blew through the open windows, clearing out the strong scent of lye soap that permeated the kitchen.

The care of William and Mary Alice's fine porcelain was Ruth's responsibility by choice. She vividly remembered the scene years ago when one of the kitchen women accidentally broke a cup. Mary Alice became so upset she ordered the woman out of the house and assigned her to work in the fields. Ruth was proud of the fact that nothing had broken during the six years she personally cared for the family china. It was Mary Alice who dropped a platter and cracked it. Still useable, she gave it to Ruth as a gift.

Sarah had asked Ruth to sent Anthony back to the cabin early because, in his excitement over the events of the day, his jabbering had become a distraction to the women.

"Lord, I thought your Anthony would never stop running his mouth. I ain't never seen that boy so excited," Hattie said.

"It's all this talk about freedom. First come Reverend Harris and that sermon he preached. Then come smart mouth Moab Jackson with all his talk about how he got free. I ain't so sure it's good for him to hear it at his age."

Jim opened the kitchen door and motioned for Ruth to come into the dining room. He shared with her what had transpired in the library. "Please don't speak to Anthony about this. After all I taught him about how to act around white folk, it would too embarrassing if he knew I forgot my place," he said.

The incident with the decanter amused Ruth. She patted Jim on his shoulder, "Come tomorrow, Master Bradley will forget all about it. After all, he's your half-" she paused, but the exchange between them was understood. She motioned for him to come to the kitchen where she poured him a cup of coffee. He took his cup, thanked her and left by the back door for his cottage.

After Ruth sent the last of the crew back to their quarters, she sat at the kitchen table reflecting on the events of the day. By candlelight, the unblemished texture of her face took on the soft hue of ripe persimmons.

She smiled with satisfaction, knowing that the dinner had gone as planned. Jim once told her that her natural smile gave everyone the impression she was happy most of the time. Men who made unwanted advances knew better. When she narrowed her dark eyes, and put her hands on her slender hips, it was a signal to stand clear. Her thoughts were interrupted by a knock at the door. Glancing up, she saw Moab peering through its small window. "Come on in."

Moab entered and strolled over to the table. "Well, how the big day go for the white folks?" he asked, looking hungrily at the sweet potato pie on the table.

"I see you eyeing my pie." Ruth smiled, cutting a slice and sliding the plate in front of him.

"I know this gonna taste mighty good," Moab said, his wide smile revealing a perfect set of white teeth. Taking the pie with his fingers, his bit off half of it. "Um, this sho' is good sweet potato pie. Best I ever had," He never took his eyes off her while eating. Ruth shook her head as his second bite consumed the remainder of the pie.

"You must be hungry, the way you gobbled that down."

"I's hungry all right, but not half as much as I am for the sight of a good-looking gal, the likes of you."

"Don't you go trying to flirt with me. You here today and gone tomorrow. I know you got lots of women in Washington City."

From the tone of her voice, he felt no hostility in her reply. "Well, there be lots of fine women in Washington City, but I swear on a stack of Bibles, none of them half as fine as you. You married?" he asked, hoping she would lie.

"I'm married, but my husband was sold some years ago. My master say he had to do it to save this plantation," she said bitterly.

"What's his name?"

"Zachariah. You hear tell of anybody by that name?" she asked, staring at him hopefully.

He had heard the name related to an incident years ago, but could not recall it. "No, not lately. If I knowed somebody with a name like that, I sho' not forget it."

Ruth sighed while wiping the last crumbs from the table. "Well, let's talk about something else. Tell me all about that Washington City you live in."

"What you want to hear about, sweet lady?" he asked, grinning.

"About how you free colored folk live," she said cheerfully. "Are ya'll really free to do and go where you want to?"

36

"Well, we somewhat free all right, but not as free as white folk. We pay taxes but we can't vote, and we sho' can't go to none of them theaters and fancy drinking places. It's like this; white folks scared of free colored folks. Scared we gonna start something. That's why they passed that law in 1818. The law say colored folk gotta be off the streets by ten every night. You break that law, you in for a heap of trouble. Several men I know got caught coming home from a Wednesday night prayer meeting. Two got flogged and nobody ever seen the third man again. We 'speck they sold him." He paused to drink a cup of water.

"That doesn't sound like much freedom to me. How many free folks live in Washington City?"

"At last count there be about three thousand, more or less. Lots of high yellow niggers in that number. I 'speck you understands that, being you work here in this house."

"I don't. I guess you'll have to tell me," Ruth replied, cryptically. Moab paused, not quite certain what lay behind the look in those mysterious eyes.

"More house niggers gets they freedom than field niggers because most related to they masters, one way or another," Moab said, sarcastically.

"Moab Jackson, I guess you done said enough on that subject for one night."

"I's sorry, Miss Ruth, don't be meaning to upset you," Moab pleaded apologetically. He sipped the coffee she placed in front of him, and for moments neither spoke.

"I saw Hattie Johnson's gals hanging out yo' master's sheets. The one named Cathy. Is that baby she be carrying hers?"

Ruth stared at Moab. "I think you know it's her baby. But I don't want to talk about her. Tell me about the schools for free folk in that Washington City of yours," she said, smiling. Moab felt a sense of relief.

"Well, few years back, all us free folks got together and started the Colored Resolute Beneficial Society. Let me think. That be in 1818. We started a school for our chillen, but the white folks don't give us one cent from the taxes we pay. We raised the money ourselves to pay the teacher we hired." He paused. The last thing he wanted to talk about was Washington City, but from the anticipation on her face he decided to continue. "Money comes real hard this year, and we don't know if we can keep the teacher we got," he said, sadly.

"My son can read and write," Ruth said proudly.

"White folks here let your boy get some book learning?"

"That's right. Miz Mary Alice and I had our babies about the same time. After our babies were born, she got deathly sick and couldn't nurse hers. I had lots of milk and I nursed them both, and took care of her. Miss Roberta,

Master Bradley's sister, loved my Anthony. She was the one that started teaching him to read and write, and both Master Bradley and his wife agreed."

"Where that son now?"

"He died from the fever back in 1814, that terrible year the English burned down Washington City. They got two other children, though. Their older son is named Henry. He's away at college, and their daughter, Louise, is married. She and her husband have two lovely children. They live in the town of Alexandria Virginia."

Moab pretended to be interested, having heard it all from the blacksmith. "Who that nigger everybody calls Uncle Jim? The one that walk and talk like he's white?" he asked, sneering.

"Moab Jackson, I don't like it when you call people niggers. I hate that word."

"I's sorry. I just don't trust high yellow nig—." Catching himself, he grinned. "Almost said it again, Miss Ruth."

"What you got against folk who half white? They can't help that."

"They think they better than us black folk."

"Moab, where you get all that anger? You got no cause to hate our folk, be they skin white, brown or black. It's white folk that makes our life hell on this earth. I think your problem is you can't do nothing about how white folk treat you, even if you are free. Is that why you take it out on our own folks?"

Moab reflected for a few moments. Taking a deep breath, he grinned and said, "Miss Ruth, you not only pretty, but you smart. Look, I'm gonna be taking the Senator, his wife, and they guests back to Washington City, come day after tomorrow. I likes you the first time I seen you." He moved with surprising swiftness around the table and placed his arms around her waist. "What you say you and me do a little sparking befo' I leave."

Her eyes narrowed as she quickly turned her head, causing his puckered lips to brush the side of her face. It was the first embrace she had experienced in years. As graceful as a cat, she slid from his embrace and backed away. He made a second attempt to kiss her, but was surprised by her agility as she glided to the other side of the table. It was clear that he was not used to women rejecting his advances. When he approached her the third time, she picked up a plate and thrust it in his hands. "Here, take your plate over to the dish tub and wash it," she said.

Looking down at the plate, Moab burst into laughter. After washing and drying the plate, he handed it to her.

"I see I gotta keep those hands of yours busy, Moab Jackson,"

"Now can I kiss you?" he said smiling.

38

"No," she said irritably. "Moab, you a fine man but I can't be doing nothing like that. I'm married, and I will remain faithful to my man because I know in my heart, the day of Jubilee coming. On that day my Zach's gonna come right through that door and take me and my boy to freedom."

"Woman, you crazy. White folks ain't gonna set you free. I 'speck that man of yours been sold down South, long ago. You ain't never gonna see him again as long as you live, and that's a fact, Miss Ruth. If he's still living, by now he done been mated up with some gal, just like they mate horses and cows. That's the truth. You gotta live for now. I needs a fine woman like you."

"You need a bath in some cold water, that's what you need," she said, staring at him sternly.

Moab studied her determined face and resigned himself to the fact that he was only making her angry. He sat down dejectedly and pouted like a little boy.

To his surprise, Ruth's demeanor softened, "I'll let you walk me to my cabin door if you behave yourself," she said.

"I sho' will, Miss Ruth," he replied, with renewed anticipation. She blew out the three lamps and motioned him to follow her. Outside the night air was sultry. As they walked together under the bright full moon, Ruth felt carefree and happier than she had in years.

"That Anthony of yours is one fine boy. I seen the way his eyes light up when I told him how I got my freedom."

"That's what been worrying me. He's smart, but I hope he don't go getting himself in trouble with all this talk about freedom he been hearing these past two days."

"He gonna hears about it sooner or later. That boy's smart, he gonna be free one of these days, mark my word."

Ruth stopped suddenly. Standing in the shadow of a tall tree was the dark figure of a man. When he stepped from under the tree, Ruth's heart froze when she recognized the scowling face of Joseph Hanks. The barrel-chested man approached and stopped only inches from Moab's face.

"Nigger, what you doing out here with this here gal?"

Ruth knew from his slurred speech he had been drinking. She pulled Moab back and stepped between them.

"You got no call to say that to him. I asked him to walk me to my door," she said angrily.

Joseph pushed her aside and pointing his finger at Moab. "Keep your black hands off her. She's the personal property of William Bradley. Get your nigger ass away from her, and don't be messing with any of our wenches, you hear me?" Joseph shouted. It angered him when Moab said nothing, but stood his ground.

"God damn it, answer me, nigger," he shouted, snatching a short whip from his belt.

"Yes sir." Moab responded quietly.

Ruth grabbed Moab's hand and held on tightly. "Stay away from him," she screamed.

Moab felt humiliated by her act of defiance. Although he carried a hunting knife in his scabbard and could easily kill this drunk, he realized it would cost him more than his hard-earned freedom. It would cost him his life. Slowly, Moab pried his hand from her strong grip. "Miss Ruth, it's best I be going."

Ruth's heart sank as he quickly turned and walked away. Suddenly the night sky turned darker as clouds shut off the soft rays of moonlight that they enjoyed for those few brief moments.

She glared at Joseph, then muttered, "The Lord's gonna send your soul to hell one of these days." It was the first time in her life that she had spoken in anger to the overseer.

Hanks smirked, "Hell Ruth, you don't want no ugly black buck like that. You want some of this. I'll ride your sweet ass anytime." He grinned, placing his hand to his crotch and lifting it.

Ruth recoiled and backed away. "The master's gonna hear about this," she hissed, defiantly.

Enraged, he drew back his whip, but hesitated, remembering who she was. She stood her ground, daring him to strike her. "I know all about you, wench," he sneered. "You think I don't know why they put you in that kitchen. You better keep that tight ass of yours in your cabin, and stay away from that black buck, you hear me? And you better keep your mouth shut if you know what's good for that little nigger of yours," he snarled.

Ruth understood the threat all too clearly. He would never touch her, but he could retaliate by abusing Anthony.

Ruth stood her ground as the pounding in her chest felt like a steel trap. She felt naked as he stood surveying her figure. He held the whip in his left hand, menacingly moving it back and forth in a snakelike motion. Slowly, she moved around him and began walking toward her cabin. She could hear his booted steps and his heavy breathing close behind her. She reached the cabin door, darted in and pulled down the wooden latch. She knew that with one kick of his boot, the latch would snap with ease. She grabbed an iron poker and stood facing the door, fearful he would burst in at any moment. She hoped Anthony would not wake up. She flinched at every creaking sound and her muscles ached from the tension. Every passing minute seemed like eternity. When two cats started fighting outside her window, she realized he had gone.

As Ruth's fear subsided, she folded her hands and said a silent prayer. After twenty minutes she relaxed. The perspiration that ran down her face and soaked her cotton dress now felt cool and refreshing, even though she found it hard to stop trembling. She felt a strange sense of pride for having stood up to Joseph Hanks. She remembered the talk among the field hands that he had accidentally whipped a black man to death before coming to Bradley Manor. They whispered that when Joseph got drunk, he often beat his wife, Sue Ellen. Ruth had never seen his wife smiling during the few times their paths had crossed. Before falling into a restless sleep, she decided she would go straight to Mary Alice and report the incident.

After going to the kitchen the next morning, Ruth found it impossible to concentrate on her work. By eight-thirty, she was sure Mary Alice was up and dressed, so she instructed Sarah to take over the kitchen duties until she returned. After muttering a prayer, she went to the parlor where she found Mary Alice chatting with Betty Cox. The men apparently were sleeping late.

"Excuse me. May I speak to you for just a moment, Miz Mary Alice?" she asked politely. Betty smiled as Mary Alice rose from her chair."

"I will wait outside in the rose garden," Betty said, leaving through the French doors.

Ruth burst into tears. "Miz Mary Alice I got something I need to tell you."

"I think I know, Ruth. Mr. Hanks spoke to me this morning and told me you were with that coachman last night. Is that true?" Mary Alice asked.

"Yes, I was. He came by the kitchen and after I gave him something to eat, I asked him to walk me to my cabin. Along come Mr. Hanks saying nasty to him and me. That's when Mr. Hanks ran him off," she said defensively.

"Mr. Hanks said that he caught you and that Coachman fooling around."

Ruth stared at Mary Alice with disbelief. Never in her life had she ever lost her temper or raised her voice when speaking to any member of the Bradley family. "You know he lied on me," Ruth cried. "Both of you know I don't fool around with nobody. I ain't so much as looked at no man since the day my husband was sold seven years ago. Master William even tried to pick another man for me. I told ya'll I will never look at no other man, unless I know for sure my husband is dead and gone to heaven. Maybe, not even then."

Mary Alice stood shocked when Ruth began sobbing uncontrollably. She suddenly felt remorseful for having mentioned what the uncouth overseer had said. How could she have been so gullible? Taking a handkerchief from her pocket, she placed her arms around Ruth's shoulder and wiped the tears from her cheeks.

"Ruth, I'm sorry you're upset. Don't cry now. I will speak to Mr. Bradley about this. Go wash your face," Mary Alice said, feeling it would be beneath her station to admit she had made a serious error in judgement. But she had. "I never believed one word he said."

"Then you should have never said it," Ruth said. "You know he ain't nothing but a polecat."

Ruth turned abruptly and walked away. She realized she had not told Mary Alice about the obscene gestures or the subtle threat he had made toward her son. She trudged despondently back to the kitchen, wondering if she would have another chance to see Moab before he left.

Betty Cox stepped through the French doors into the rose garden. Having observed Ruth's worried expression, she decided to give both women some privacy. Here among the rose arbors, she was pleased to find it in full bloom. Mary Alice said the flowering would not reach its peak for another week. Betty felt her hostess seemed somewhat frivolous, but there was nothing frivolous about the way she arranged and cared for her garden. She made her way along the winding brick path, admiring the wide variety of healthy bushes that Mary Alice had carefully spaced in mulched beds. From time to time, she paused to read the hand-printed signs that identified the Yellow Briers, Damask and Moss roses in addition to a number of climbing vines supported on two wooden trusses that arched across the path. As she stepped through it, she saw a young woman sitting on a bench nursing a newborn infant. Betty recalled seeing her washing windows in the parlor and had found it hard to believe such a beautiful person was one of William Bradley's slaves.

"Good morning," Betty said politely. "May I ask your name?"

"Cathy Johnson, ma'am," she replied shyly.

"You are Hattie Johnson's daughter?"

"Yes ma'am." Cathy removed the baby from her breast and buttoned her blouse.

"May I hold your baby? Is it a boy or girl?" Betty said, taking a seat beside her.

"He's a boy, ma'am." Cathy squirmed nervously, not use to white people speaking to her in such a respectful manner.

"I just love babies. Reverend Cox and I hope to start our family soon."

Cathy reluctantly handed her the baby. Taking it gently, Betty removed the covers from the child's face. She found herself looking into the bright blue eyes of a white child, its head crowned with blonde curls. Shocked, she stared at Cathy.

"How old is your baby?"

"He's four weeks old, today."

"What's his name?" Betty smiled, trying to regain her composure.

"Henry, ma'am,"

Betty stared at the baby, then at the mother. Cathy's caramel-colored complexion and hazel eyes reminded her of the Egyptian women she had met in Cairo.

"Is he named after your husband?"

"No ma'am, I ain't married," Cathy stammered, clearly embarrassed.

Betty felt remorseful. For years she had heard whispers in Boston's polite society about slave owners and their overseers taking advantage of slave women, but never in her wildest dreams did she ever think she would see such clear evidence of it. Looking at the child's features, she suppressed her anger. She recalled Mary Alice telling her that her son, Henry, was a student at St. John's College in Annapolis, Maryland. Was a coincidence that Cathy had chosen that name for her child? Mary Alice had gone to great lengths to explain that it was not unusual for slaves, who 'dearly loved their masters,' to take their master's first or last names. She tried to put the thought out of her mind by rocking the child and making small talk about the care of babies. Looking up, she saw Mary Alice walking toward them.

"Oh, here you are," Mary Alice called out. She stopped short when she saw Betty holding Cathy's child.

"Cathy, have you properly introduced yourself?" Mary Alice asked, nervously twisting her handkerchief.

"Yes ma'am."

"Take your child and be along now. Your mother needs you in the sewing room. She's putting the finishing touches on the dress she's making for me. It must be done before Sunday," Mary Alice said, smiling nervously.

As Betty handed the child to Cathy, she turned to Mary Alice. "Have our husbands come down for breakfast?"

"They will be there soon. My dear, you are in for a treat. Ruth has prepared her special egg omelette. Her secret is the fresh Maryland crabmeat she puts in it. We bring the crabs here live right from the Chesapeake Bay. It's simply marvelous," Mary Alice said, regaining her composure.

When Cathy turned to leave, Betty called out, "Cathy, you have a beautiful baby. He looks just like my sister's child when he was that age."

Mary Alice reached into her pocket, took out her pearl-handled fan and began to fan herself briskly.

"After breakfast, you must come to the sewing room to see the dress Hattie is sewing for me. She is a marvelous seamstress. All the patterns I've ordered from Paris, she improves on them." Mary Alice failed to mention that one of the women in her sewing circle had commented that Hattie could have been a fashion designer in her own right, had she been born white and free.

While returning to the Manor house, Mary Alice babbled on and on about her prize roses, all her first place ribbons, and how her circle of friends all wanted to know the secret of her success with roses. She was determined not to give Betty an opportunity to ask questions that were none of her business.

At the hallway, Betty paused when she saw Anthony seated near the top of the circular stairway dusting the woodwork.

"Isn't that the boy who served us last night?" Betty asked, pointing to Anthony. "He is a handsome lad."

"Yes. That's Ruth Bowen's child. He was born right here." Mary Alice whispered. "You know, we taught him to read and write. Why, he could read parts of the Bible by the time he was four."

While impressed, Betty could not help but wonder what possible future this lad would have as a slave, even if he could read and write. "After breakfast, I would love to see more of Bradley Manor. Could it be arranged?" Betty asked. She had resented the fact that William had taken her husband and Gerald Calvert on the tour and left the women behind.

"Why, of course. Would you like Anthony to escort you? I would go with you myself, but my doctor does not want me to expose my delicate skin to the sun. When my mother was in her thirties she came down with a skin problem and later died. I will always believe it was caused by too much sunlight. Whenever I spend too much time in the sun, it caused blisters," Mary Alice said, placing her gloved hand to her cheek.

"I would be delighted to have Anthony escort me."

Mary Alice called out, "Anthony, Mrs. Cox wants to see our farm after breakfast. I want you to escort her, so don't go running off, you hear?"

"Yes ma'am," he replied, his eyes lighting up with excitement.

Anthony could barely restrain himself while running down the stairs and into the kitchen. His thoughts raced as he recalled the dinner conversation. If only he had the courage to ask Mrs. Cox about the people in Africa. He suddenly remembered the warning Uncle Jim had given him about keeping his place around white folks. It would be safer not to ask questions, having been taught to speak only when spoken to. He slowed his pace as he entered the kitchen. He was tempted to blurt out his good news, but quickly realized

Ruth and Sarah were busy planning the next meal, so he wisely kept silent. When he finally told Ruth, she only smiled.

Sarah chucked. "Hope she don't go falling off no horse with her fancy self."

Jim brought Betty to the kitchen an hour later. "Anthony, it's time for you to take Mrs. Cox on a tour of the farm. Follow me to the stables. Moab has one of our horses saddled for you, madam."

"Will I need a horse?"

"This farm covers more than four thousand acres. If you want to see it, you best ride."

"And young Anthony. Will he be riding?"

"We have a mule for him," Jim replied, tapping the top of Anthony's head. Betty followed Jim and Anthony the fifty yards to the riding stables. Moab had just placed a side-saddle on a beautiful brown filly.

"This is Lady Delight. She likes ladies to ride her," Anthony said excitedly, patting the horse's head. "I'm riding this mule name, 'Kick Me Quick'. He got that name 'cause when he was young he liked to kick at folks. One day he kicked Big George. Big George picked up a pole and hit him in the head and from then on he never kicked nobody ever again. He said that was the only way he could get that mule's attention."

"If you say Lady Delight is gentle, Anthony, I know we are going to have a delightful ride." Betty stepped up on a wooden platform and mounted the horse while Moab held the reins.

Anthony led the way to a section of the farm where tobacco was growing. "Master Bradley's got more than three hundred acres of tobacco growing this year. Next year he won't plant nothing here. That's because tobacco fields need to rest for a year or two after the crop comes in," Anthony said, eager to impress her with his knowledge of farming.

"Anthony, have you ever been to Washington City?" Betty asked.

"No ma'am, only place I've been to is over to the Johnson farm. That was to help my mama who did the cooking for a big party farmer Johnson's had last year."

"Mrs. Bradley tells me you can read the Bible."

"Yes ma'am, Miss Roberta and Uncle Jim taught me. I read the Bible at our Sunday church service, when asked." His eyes lit up with special pride.

She reached into her saddlebag, removed a small Bible with a white leather cover and handed it to him. "Will you read me a passage?"

Anthony hesitated then smiled. Taking the Bible, he thumbed through the pages, cleared his throat, and began reading in a clear soft voice, "There is a river, the streams whereof shall make glad the city of God, the holy place of the tabernacles of the most High. God is in the midst of her; she shall not be moved…" When he completed the passage, he handed the book back to her.

Betty sighed and smiled. "Anthony, you read that beautifully," Betty said, trying to compose herself while guiding her horse to the fence. The thought of such an intelligent child being a slave depressed her. "May I ask you a question?"

"Yes ma'am," Anthony replied, surprised that a white person would need to ask such a question.

"Are you happy living here?"

"Yes, ma'am," Anthony replied quickly.

"Would you like to be free some day?"

Anthony felt a knot tightening in his stomach. He opened his mouth, but found it impossible to speak. His survival instincts surfaced as he lowered his eyes so she could not see his tears.

Betty Cox felt foolish, watching the anguish boiling up in his youthful face. She realized she had placed him in an untenable position. "It's all right. It's all right. I understand, Anthony. I should not have asked such a question."

Her words only compounded his uneasiness. For a brief moment, he felt as though he was outside his body. He turned his mule to avoid facing her. They did not speak as he guided Betty past a marshy pond to another cultivated field where young corn was growing. As they rode past the cornfield, Anthony reflected on his fear and all that Jim had taught about how to act around white people. Suddenly, he felt no longer fearful of this kind woman. Mustering all of his courage, he turned the mule and faced her.

"I heard your husband say last night that ya'll been living in Egypt?" Anthony stammered, his voice quivering. Betty pulled the reins of her horse and gazed into the dark pools of his eyes and smiled. Anthony knew this was a defining moment in his short life. "Are there folks like me living over there?"

Betty's excitement grew, for she had perceived what her hosts would never allow themselves to perceive. There were unseen guests in that dining room last night. They not only heard the discussion, but also possibly understood its implications for their future.

"Help me down, Anthony." Betty extended her hand to him. Anthony jumped from the mule and gave her his hand as she dismounted. He tied the horse and mule to a fence. Betty removed her sunbonnet, walked into the shade of a tree and sat on a stump. "We will rest here. Now to answer your question. Yes, there are millions of people in Egypt that look just like you and your mother. Egypt is a wonderful nation and is one of oldest in the world. When it was young, white people lived in caves and many were slaves."

Anthony sat on the grass, a respectful distance from her. He found it hard to believe that white folks were once slaves. "Do people in Africa believe in God?"

"O' yes. Most people throughout the world believe in God. There are many Christians in Africa, but most of the people do not believe in our God. They call their religion Islam. In fact, in some parts of Africa they have never heard of our God."

"By what name do they call their God?" he asked puzzled.

"That's a very good question. Different groups of people call him by different names. We have heard him called by the name *Allah, Mulungu, Nyambe, Ol-orum*, just to name a few. People who speak different languages all have different names for God."

"But is he God, only with a different name?"

"Many Christians would say no, but I believe God made the earth and everything in it, and that he speaks and cares for all the children of the earth, but in many different ways. Has your preacher told your people the story of how our God made the heavens and the earth?"

"Yes ma'am. It's in the Book of Genesis."

"My husband told me a wonderful story that the black people from the West Africa country of Mugambo tell their children. Would you like to hear it?"

"I sure would," Anthony said grinning, now totally at ease.

Betty folded her hands and leaned closer to him, "Well, these people called God by the name '*Nyambe.*' For this story, that's what I will call him."

"Nyambe," Anthony repeated, his eyes glowing with excitement.

"Now, like in our Bible, the people believe that when Nyambe made the world, there were no plants or animals. One day Nyambe climbed down from heaven on a spider web, bringing with him a giant turtle, three hens and a bag filled with all kinds of seeds. Nyambe sat on the turtle's back as it swam about in the dark muddy water. Nyambe, said to the turtle, 'Open up your shell.'"

"I once caught a turtle and it tried to bite my hand," Anthony said, laughing.

"Well, this was a giant turtle, the size of the barn we just left. It had two gates on each side of its shell. The turtle opened its gates and lo' and behold, out poured rich black dirt. There was so much dirt it rose above the water and soon become dry land. Nyambe stepped out on the land, took the bag and scattered seeds on the ground. He turned the hens loose and told them to scratch the soil and plant the seeds."

"We got more than a hundred hens and it's my job to feed them every morning and evening," Anthony said proudly.

Betty smiled, "Now, the hens were very hungry and wanted to eat the seeds, but they obeyed Nyambe and planted the seeds. When they finished, there was enough left over for their dinner. Soon the dry land was green with plants and trees of every kind. There were beautiful flowers, and all kinds of fruits and vegetables. Others grew to become tall grasses, bushes and lovely shade trees. The hens made nest and when their eggs hatched, out came all kinds of beautiful song birds that soon filled the air."

Betty adjusted her bonnet when a gust of wind blew it sideways. "It's clouding up. I'd better hurry and finish. Not long after that, the great turtle died. His shell became the first mountain on the dry land. Nyambe was sad and very lonely. He said 'I gonna make me a man and a woman.' So one fine day, Nyambe reached down and scooped up the rich black soil in both of his hands. From the soil in his right hand, he made the first man, and from the soil in his left hand, he made the first woman. Their skin was black and very beautiful, just like the dark soil of the earth. Nyambe blessed them, then sent them up the mountain to live happy and free." She hesitated to observe Anthony's reaction. It thrilled her when she saw him sitting transfixed with his mouth wide open, totally absorbed in the story. "With his work now finished, Nyambe climbed back up the spider web to the spirit world called heaven," Betty concluded, taking a deep breath. "How do you like that story, Anthony?"

"It's different from the story in the Bible. I think I like the one you told me better."

"And why is that?" she asked curiously.

"Because when God took that rib out of Adam's side to make Eve, I know it hurt him an awful lot. I saw what happened when Master Bradley had to cut off a man's toe when it got rotten. I would hate walking around for the rest of my life with one of my ribs or any part of me missing."

Despite herself, Betty could not suppress her laughter. After catching her breath and wiping tears from her eyes, she said, "Now Anthony, it's your turn. Tell me what story you like best from the Bible."

Anthony reflected for a few moments then his eyes sparkled. "I like the story about Moses and how he freed the Hebrew people. Reverend Harris preached about it this past Sunday."

She shook her head in amazement. Never in her wildest dreams did she think she would encounter a slave child that could converse so intelligently, and who was knowledgeable about the Bible. Had God given her this opportunity for a purpose? Was that purpose to plant the seed of freedom in his mind?

A sudden gust of wind blew her straw hat off. As Anthony jumped up to chase it, she placed her hands over her eyes and glanced at the sky. "It looks like rain clouds are heading this way, Anthony. I think we should head back."

Anthony handed her the hat. "Are our people slaves where you come from?"

"Once they were, but I am proud to say that there are no slaves in the city of Boston now." She stood up and brushed the dry grass from the back of her skirt. "Never forget that your people were not always slaves. Thousands of years before Jesus was born, colored people in Africa were some of the greatest teachers and builders on earth. Some day the true history of your race will be told," Betty said, placing her hand on Anthony's shoulder. "Reverend Cox and I will be leaving tomorrow. We will be praying every day for you, your mother and all the people here."

"Thank you, ma'am. My ma and I pray my papa will come home someday and we will be free, come the day of Jubilee. Master Bradley sold papa when I was four-years old." Anthony stood tall and looked directly into her eyes. He could speak freely now, proud that he felt not the slightest trace of fear.

For Betty Cox, the weight of his revelation was as much as she could bear for one afternoon. "God will be your refuge and strength, Anthony. He will show you the path to freedom." They walked to the fence and untied the horse and mule. After he helped Betty mount, the two friends rode in silence back to the stable at Bradley Manor.

CHAPTER 6

Ruth awoke to the sounds of thunder, followed by the screech of a night owl perched in the willow tree beside her cabin. A second bolt of lightening, followed by thunder made sleep impossible. She instinctively knew it was four in the morning and now her thoughts filled with the events of the past day. Anthony had kept her awake jabbering about the wonderful story Betty Cox had told him. It was hard to suppress her anger. That white woman had no business filling Anthony's head with mess that would only confuse him. She and her husband would soon be returning to where they came from, and the sooner the better. Nothing would change for her or Anthony. She clenched her fist and pounded the thin blanket, but stiffened when she heard a scampering sound near the wood box. She knew the sound all too well and it terrified her. When she was a child, she recalled being awakened with pain in her left foot. A rat had bitten the tip of her toe when she was only three. Memories of her mother's screams and her father's curses came flooding back. He had cornered the rat and clubbed it to death.

"Anthony, wake up. That rat's in here again," Ruth said, shaking him, only to have him bury his face in his pillow.

"Wake up, son. You gotta help me. That rat we saw last week is back in here. You know I'm scared to death of rats."

Anthony sat up and rubbed his eyes. He reached under his bed for a club, ran to a table and lit a candle. After dropping to his knees, he crawled around the cabin floor searching under their beds and behind the wood box next to the fireplace. "He's gone, mama, but I see where he got in. He came through this crack in the floor. See where he's been nibbling on the wood?"

Ruth shuddered, covered her face and refused to look. He sat beside her and put his arms around her shoulders. "Don't worry, Mama. I'm gonna catch that rat and kill him." Both flinched when they heard a knock at the door.

"Who's that at my door this time of the morning?" Ruth called out, fearful it might be Joseph Hanks.

"It's me, Moab Jackson," the coachman whispered.

Ruth's heart skipped when she recognized the coachman's low husky voice. Despite her fear, she slipped on her shoes, hurried to the door and opened it. There was enough moonlight for her to see him smiling down at her. He looked anxiously over his shoulder as she reached for his hand and pulled him inside the cabin.

"Miss Ruth, I just had to see you before I left," Moab whispered, glancing at Anthony. "I's glad to see you, boy. I didn't 'spect you to be up this time of the morning."

"Mama got me up 'cause a rat been running around in here."

Moab looked around the floor, then at Ruth. "Now you sho' don't need no rats in here, nice as this place be. Anyway, I's glad to see both of you."

"Well, we are wide awake now," Ruth replied. "Come over here and sit yourself down while I light a fire." She picked up a stool and handed it to him. "Anthony, you need your rest, so go back to bed."

Anthony frowned. Surely she knew he was too excited to sleep.

"About what happened last night. I just wanted to tell you-," Moab whispered haltingly.

Ruth placed her finger to his lips. "Moab, don't say one word about what happened. You just sit right here. I'm gonna make us some coffee." Having access to the kitchen supplies, she was one of the few of William's people permitted to have a ration of coffee now and then. Within minutes the fire began to blaze and the light from the fireplace cast its flickering glow throughout the cabin. As the pot brewed, Moab sat quietly admiring her.

"Did that white trash hurt you?" Moab whispered.

"Joseph Hanks knows better than to put his hands on me." Her eyes narrowed as she spoke.

"I come close to killing that drunk fool, Miss Ruth. I never wanted to kill nobody in all my life 'til now, and that's the honest truth."

"I'm glad you didn't. I know how you felt, but the Bible tells us not to kill, Moab."

"Miss Ruth, somewhere that good book also say there be a time to kill and a time not to kill, but I don't come here to talk about killing. I comes to say you the finest woman I ever met in my whole life."

Ruth smiled as she observed the broad grin on his face. There was a tenderness and sincerity in him that she had not seen when he first approached her in the kitchen. She reached out and placed her hands over his rough calloused hands. "Moab Jackson, you are a wonderful man," Ruth whispered. "I'm glad you came to say goodbye. I was wondering if I ever get a chance to see you again." She looked into his pleading eyes, knowing what he wanted from her. "Like I say, I'm a married woman. I know they sold my husband and I may never see him again, but I gotta keep hoping."

"There you go again, Miss Ruth. Please listen to me. I loves you and someday I's gonna find a way to set you and Anthony free. You gotta know by now your man ain't ever coming back," he whispered.

"Don't ever say that again. I can't love no other man, Moab," she whispered, pleading for understanding. For a brief moment he stared at her, knowing she spoke the truth. The depth of her commitment to a man who was beyond her reach left him bewildered. In their precious final moments, all he could do was gaze at her admiringly.

"Miss Ruth, I needs to talk with Anthony before I go." Ruth regained her composure and nodded. Moab strolled over to Anthony's cot and gently shook him. Anthony sat up and smiled.

"I hate to wake you, late as it is."

"I wasn't sleeping."

"Yo' mama one of the finest women I ever met, and yo' pappy must be some man for her to love him the way she do. If she ever change her mind, I be proud to have you for my son."

"Will you come back to see us someday?"

"Well, I sho' got good reason too. Now you listen up, boy. Don't forgets what I tells you about freedom. You gotta gets you a plan, and always take it to the Lord in prayer. The good Lord will tell you if it's a good plan or not."

"Moab, I'll never forget you as long as I live," Anthony said, choking back tears. Both turned when they heard sounds coming from behind the wood box.

"He's back," Anthony whispered. Moab removed his knife from his sheath. There was now just enough light from the fireplace for them to see something scampering across the floor. Moab's sudden movement, and the reflection of cold steel flashing across the room caused Anthony to flinch. Sharp squeals came from one corner of the cabin. Ruth placed her hand over her mouth to stifle her scream.

Moab went to the corner and picked up his knife. Impaled on the blade was the largest rat Anthony had ever seen, and he'd seen dozens. "Miss Ruth, this here rat ain't gonna scare you ever again," Moab said, proudly holding it up.

Ruth turned her head and waved Moab away. "Take that critter out of here. Anthony, show him were we keep the shovel."

Moab took the shovel and buried the rat behind the cabin. When he returned, Anthony showed him the hole where the rodent had entered through the floorboards. Taking his knife he knelt and pried the board loose. "That was a mama rat, for sho'," Moab said. He lit a match and peered through the opening. Anthony watched as he reached under the floor and pulled out a nest of torn paper, straw and old rags. In the center of the nest were six hairless baby rats. None had its eyes open, and all were the size of Anthonys' little finger. Anthony carefully placed the tiny rats in his straw hat. As he watched them squirming, he turned to Ruth with pleading eyes. "Mama, can I keep them for just a little while?"

Ruth stared at Anthony with disbelief as Moab snickered.

"Anthony, I know you like to catch tadpoles, birds and snakes, but if you ever bring such critters in this cabin you gonna be in a heap of trouble. Now take those rats outside and drown them this very minute, you hear me?" Ruth shouted. "Do you hear me?"

"Yes mama," Anthony replied, his ears ringing. He left the cabin, knowing he dared not look back. After filling a bucket with water, he dumped each of them into it. As much as he hated rats, it saddened him to watch them drown.

When he returned, Ruth walked to the window. "It will soon be getting light, Moab. It's best we all say goodbye. You need to be going now." She took Moab by the hand and led him to the door. He turned and tried to kiss her, but she placed his hands to his side, then rose on tiptoe and kissed his cheek. They looked into each other's eyes for a few moments, then he turned and disappeared into the dim light of a quarter moon.

At six a.m., William, Gerald and Samuel walked to the barn where Anthony stood waiting. He handed each man a fishing pole. The air was cool and the landscape had been washed clean by the storm. William was relieved that the strong winds had not damaged any of his trees and buildings. Most important, his pastures and trout pond received much needed rain.

"My pond is only a short distance from here. I had my people dig it out five years ago and I stocked it with a few dozen finger-length trout. Now we have my favorite fish once a week," William boasted.

"What do you use for bait?" Samuel asked.

"Tell them, Anthony," William said, patting his head.

"Worms and caterpillars. Not many caterpillars around this time of the year, so I got up early and dug some worms from our worm pit outside the hog yard. We call it our worm farm because us boys catch worms during plowing time and put them in a pit, cover them with lots of dirt, dead leaves and slop from the hog pen. That make them grow fat, like the ones you are fishing with today."

"Anthony's a bright boy. He will put the worms on your hooks if you don't want to get your hands dirty."

"That's part of the fun, uncle," Samuel said laughing. "I will bait my own hook."

William guided them to an oak tree whose branches shaded part of the pond. The pond was about twice the size of William's living and dining rooms. The surface of the water seemed so peaceful and calm, Samuel guessed there were only a few fish in so small an area.

"Watch this," William said, reaching in his pocket and tossing a chunk of dried bread in the water. Suddenly the surface of the water rippled as dozens of hungry trout came to the surface and fought for the prize.

"This morning our limit is four each. That will be enough for our breakfast."

Anthony baited the line, cast it into it into the pond and immediately pulled out a trout. Samuel shook his head. "There is not much sport to it."

"Not from my pond. The sport is in the eating. These trout will grace your plate shortly."

It did not take long for the men to catch their quota. As fast as they pulled the fish in, Anthony gutted, cleaned and scaled them.

"Anthony, take the fish to the kitchen and tell Ruth I want this mess of trout on my table for breakfast." Anthony took the bucket of fish and trotted off toward the Manor house.

"I'm glad the boy's gone. I wanted to finish our conversation about that slave ship, *Antelope*. There is a scandal brewing at the capital concerning John Morel, the Marshal of the District of Georgia," Gerald said.

"What sort of scandal?" William asked.

"I have it on good authority that Morel has accumulated a small fortune working the slaves taken from the *Antelope*. Simultaneously, he is billing the government for their maintenance."

"That's outrageous!"

"What's worse, he's swamping them. They will be worked to death before the matter is adjudicated in the courts. The man's cruelty is notorious. Several years ago he was tried for murdering a slave, but the good people of Georgia acquitted him."

"Who is aware of this?"

"The matter has been brought to the President's attention, but as of this date he has not acted on it."

"This sort of thing must not be tolerated. Such behavior brands us southerners as being little better than barbarians. I will address a personal letter to Monroe this very day. Will you post it when you return to Washington?"

"I'll do better than that. He will receive it from my hand," Gerald said. Samuel reached out and shook William's hand.

At nine-thirty, William and Mary Alice led their guests into the dining room. Anthony entered carrying the platter of fried trout surrounded by scrambled eggs mixed with red and green peppers.

"Uncle Jim, you may serve the coffee now. Anthony, you may be dismissed," William said.

"Will you be staying in Washington City or returning right away to Boston, Samuel?" Mary Alice inquired.

"We will remain in Washington through Sunday. Unitarians have invited me to preach at their church."

"I've read that Christian church leaders in Washington City are not happy about Unitarians forming a church in our nation's capital. They charge that Unitarians reject the trinity and the divinity of our Lord, Jesus Christ. Is there any truth to the charge?" William asked.

Samuel reflected, while wiping his mouth with his napkin. "We believe Jesus is divine but so are all of us. Jesus Christ teaches us how to access the divine within ourselves."

"William, you promised that there would be no discussion of religion at this table," Mary Alice interjected.

"I know what I said," William replied calmly. "Samuel, talk straight when I ask you a question. Do Unitarians reject the trinity?"

"Uncle, we do have religious freedom in this country. We Unitarians believe in the unity of one God. Nowhere in the Bible is there any reference to a trinity. The concept developed at a conference called by the Roman Emperor Constantine three hundred years after the death of Jesus. It passed on a split vote. It may interest you to know Senator John Calhoun of South Carolina and John Quincy Adams are two of the founders of the Washington Unitarian church."

"Calhoun and John Adam's son are Unitarians?"

"They are, as are a number of other distinguished Washingtonians, including Charles Bullfinch, the architect who designed many of our nation's government buildings.

"Your eggs are getting cold, and I insist you finish eating your fish," Mary Alice said.

"Yes William, you don't want Unitarians to give you indigestion," Gerald said with his mouth full.

Betty waited until everyone had finished eating before reaching in her purse and removing a small book.

"Mary Alice, may I have your permission to give this gift to Anthony. He was so courteous and helpful during the trip yesterday. It is a little book of poetry written by a colored woman of Boston."

"A book of poetry?" Mary Alice replied, astonished. "Our people don't read poetry, my dear. I'm sure it would be of no interest to Anthony."

Despite the rebuff, Betty handed Mary Alice the book. "This book was written by a remarkable woman named Phillis Wheatley. She was brought to

Boston from Africa when she was only six, and sold to John Wheatley, a tailor in our city. I believe the year was 1759. Just as you taught Anthony to read and write, the Wheatley family taught Phillis. She was so bright they encouraged her to study geography, history and Latin."

"Latin?" William said, laughing. "Why would they do a fool thing like that?"

"Mr. Bradley, please," Mary Alice pleaded.

"Bill, you know Yankees are peculiar. All that cold weather messes with their judgement," Calvert said.

Deeply hurt by William's remarks, Betty was determined to tell them about the remarkable woman who had become the poet laureate of Boston during the American Revolution. "This book, entitled 'Poems on Various Subjects, Religious and Moral,' was published in London in 1773. During our American Revolution Phillis was introduced to General George Washington," Betty said proudly.

Mary Alice took the book and thumbed through the pages, then handed it back to her. "I'm afraid I can't allow Anthony to have such a book. The only book we allow our people is the Bible." She smiled, feeling satisfied she had put this foolish young woman in her place.

"I would like to hear one of her jingles," William said, amused. "Blacks are good at making rhymes."

Betty thumbed through the pages before placing the book beside her plate. "The poem I shall recite is not in this book. I know it by heart," Betty said, taking a deep breath. "'Should you, my lord, while you pursue my song, wonder from whence my love of freedom sprung, I young in life, by seeming cruel fate was snatched from Africa's fancy'd happy seat: What pangs excruciating must molest, What sorrows labor in my parent's breast? Steeled was the soul and by no misery moved that from a father seized his babe beloved. Such, such was my case. And can I then but pray others may never feel tyrannic sway?'" Betty looked directly at William during the silence that followed.

Samuel reached over and patted her hand. "Thank you, darling," he whispered.

"I will go to my room and finish packing," Betty said, rising and walking proudly from the room. Upon entering the bedroom, she sat on the edge of the bed trying to regain her composure. After completing her packing, she stood by the window looking down into the rose garden. "How can people who profess such love for Jesus be so blind to the truth?" she muttered, while pulling the cord to summon a house servant. Jim entered the room.

"You rang, Madam?"

"Yes, will you be so kind as to take my bags to the carriage."

"May I speak, Madam?" Jim asked. Betty nodded in the affirmative. "I would be more than glad to keep the book for Anthony and give it to him at the proper time."

Betty's eyes lit up. "You will? Are you sure you will not get yourself or Anthony in trouble? I would never forgive myself if anything happened to either of you," she whispered, removing the book from her purse and holding it to her chest.

"Do not worry, madam. I will see to it that nothing happens," Jim whispered reassuringly. "Anthony asked me to give you this gift. He named it Lady Delight." Jim handed her the small hand-carved wooden horse.

She took it and placed it in her traveling bag. "Tell Anthony we love him and will never forget any of you," she said, handing the book to Jim.

Jim turned his back to her, unbuttoned his jacket and placed the thin volume under his vest. As he left the room, Betty closed her eyes and prayed that she had done the right thing.

When Jim arrived at the carriage, Moab helped him secure the luggage on top of it with ropes. Anthony assisted by holding the reins of the horses.

"I's gonna come back here some day," Moab said.

"Why would you ever want to risk your freedom by coming here?" Jim said quietly.

"Got my reasons," Moab said carefully, not knowing how far he should trust Jim.

"Don't let reasons get you killed," Jim whispered. Both remained silent when they saw William and Mary Alice escorting their guests to the carriage.

After the carriage pulled out of the driveway, Anthony overheard William whisper to his wife, "That's one beautiful young lady, but I just can't stand women who butt into the affairs of men." Mary Alice smiled. They were in agreement that these young relatives had been very vexing guests.

Several weeks later, Mary Alice summoned Ruth to the parlor. "Mr. Bradley received a letter today from Senator Calvert. Mr. Bradley would like to speak with you concerning its contents. He is in the library."

"Yes, Miz Mary Alice." Ruth wondered what the letter had to do with her? She found William standing by the window, his hands locked behind his back.

"You want to see me, Master William?"

William motioned for her to close the door. "Ruth, I have received word that the coachman that came here was so smitten with you that he has made an offer through my cousin to buy both you and Anthony. I have replied that you are not for sale. I could never sell you. Mary Alice and I consider you and Anthony a part of our extended family."

"I understand," Ruth replied quietly.

"Ruth, if you want to marry, we have fine men here that would make good husbands. I know Walter Johnson-" Ruth raised her hand and cut him off. Her defiant look did not surprise him.

"I told you long ago I don't want and don't need no man, for reasons you know." Surprised by the tone of her voice, he said nothing more. They stared at each other for a few tense moments, then William waved her away. Ruth did not move immediately, recalling painful memories she had blocked out long ago. She left the room and hurried to the kitchen.

Ruth kept busy the rest of the day, but she kept thinking of Moab. It was ten-thirty that night when Ruth entered her cabin. She found Anthony sitting at the table reading his Bible.

"I got something for you," she said smiling. He knew it was left over from the kitchen. "Here, eat this meat. Master William had two steaks for dinner and he hardly touched the second one. He said it's a T-bone steak. That's a funny name for a piece of meat."

"That's because the bone in the middle is shaped like a 'T', Mama," Anthony said, holding the steak up with his fork.

"Don't forget to say your prayers before you sleep. Remember, praying is talking to the Lord. I talk with him three times a day."

"Does he ever talk back?"

"Now and then, but always in my dreams," Ruth said thoughtfully. "Other times the Lord speaks to me through the words of the Bible."

"You can't read, Mama. So how does the Lord speak to you?"

"Preacher Harris reads words to me. This is how we do it." She took the family Bible and handed it to him. "Turn to that part of the Bible called Zachariah."

Anthony opened the book, thumbed through its pages and handed it to her. Ruth closed her eyes and placed her finger the pages.

"Read what the words say for me."

"Your finger is on verse twelve in chapter nine. It says, 'Turn you to the stronghold, ye prisoners of hope, even today do I declare that I will render double unto thee." Anthony stared at Ruth. "What does it mean to you, Mama?"

Ruth closed her eyes and did not speak for several minutes. Her face glowed when she reached out and held Anthony's hand. "The Lord says he knows we are prisoners. He telling us to keep hope alive, because one bright morning he gonna do double right by us. And I'm gonna keep hoping that my Zach will be coming home one day. That's what I hear in those words, son."

Anthony leaned over and kissed her on both cheeks, then they knelt and prayed silently.

After Ruth blew out the candle and stretched out on her cot, she closed her eyes and began drifting back, back to that dreadful summer of 1814, the year she could never forget.

"Zach" she muttered. Was she dreaming or was her husband standing at the foot of her bed, smiling down at her. Suddenly she found herself being lowered into the well of remembrance.

CHAPTER 7

March 1813 *Remembrance: The War of 1812* -

Ruth stood at the library doorway and watched with pride as four-year-old Anthony trotted over to William and his father, James Oliver Bradley, the eighty-two-year-old patriarch of Bradley Manor. Anthony stood at attention and waited to be acknowledged.

"What you got, boys," William said, motioning for the child to step closer.

"Mails come, sir," Anthony said, handing two letters and a newspaper to William.

"Big George just come from the village with these letters," Ruth said. "The man at the general store says they are very important."

William took the letters, noting that both were from James Madison, President of the United States. He handed one to his father.

"Why the hell is Madison writing us?" James Oliver said, tossing his letter into the fireplace.

William opened his letter. "We've been invited to a meeting with members of his cabinet. It seems the British are getting the upper hand in this war that Congress started," William said, patting Anthony's head. "Thank you, Anthony. Go with your mother now."

James Oliver waited until Ruth closed the door. "I knew it. None of those damn fools at the Capitol would listen to me. Now there will be hell to pay, mark my words."

"Papa, don't upset yourself. I will go represent us. You must not put any strain on your heart. You know what your doctor told you after your last heart attack."

"Strain my ass. I'm going and I won't take any back talk from you. This may be my last chance to tell those idiots what I think of them. Have Jim prepare the carriage," James Oliver shouted.

William knew it was useless to argue when his father's temper was up. As a Federalist, James Oliver had decried the war effort from the start and had stated publicly that Madison was a damn fool for allowing the country to be dragged into a war with England. William called for Uncle Jim and instructed him to prepare for a three-day trip. James Oliver insisted that his slave son be their driver.

William opened the Washington newspaper, *The Intelligencer*, and read a feature article on the outcome of the Battle of Leipzig. It reported that the English had introduced a new weapon into the battle, the Congreve Rocket.

It alarmed him when he read that Napoleon's army had been defeated, and the dictator was now in exile on the island of Elba. If France was no longer at war with England, it would have serious implications for America's war effort. He read aloud that war hawks in the English Parliament were charging that the United States had stabbed England in the back while she was fighting France, and all were clamoring for revenge. Units of the Duke of Wellington's army were reported being prepared to set sail for America. William suddenly realized why Madison wanted to meet with them.

The next morning, William, James Oliver, and Jim began the twenty-mile trip to Washington City. While Jim drove, William was forced to listen to James Oliver's ranting over how the country had gotten into war with England.

"Those god-damn war hawks in Congress were convinced that, with England and all of Europe bogged down in a war with France, they could take over Canada and expand our western boundaries. They used the raids by the England navy on our shipping as their excuse, ignoring the fact that France had been guilty of the same thing. Madison calls himself a Quaker and a man of peace. He did not have the backbone to stand up to those idiots. He caved in to their demands, and I'm going to give all of them a piece of my mind."

On March 24, 1813, a grim-faced James Madison and members of his cabinet met with a select group of congressional leaders, businessmen and influential planters. The room grew quiet as Madison reviewed the situation.

"Gentlemen, I regret to inform you that our armed forces have suffered setbacks at the Canadian border. Detroit has fallen to the British, and the Chesapeake Bay has been blockaded by the British fleet," Madison said in a low monotone. "Our ships have won several naval battles, however. For now, there is little we can do to relieve the situation in Maryland. Exports have dropped from five million dollars in 1811, to under a million this year. All trade out of the port of Baltimore has come to a halt. In the western territories, the Indian tribes, under the leadership of Chief Tecumseh, have allied themselves with the English and are engaged in hit and run battles."

Brigadier General William Winder of Baltimore approached the podium and handed a letter to Madison. Madison paled as he read it.

"Gentlemen, I have just received the latest dispatches. The British Rear Admiral George Cockburn and General Robert Ross have landed troops on Maryland soil."

Men sprang to their feet with angry shouts and calls for action. James Oliver rose from his chair, and pointed his cane directly at Madison. "I warned you we should never have gotten into this war. You allowed those fools in Congress to drag us into this mess. Before this war is over, we will all regret it. That sniveling coward, William Hull, gave up Detroit without a shot being fired, and Buffalo has been burned to the ground. What you need to do is put those idiots Henry Clay and John Calhoun on the front line." As his words ricocheted throughout the room, James Oliver pounded his cane into the floor, turned and limped out of the room.

William considered leaving, but decided to stay despite his concerns for his father's health. He feared there was more news that could have serious consequences for Bradley Manor. With Jim waiting outside, he felt certain his father was in good hands.

Madison raised his hand and called for order as the room grew quiet. "Gentlemen, this is not the time to place blame. I have asked Brigadier General William Winder to speak about our plans to break the blockade and defeat the British."

A man seated next to William whispered, "Winder's not the man for the job. The only reason Madison appointed him is because his father is governor of Maryland."

An ashen-faced Winder approached the podium. "The latest dispatches are grave. British marines have sacked and burned the town of Havre de Grace. They are encouraging our slaves to revolt and join them."

Pandemonium broke loose as men rose to their feet and shouted at Madison, demanding to know what action would be taken to protect their property.

When Madison returned to the podium someone in the rear of the room shouted, "Is it true that swagger Cockburn sent a message to your wife, Dolly, that he will be making his bows in this house soon?"

"Gentlemen, we must remain calm. With your help we will make him eat his words," Madison replied, appealing to their patriotism. "General Winder will share with you our plans for the defense of the city."

Winder held his hand up for order. "Our first priority is to strengthen the defenses of Washington City, Georgetown and Alexandria. We need all the skilled brick layers, carpenters and laborers we can get to strengthen Fort Washington."

William stood and shouted, "Several of my people have skills, both as brick layers and carpenters. I will make them available."

Winder pointed to William. "That's the kind of spirit we need." Soon others grudgingly joined in with pledges of support.

"What are we going to do if we are away fighting and our slaves begin a rebellion right here in the streets of Washington City? There are also several thousand free blacks living among us. They could stab us in our backs," a cabinet member yelled.

Parker Elison, a local banker, stood up and shouted, "Let me speak on the question of free colored people, as I know their leaders. I have no fear of a revolt among them. If we ask for their help, I am confident they will be more than glad to join us in preparing the defenses of this city. I am more concerned about the defective classes of poor whites whose vice and crime has almost been the ruination of this fair city. If there is no force to preserve law and order, I fear they could be among the first to run amok in our streets."

Winder replied, "I think it highly unlikely that our folks, whites or black, would turn against us in our hour of peril. However, I will instruct my officers to form a volunteer home defense corp. These folks will be charged with defending the city if it is needed. Every man between the ages of eighteen and fifty-five will be subject to service, be he rich or poor."

"What about volunteers to fight if the British attack Washington," William shouted.

"We will need to expand and train the district's militia. This is where you men can help. Earthworks must be constructed for our heavy guns at Greenleaf's Point and at the Navy Yard. Here are sign-up sheets for those who wish to volunteer." As Winder concluded his remarks, he was relieved that those present seemed satisfied with his defense plans. William was the first to sign as a volunteer.

On the lawn of the presidential building, Jim waited beside the carriage. This was his third visit to Washington City and on each visit he marveled at its impressive buildings. He took a short walk down Pennsylvania Avenue, but suddenly felt uneasy and hurried back to his post. Just as he arrived, he saw James Oliver walking laboriously down the driveway.

"Ah, there you are, Jim. Get me out of this infernal heat and back to the hotel. I'm not feeling well."

Jim opened the carriage door and assisted James Oliver. He noticed that the old man's hands felt clammy and cold to the touch. After placing a thin blanket over his lap, he drove two blocks to the Capital City Hotel. When they entered the lobby, James Oliver demanded he be taken to the lounge where he ordered a double whiskey. Ten minutes later Jim called for a porter to help him carry James Oliver to his room. After helping him undress, Jim lifted him into bed. James Oliver motioned Jim to come closer.

"Go get your brother," James Oliver said, his speech slurred. "Tell him to come now. Be quick about it."

Jim stared at James Oliver and for seconds was speechless. It was the first time James Oliver had acknowledged his relationship as a member of the Bradley family. What could it mean?

Jim's heart beat rapidly as he rushed to the carriage and drove back to the presidential building. When he reached the entrance, the guard told him the meeting was still in session and no one could enter. Jim requested that a message be sent to William. The guard took it and ordered him outside. Feeling helpless, Jim made his way to the hitching post where other black coachmen were resting in the shade of a willow tree. Jim nodded and sat beside them.

"I'm Willie," said a tall bearded black man. After shaking hands with Jim, he offered him some chewing tobacco. Jim politely refused.

"White folks in there talking about them Brits being in Maryland. Never thought I see white folk be as scared as they is now. They say some of our folks on the Eastern Shore done join up with the Brits," Willie whispered, cupping his hand over his mouth.

"Do you think there's any truth to it?" Jim asked.

"Some of them folks they brung here from Africa sho' might, but I 'spect most won't. This much for sure, us free niggers ain't going nowhere. We staying put," Willie replied. "I'm a free man today because my pappy fought with George Washington in the revolution."

"Are you all free?" Jim asked the other two men seated next to him.

"Sure, we free. Ain't you?"

Jim looked down and did not respond. The men observed him closely, noting his olive complexion and the quality of his dress. They knew he was no common field slave.

"You be one of those high yella house niggers, ain't ya?" Jellie said, which set off a howl of laughter.

Jim stood up. "I will take leave of you."

"Now ain't that something. This nigger's ah' slave, sitting here talking all proper, like white folks," Jellie said sarcastically. "You best take your yella ass away back to the plantation."

Jim showed no emotion and remained calm as he walked away. He had grown accustomed to racial insults from whites and field blacks. Upon arriving at the entrance of the building, he was relieved to learn that the meeting had adjourned. He saw William, accompanied by General Winder, making their way through the crowd. Jim rushed to meet them.

"Master James is not well. I took him back to the hotel and put him in bed. He insists that you come at once."

The urgent tone in his voice alarmed William. "General Winder, this is my servant, Jim. I fear I must leave at once and go to my father. I will accept the commission to serve as captain with the district militia. You understand, of course, I must return home to set my affairs in order. Expect me to report to your headquarters with my men within two or three days." After shaking Winder's hand, William slapped Jim's back. "Let's go."

Although they were only a short distance from the hotel, the carriage almost collided with a wagon as it made a sharp turn onto Pennsylvania Avenue. When the carriage pulled up in front of the hotel, William jumped out and ran upstairs to their room. When he saw the old man's face, he knew something was terribly wrong. James Oliver was awake, but his face was drawn to one side, and he could not speak. William rushed to the lobby, shouting orders to the clerk to find a doctor. When he returned, Jim was applying cold towels to James Oliver's forehead. The old man tried to speak but made only garbled sounds.

"Papa, everything is going to be all right. Don't try to talk, you'll only make yourself worse. Listen to me. I have received a commission to serve as captain to the district militia. I won't let the British destroy this city, or your life's work. They will never set foot on our property. Do you hear me?" he asked.

James Oliver blinked his eyes in appreciation. He made a feeble attempt to point to Jim with his left hand, but was too weak to raise it more than a few inches. The words he desperately wanted to say were locked in his damaged brain. William nodded to his father that he understood. "Don't try to speak, father."

James Oliver opened his mouth but made only garbled sounds as pools of saliva dribbled into the stubble of his unshaven face. As the brothers watched, James Oliver Bradley suffered another seizure. He took his last breath just before the physician arrived.

William had known since he was twelve that Jim was his half brother. He felt certain that his father intended to communicate that he wanted to free Jim, but the words were never spoken.

When Jim stared into the swollen eyes of his half brother, his heart sank. He saw only the cold blue eyes of the new master of Bradley Manor.

On the return trip, Jim and William sat beside each other on the driver's seat, with the body of their father wrapped in sheets inside the carriage. Each felt the physical closeness of the other, but knew they would remain worlds apart.

"Jim, I'm not sure how long I will be away. I'm placing the welfare of Bradley Manor in your care. When I return, you will serve as my personal valet as you so faithfully served my father. I will take five of the boys back with me to help with the defenses."

"Yes, *master,*" Jim replied softly, keeping his eyes on the rutted road.

"With the British fleet blocking the bay, we will not get paid for the tobacco we delivered to the warehouse in Alexandria. If we don't get the money for that crop, this will be a long hard winter."

Jim half listened as William spoke. His thoughts were on that final scene at the Capital City Hotel. He knew their father was trying to communicate an important message. It was now clear that the old man had taken it with him to his grave.

On a cool spring evening, the carriage approached Bradley Manor. The day turned out to be a fitting tribute to the elder Bradley. As the carriage passed through the peach orchard that the old man had personally planted, it was in full bloom. The pink flowers and light green leaves spoke of rebirth as the old passed away.

William placed his father in the family burial plot next to his beloved wife, Jane. His mother had died giving birth to him in 1765. As he remained at the gravesite, William reflected on his father's life. James Oliver had been so heartbroken over Jane's death, he never took another wife. William knew his father loved him, but for years he never understood why he always turned away when he cried as a child. It was his Aunt Roberta who later explained that his tears always brought back memories of the final hours of Jane's agony. Five years later, James Oliver had found solace in the arms of an attractive slave girl named Barbara Hill. When Barbara became pregnant and bore him a son in 1769, she named him after his father. James Oliver grew fond of his slave son, and instructed his daughter, Roberta, to teach him to read and write. As Jim grew into young manhood, James made his son his personal valet and bookkeeper.

William waited until after the burial to break the news of his commission to Mary Alice and Roberta. When Mary Alice was told, she became hysterical and it took him hours to calm her down.

"Why can't you stay here and protect us?" she pleaded.

"It's a matter of honor, my dear. We must protect our home and our nation's capital," he said, hugging and kissing her.

Roberta placed her hand on Mary Alice's shoulder. "She'll be all right. Do what you must do, brother," Roberta said proudly.

William instructed Big George to bring Zachariah Bowen, Hardy Jones, Daniel Bradley and Amos Johnson to the parlor. When the five men arrived, to their surprise he poured each of them a shot of whiskey.

"As my father's most loyal workers I give each of you a shot of his whiskey." As the men drank the toast, several coughed. The strongest drink they were permitted was beer on special occasions. They smiled at their good fortune.

"Boys, our country is at war, and there is the chance it may be coming close to Washington City. I have chosen the five of you to leave with me in the morning," William said, watching their smiles vanish. "You will be assigned to help build earthworks for gun emplacements for our troops. I am now a Captain in the District Militia. I expect the best report from all of you. If you do a good job, each of you will be rewarded when we return."

Zachariah raised his hand. "Master, you think them Brits be coming near here? What we gonna do to protect our wives and chillen if they do?"

"I don't intend for them to get anywhere near here, Zach. Now you boys go to your cabins and say your goodbyes to your families. We may be gone for quite a spell."

Zachariah ran to the kitchen, only to find Sarah alone washing pots. "Where Ruth?" he asked.

"She be sitting on the front porch with Miss Mary Alice and Miss Roberta. What you want her for?"

Zachariah turned and ran out the kitchen door and sprinted around the house to the veranda where he found the three women knitting and chatting. Anthony and Abner played happily together on the front lawn. Four-year-old Abner was the youngest of the Bradley children.

Zachariah took off his hat and bowed. "Excuse me, Miz Mary Alice. May I speak to Ruth?" When she smiled and nodded, he took Ruth to the shade of a willow tree.

"Master Bradley say I gotta go with him first thing in the morning."

"Where are you going?" Ruth asked.

"There be a war going on, and we gotta help the white folk. That's all I know."

"Zach, you think that war gonna come anywhere near here?" Ruth said, gripping his hand.

"Now don't you go worrying none. We gonna help Master William send them Brits back where they come from. Anybody come messing around here, I'll kill em' with my bare hands, be they white or black. Don't be going sad on me. I needs to see yo' face happy."

"How can I be happy if you going away?" Ruth said, resting her head on his shoulder.

"Let's you and me go to the cabin and say our good byes the way I likes best."

Ruth smiled and gave him a gentle slap on his cheek. "We got time for that tonight. You best go now and get what you need for that journey, come tomorrow."

Zachariah stood, pulled her to her feet and kissed her. Mary Alice and Roberta smiled as they watched from the porch. As he left, Ruth felt a chill come over her. "There be an evil spell in the air and I don't like it," she whispered.

At eight o'clock, William added several logs to the fireplace in the parlor. Mary Alice went to the hall and called to the children, "Louise, Henry, bring Abner to the parlor. It's time for our family altar." William read several passages from the Bible, then said, "Children, while I am gone, I want you to pray for victory."

"Papa, how long will you be away?" thirteen-year-old Henry asked.

"Not long I hope. You will be the man of the house while I'm gone. Take good care of your mother and don't tease your sister."

"I promise, sir," Henry said dejectedly. "But I sure wish you wouldn't take Zachariah. He's my best friend."

Mary Alice rang for the twelve-year-old servant, Cathy Johnson, to serve tea and cookies. Neither parent noticed when Henry playfully pulled the bow on her apron.

In the dim light from the cabin fireplace, Ruth rested contentedly as Zachariah played with Anthony on the cabin floor.

"Make shadows on the wall, papa," Anthony said, holding up his hands. Zachariah moved the table and two stools over to the door and placed the candle on the table. Clasping his hands together, he cast a shadow on the wall.

"Who that?" Zachariah asked, forming a shadow that seemed to open and shut its mouth.

"That's Wishbone, our dog," Anthony shouted, clapping his hands. "Make me another one."

"I gonna make one more then you gotta get to bed," he said, shaping his hands to form the shadow of an animal. "What you see?"

"That's a bear," Anthony said, clapping. After saying his prayers, Anthony kissed Zachariah and Ruth then climbed onto his cot. Ruth sat beside him, humming tunes.

In the soft glow of the fireplace's last dying embers, Zachariah whispered, "I sure wish he would go to sleep. Just look at those bright eyes, all wide awake. When I gets to loving you, woman, that's when he starts calling us."

"That's cause you so noisy" Ruth whispered.

"Can't help it. You do that to me."

"I love you, Zach. I remember that day Master Bradley brought you here just like it was yesterday. I say to myself 'that sure is one fine man,' but I never dream Master William would let you marry me."

"And the first time I seen you looking out that kitchen window, I say to myself, 'Who that fine looking gal?' The next thing I knowed, Master William say he gonna give me one of his gals if I do my work real good. I tells him I had my eyes on you."

"Don't know why I waited this long to ask you. Didn't your pappy have a last name?"

"Well, my pappy comes from Africa. His name was N'kula. His Massa named him Paul. He say the white folks call him what they want, but he always be N'kula. When we got married, I took your last name but in my heart, my real name's N'kula," he whispered proudly, pulling Ruth into his arms.

"I think Anthony's asleep. He just closed his eyes," she whispered.

"I sho' am glad, 'cause I can't wait much longer," he whispered.

Ruth covered Anthony with a sheet, walked over to the table and combed her hair. She watched the quivering embers from the fireplace with mixed emotions, knowing this could be their last night together. After removing her gown, she stood before him, knowing the pleasure he derived from the sight of flickering candlelight on her shapely body.

Zachariah swept her into his arms and carried her to their bed. She tried to remain quiet when he kissed her breast.

"Ruth, you the sweetest rose God put on this earth," he whispered. He did not resist when she pressed him on his back and straddled him. He moaned as jolts of pleasure rippled through his loins. Shortly thereafter, Anthony sat up and rubbed his eyes.

"Mama, I'm scared. I hear a bear growling in here."

CHAPTER 8

August 1814 *Remembrance: The Burning of Washington*

Ruth put on her work gloves, walked to the garden and began digging up sweet potatoes for the evening meal. She paused when she heard what sounded like distant thunder. Placing her hand over her brow, she searched the sky but found not a single cloud. Just as she put her foot on the shovel, the thunder sounded a second time, but with a continuous roar. Her heart beat rapidly as she placed the potatoes into a bucket and hurried toward the Manor kitchen. Upon approaching the house, Mary Alice called to her from the second story bedroom window. "What's that noise?"

"Miz Mary Alice, you hear that thunder too?" Ruth shouted. "Ain't any clouds in the sky."

Mary Alice reflected for a moment. "I fear that is not thunder, Ruth. Those are guns we hear. Our dear men are fighting the British. Call all the servants into the living room for prayer."

After all had assembled, Ruth only half listened to the prayer Mary Alice delivered, calling on God to grant their men victory over the evil English King that wanted to re-enslave America. She rocked Anthony on her lap and said a silent prayer for Zachariah's safe return. They had never been separated during their five years of marriage. Ruth could not imagine life without him. After the prayer service, everyone returned to their work stations. Ruth took Anthony's hand and led him to the back porch where she listened for the strange thunder. The only sounds were those of crows making their yawing calls in the nearby oak tree. She took Anthony to Sarah's cabin where Cathy was caring for several children. After returning and serving the evening meal, she followed Mary Alice and Roberta to the parlor.

"Can I bring you anything before I go to my cabin?" Ruth asked.

"No. Just ask the field hands to pray for victory," Mary Alice said.

Ruth closed the door and returned to Sarah's house to fetch Anthony. She found him sleeping on the cow hide rug that covered the pine floor of the two-room bungalow. Cathy was sleeping in a chair beside him.

"Little Anthony tried to wait for you, but he just tuckered himself out playing with my boys. He sho' miss his papa. When you think they be coming home?" Sarah said, handing Ruth a slice of apple pie.

"I wish I knew. That was sure some evil sound I heard this afternoon. I don't know why white folks got to go killing each other. They suppose to be

Christians, or so I've been told. All they talk about is loving one another, but don't seen to mean a thing when wars come."

"I don't mess my head up thinking about it."

"Well, I think about it all the time. The good Lord gave us brains to think with, didn't he? I use mine, girl. Some time I pray my son gonna be a free man some day," Ruth said, gently picking Anthony up.

"You scare me, talking like that. One of these days somebody gonna hear you."

"Ain't nothing to be scared about if you take it to the Lord in prayer. See you in the morning."

Ruth sat up in bed and listened to the faint sound of voices outside her cabin window. She pushed her curtain aside, looking into the faint dawn light. She could just make out two dark figures walking toward her cabin. Who could be coming so early in the morning? Not daring to hope, she ran to the door and opened it. Ruth placed her hand over her mouth when Zachariah entered and swept her into his arms. Unable to restrain her tears, she sobbed as she hugged and kissed him.

"Don't cry, sugar," Zachariah said squeezing her tightly. "Let Anthony sleep."

"I just knew you would be coming back home to us," Ruth whispered between breathless kisses. "I prayed night and day that the Lord would keep you safe."

"Big George and me just come back, but there be a heap of trouble in Washington City. Them Brits done burned the whole city down. Master Bradley almost got killed, but we saved him. He sent us here to protect ya'll."

Ruth stared at Zachariah, not fully understanding what she had just heard. "What you telling me?" She watched as Zachariah dragged himself to their bed and stretched out on his back, staring at the roof of the cabin.

"Lord, I's so weary," Zachariah said.

"You wanna tell me about it in the morning?"

"Gotta tell it now, Ruth," Zachariah said, pulling himself up on one elbow. "Master Bradley and us reached Washington City day before yesterday. We went to a place he call the War Department. This soldier who called himself General Winder come out to meet us. Master Bradley tell us to do what the white soldiers tell us. They took us to a place where lots of white men with guns were marching. They put us to work digging trenches. Next day we see Master Bradley giving orders to them soldiers. Then we hear them say Brit soldiers was headed toward Washington City. The white boys say they gonna whip their butts and send them back where they come from. But they looked scared when word come that them Brits was only five miles down the road."

"Were you scared?" Ruth asked.

"To tell you the truth, I was. But every time I think about you, it left me. I hear Master Bradley say that we got the high ground at a place called Bladensburg. We was working side by side with white folks, building them earthworks. Massa Bradley comes and gets me. He say he wants me to do his cleaning. This what Master Bradley say happening during all that fighting and I seen part of it:"

General Winder and his officers prepared for the attack in a scene of utter confusion. Scattered units of cavalry and various companies of troops arrived near the village of Bladensburg throughout the day. President Madison and members of his cabinet rode out to Winder's field headquarters in the hope word of his presence would inspire the troops.

Zachariah was shining William's boots when General Winder began screaming at his officers, "How can I command when I have all these damn self-constituted contributors of advice. These damn politicians should know there is no such thing as a democracy of commanders."

William attempted to calm his commander, "General Winder, what's the problem?"

"Look at that fool Washington lawyer, Francis Scott Key. He's issuing orders to my officers where to post their troops. Get him out of here before I have him arrested and shot."

"Calm down, let me handle this," William said. He ordered all civilians to leave the area.

As troops took their places behind the earthworks, Big George saw William at a distance but failed to get his attention. He approached one of the officers. "Massa sir, Amos, Zach and me belongs to Captain William. He the one who taught us to shoot squirrel guns real good. Any way we can join in and help ya'll fight them Brits?"

The officer stared at Big George then laughed. "Nigger, this is a white man's war. When the shooting starts, you best get your black butt out of the way before it gets shot off."

Big George nodded, picked up his shovel and continued working on the entrenchment. He wondered what had happened to Hardy and Daniel. They worked side by side the first day, but that night both men disappeared. Maybe the white boss took them to another site.

"I hear folks saying that during the war for freedom, President Washington was glad to have black folks fighting for him," Big George said, pausing to stretch his back. "They done so good the government set they free after the war."

"White folks here in Maryland ain't 'bout to free us niggers. So you can forget that," Amos said, as he angrily drove his pick into the hard earth.

"Well, if things get bad enough, maybe they change they mind," Zachariah said.

A white officer approached and ordered them to the rest area set aside for blacks. After working for twelve hours without food, they gathered their tools and hurried past newly arriving troops. Zachariah took the horses to a trough. Two black men came over and sat beside him. One was holding a small poster.

"What that paper say?" Zachariah asked, inquisitively.

"It say that people of color who free ain't as free as white folk, that's what it says."

"Read him what it say, Jesse," the second man said.

"This here paper was printed by the Baltimore Committee on Vigilance and Safety."

"If it come from Baltimore, how you get it?" Zachariah asked.

"I live in Baltimore. I come here to visit my sister and got picked up and sent out here. I'm a free man and I reads."

"Well, read what it say."

"It reads here in this first part, 'Resolved, That all free people of color are hereby ORDERED to attend daily, commencing with Wednesday morning, the Tenth, at the different works erecting about the city for the purpose of laboring therein, and for which they shall receive an allowance of fifty cents per day together with a soldier's rations."

The man's companion looked at Zachariah without smiling. "That's what it say we colored folks gotta do, and we ain't got no choice in the matter."

"What it say about the white folk?"

He put the paper close to his face again, and read, "Resolved, That our fellow citizens who are exempt from military duty, are hereby earnestly invited to labor on the fortifications, either in person or by substitute, and in the latter case, to furnish the substitutes with notes to the superintendents, requesting them to certify therein that the bearer had performed this duty."

"What they mean by substitute?"

The two men laughed. "It means if you white and rich and you can pay some fool to get his ass shot off in you place. Now white folks scared of us free niggers. We hear white folk talking about slaves running off to join up with them Redcoats. They say the Brits take our folks to one of those islands in the bay and they training them to fight. White folks here in Washington and Baltimore are scared we free people will join them too, so they makes all of us work on them fortifications. That way they can keep an eye on us. That's what it's all about."

White folk tells us that the Brits just using us. They say all they gonna do is take colored folks to the islands and sell them after the war's over. They say that just to scare us."

Zachariah shook his head. It never dawned on him that whites would fear blacks. He decided it was best not to think about it too hard because it could mess up his head.

Zachariah was suddenly aware of Ruth's hand on his cheek. He had closed his eyes and drifted into a troubled sleep. Ruth kissed his cheek and placed a thin cover over him. She sat looking down at him until the first rays of sunlight lit her cabin. There was a soft knock at the door. When she opened it, Ruth smiled at Big George who looked anxiously beyond her.

"Wake yo' man up, Ruth," Big George said. "We got lots of work to do."

"Well, you may have lots to do, but my man's gonna have some breakfast, so come on in and sit yourself down," Ruth said, pointing to a chair. She went to the fireplace and placed sticks on a pile of straw. "Zachariah started telling me what happened, but he fell asleep. Now it's your turn, and don't wake him until my eggs and grits are on your plate."

Big George knew it was useless to argue with her. Besides, he wanted some good home cooking. "Well, us black folk were watching from a hillside when the fighting started. We was sitting in the shade when them guns start shooting. That's when we hear a whistling sound and see a trail of smoke coming near us. When it hit the ground, it went 'boom.' Not long after that, white boys started running like they seen the devil. This white General come riding up and yelled, 'Turn back you cowards, the battle is not lost.' This white fellow yelled back, 'The hell it ain't.' He made tracks of dust across the field like a scared rabbit. We jumped up and ran with them all the way back to Washington City. White folks was running each which way, trying to get out of town, 'cause they know them Brit's be coming."

"What happened to Master Bradley," Ruth whispered, her hands shaking as she broke eggs in a bowl.

"Zach, Amos and me saved his life," Big George said quietly. We learned what happened later.

When the British guns opened fire, William's corps held its position on the right flank of the battle formation. He rode his horse along the battle line, repeatedly exposing himself to hostile fire. His troops, inspired by his courage, continued to fight valiantly. When the center and left flank of the American line began crumbling, William's officers realized the situation was growing hopeless. William sent his aide, Robert Lewis, back to Winder's headquarters for instructions. By the time Lewis reached the camp, Winder and his senior officers had already fled. Realizing the battle was lost, he turned his horse and made his way back through the mob of retreating men running in the opposite direction. He rode within twenty feet of William, when both men heard screaming sounds that engulfing the area. To William's horror, Lewis' head exploded like a pumpkin dropped from the loft of a barn. Brain tissue splattered William's face and onto his uniform. He dismounted, dropped to his knees and lifted the decapitated body of his young officer into his arms. When he saw only the back of the skull attached to the body he crawled around searching for the missing parts. Another officer placed his hand on William shoulder.

"Take cover, sir. He's dead."

In a blind rage, William drew his saber and mounted his horse. When he attempted to ride toward the charging British troops, two of his officers restrained him.

"Captain Bradley, control yourself. We need you to help us defend Washington City. It must be saved."

The burst of a shell brought William to his senses. He turned his horse and led his troops to the last escape route open to them. Stunned and dazed, William rode into the city and found himself in the chaotic streets where men and women were running in all directions. As the magnitude of the defeat dawned on him, he pressed his spurs into the sides of his horse and rode until the presidential house came into view. He appeared to be dazed as he sat motionless in his saddle. The trance was broken when he heard his name being called.

"Massa Bradley, Massa Bradley, we over here." Turning his horse, William was overcome with relief to see Big George, Zachariah and Amos standing on a porch. The sign above them read, 'Rhodes Tavern.' They ran to greet him.

"Massa Bradley, we sho' glad you safe. All the folk in this town done gone crazy, they so scared," Big George shouted over the congestion of screaming women, shouting men and the roar of wagons.

"What them Brits gonna do if they catch us?" Amos asked, shaking uncontrollably.

"Master Bradley, you gotta gets us back home. Get us some guns and we'll stop them Brits fo' they come and burns us out," Zachariah shouted.

Before William could respond, he heard glass breaking. Out of the tavern door came six shabbily dressed white men carried cases of wine, whiskey, furniture and the tavern's small safe to their wagon.

"What the hell do you think you are doing," William screamed at the looters.

"Hell, the Brits just down the road. We ain't leaving nothing for them." Without thinking, William pulled out his sidearm and shot one of the looters in the leg. Several men dropped their loot and ran. One managed to get behind William's horse.

"Watch out, Massa," Big George yelled. The vagrant struck the back of William's head with a club. He fell from his horse into the dusty street. Big George snatched the club just as the looter raised it to strike him again.

The man screamed, "Nigger, get yo' black ass out of here." Big George stood his ground, positioning himself over William's unconscious body. The man took one look at Big George's determined face, cursed, then grabbed the reins of William's horse. Big George made no attempt to stop him as he climbed on the horse and made his escape. Zachariah and Amos could not believe what they just witnessed. Big George had evoked fear in a white man.

Big George and Zachariah picked William up, carried him into the tavern and placed him on the carpet.

"Massa, Massa, is you all right," Big George said.

William opened his eyes and shook his head. He saw two images of everything. "Who are you?" he muttered.

Zachariah and Big George stared at each other. "He don't know us. He hurt in his head real bad," Big George said anxiously.

"We best not move him for a spell," Amos replied. "We take care of you, Massa." Sensing they were at risk, Amos walked to a corner of the room and opened a door leading into the basement of the tavern. "I think we best take Massa Bradley down in this cellar 'til he feels better."

They lifted William and carried him down the dark stairs, finding themselves in a large area filled with barrels of wine and whiskey. Big George opened a small storage room and placed William on the floor. Amos searched the cellar and returned with five empty feed sacks and two bottles of wine. "This has to do fo' our dinner," he said grinning. He arranged the sacks on the floor and placed William on them, using one to make a pillow for his head. Satisfied that William was comfortable, they broke the top of the bottles and drank the wine, then slept for several hours while Zachariah stood guard. He woke them when it was dark.

"You think we can get out of here now that it's night," Zachariah whispered. Big George felt William's face and head.

76

"Don't think so. Massa still sleeping. He got a lump on his head the size of a egg. Ya'll stay with him while I go outside to see what's happening." Big George carefully opened the storage door, but stopped when he heard heavy footsteps above him. "Lot's of folk up there," he whispered.

They heard the cellar door open and footsteps coming down the stairs, followed by laughter.

"Gentlemen, what have we here?" The voice spoke in a odd accent.

"Ah, wine to celebrate our glorious victory. Compliments of the American government, no doubt," a second voice chimed in.

William opened his eyes and uttered a soft groan. Big George clamped his hand over William's mouth and whispered. "Massa, don't move. Them Brit soldiers right outside that door."

In the confusion, William tried to remove the powerful hand from his mouth, but Big George's grip was unyielding, leaving him with no choice but to relax and remain quiet.

They remained in the little storage area for what seemed like eternity, as the sound of footsteps up and down the stairway continued. When it became quiet, Zachariah peeped out the door. The wine cellar had been emptied of its wine bottles and barrels. The sound of raucous laughter could be heard from above. He turned and whispered, "I think them soldiers getting themselves drunk. They took all them kegs of wine upstairs and they having themselves one big party."

William stirred and tried to sit up. "Massa, how you feeling?" Big George asked.

"Is that you, Big George?"

"Thank the Lord. It's us, Massa Bradley. Zach, Amos and me here with you," Big George whispered.

Groping in the dark, William said, "Where are we?"

"We hiding down in this cellar of this drinking place. Them Brits upstairs in this very building, Massa. They come down and took all the barrels of wine and from the way they carrying on, they must all be drunk," Amos said.

"We ain't seen Hardy or Daniel after the shooting started," Big George said.

William tried to stand up, but had to be assisted by Big George. Groping in the dark, he slowly opened the door. All he heard was the sound of thunder and rain. The cellar was lit by a strange red glow coming from the two narrow windows. He made his way to the windows that were too high to see out. The flickering glow provided enough light in the cellar for him to find a small stepladder. Placing it against the wall, he stepped up and peered out into the night. To his horror, the Presidential Building, a block away, was a raging inferno and its flames turned the night sky blood red. William closed his eyes and sank back into the arms of Big George. Zachariah stood on the ladder. "Lord, they burning down the whole city."

Big George managed to get the cellar window open. The four crawled out and made their escape in the blinding rainstorm. William realized later that, had it not been for the heavy rains, the sparks from the burning government buildings could have ignited thousands of frame houses.

Moving from building to building, they made their way undetected through clusters of British troops. After crossing the District line they finally connected with other refugees.

"Captain Bradley, am I glad to see you," The friendly face was a welcome sight to William. It was Sergeant John Boggs, a man from his unit. The two men saluted, then Boggs took them to a shed which gave them some shelter from the rain.

"Has General Winder made any effort to regroup our forces?" William asked.

"I'm afraid we don't have much of an army left, sir. Reinforcements are on the way, but most of our men are putting as much distance as they can between themselves and the British."

William felt depressed as he stood up and looked at the clogged road with its miserable horde of displaced people. A wagon, driven by a white-haired man, pulled up beside the open shed. He stared at William and Boggs for several moments.

"Well, well, you fellows call yourselves soldiers. I seen it all. When you fellows rode past my house it looked like everybody was off to the races. Then come the boys on foot, running like a bunch of scared rabbits. I got a good name for the bunch of ya'. 'The Bladensburg Races'," he shouted, laughing hysterically. After shaking his fist, he steered his wagon back onto the crowded road.

Big George whispered, "Massa Bradley, don't you mind the likes of him. See if you can get us some horses so we can get back to Bradley Manor before them Brits gets there."

William stared at Big George with admiration. It dawned on him that here was a man of raw courage in the face of adversity. As master of Bradley Manor, he had to overcome his feeling of defeat and depression, for he could not afford to show his people any sign of weakness.

Sergeant Boggs led William and Big George to the makeshift headquarters of General Winder. As the men entered the tent, Winder rose to his feet.

"Well, I'll be damned. They told me you were dead or captured. Am I glad to see you. If there ever was a hero in that battle, it was you."

The compliment did little to relieve William's humiliation. "You saw what they did to our Capital?" William asked sadly.

"Couldn't help it. The fires lit up the whole area for miles around. I do have some good news, however. My sources tell me the British have left the city and are returning to their ships. I want you to return with General Walter Smith and restore order," Winder replied apologetically.

"Do we have any army to return with?"

"Several hundred officers and men have just arrived, and more are due tomorrow. Other forces from the northern states are heading for the defense of Baltimore. I will be leaving tonight and will be reporting to General Samuel Smith. He has been placed in command of all military forces in the city. It is my wish to face General Ross in one final battle," Winder said bitterly. William realized the magnitude of Winder's defeat was not fully apparent to him. Remembering the disorder and the lack of coordination before the battle, William was relieved that Winder would not command the forces defending Baltimore.

"You can count on me, General," he said reluctantly. As much as William wanted to go to Baltimore, he felt he had no other choice but to return to Washington City and maintain order.

After securing horses for Big George and Zachariah, he instructed them to return to Bradley Manor and begin preparations for what little harvest there would be as a result of the drought. Amos would remain to attend to his personal needs. Both men were given letters to insure safe passage.

"Massa, don't you be worrying about home. We do our best to save the crops and keep it safe fo' us all, "Big George said. William stood beside the road in the blowing wind and watched his men ride away. For the first time he saw them, not as his personal property, but fellow human beings fighting for the survival of the nation.

CHAPTER 9

Fall and Winter 1814-15 *Remembrance: The Aftermath*

William received a communique from General Scott, ordering him to bring his brigade to Baltimore immediately. British forces, under the command of General Ross, were preparing to attack the city. He gave orders to his officers to begin the march. He would join them after making a quick trip to Bradley Manor. Upon their arrival, Roberta took him on a tour of the fields.

"It's good you sent Big George and Zachariah back when you did. They have twice the brains of that overseer you hired. Do you have any idea of where Hardy and Daniel are?"

"No, but I hope they will make their way home before the British take them captive."

"There have been rumors of slaves on the Eastern Shore fighting with the British. Hattie tells me it is being whispered among our people, but all have remained loyal and are performing their duties."

"I expect no less," William said, picking a squash that should have been twice its size. "I received word that the British raided the warehouses in Alexandria and removed the tobacco crop we had just sent there. We will not receive one cent for this year's crop."

"Dear God! Don't speak to Mary Alice about it until you return. We've had enough bad news for now," Roberta said, shaking her head sadly.

After a quiet dinner, William informed Roberta and Mary Alice that Zachariah would accompany him to Baltimore to serve as his personal aide. "Big George saved my life. He will remain and help the overseer keep our people working while I am gone. Zachariah and I will be leaving before you wake. I think we will be better prepared for the British under General Scott's leadership." For the remainder of the evening, they drank coffee and read books in silence.

Hattie rushed to Ruth's cabin and told her that she had overheard Master Bradley say Zachariah would be leaving with him before sun up.

"Hattie, watch Anthony for me while I go find him," Ruth cried. She ran to the barn where Zechariah was grooming William's horse.

"Hattie say Master Bradley gonna take you to Baltimore with him," Ruth said, reaching for his hand. "I don't want you to leave us again."

"Now don't you go getting sad on me. Just keep praying the white folks wins the next time they gets in a fight with them Brits."

Ruth stood on tiptoe and kissed his lips. "All the time you was gone, I pray for you night and day. Now I'm gonna have nothing but misery until you come back. I can't sleep worrying about you."

"Stay close to Sarah and Joe. Sarah's good at chasing misery away."

"Hurry and finish with that horse. I got something real special for you," Ruth said, grinning.

"It's as good as done, sweet sugar," Zachariah said, giving the horse a final brush.

William and Zachariah left at 4:00 a.m. and arrived at the outskirts of Baltimore five hours later. They paused at a shallow stream to rest and water their horses.

"Master Bradley, I truly believe if your general had let Big George, Amos and me fight, we could have helped you whip them redcoats," Zachariah said.

Zachariah's unsolicited remarks caught William by surprise. "You boys are fine marksmen, but it was not up to me," William said, tossing Zachariah an apple. "While you were in Washington, did you hear talk that some of your people joined the British?"

"Yes sir. Them Brits put 'em up to it by telling them they gonna set 'em free."

"Many whites will now feel their folks can't be trusted."

"You know you can trust us."

"I'm certain of that." Reflecting on the battle, it upset William to think that he had put his trust in white trash that broke and ran when the first shots were fired. He had no doubt that his men would have stood and fought beside him.

"I hear this man in Washington City say that during the revolution, colored folks fought on both sides. He say he fought with President George Washington, and that's how come he free today."

William stared at Zachariah. It was the first time he had heard any of his people speak openly of freedom. How might this talk affect him in the future? He hoped his master brick layer had not been contaminated by freedom talk, for if he had, he would have to sell him. It would be a serious loss.

William and Zachariah reached the District Brigade's camp on the outskirts of Baltimore. Scouts escorted William to General Winder's headquarters. Before William left Washington there had been talk on Capitol Hill that Winder might be court-marshaled.

The two men saluted and shook hands. "My brigade is ready for battle," William said.

"They won't be needed. The battle for Baltimore has been won," General Winder said, lighting his cigar as though he was the victor. "General Ross was killed in a skirmish near here. I regret that, for I wanted the opportunity to face him again. You will be pleased to know General Scott has assembled a larger force that is well trained and equipped. The other states, except for several in New England, finally sent us the men and supplies we needed. They are spoiling for a fight to revenge the burning of Washington City."

"Who took command after Ross was killed?"

"Their four thousand troops were placed under the command of Colonel Andrew Brooke. When they approached Baltimore, they found themselves facing a force of more than twelve thousand of our troops, entrenched on high ground. After assessing his chances for success, Brooke retired from the field and returned to Cockburn's ships without firing a shot."

"So we won by bluffing them with overwhelming odds," William said.

William was ordered back to Washington City to assist with the restoration and rebuilding of its defenses. Three days after their arrival, he received a letter by special courier. He dreaded opening it.

"Dear Brother, Mary Alice and little Abner are critically ill, as are several of our people. It is the fever. You must return at once. Your sister, Roberta." William's hands trembled as he rushed to General Smith's office.

"I've just received word that fever has struck my plantation. My wife and son are seriously ill. As much as I regret it, I must give up my commission and return home."

"I understand. You have only two weeks remaining on your enlistment. We will treat it as a medical furlough. Bill, I have nothing but respect for the courage you showed at Bladensburg. You were truly one of our heroes that day. You are a gentleman and a fine soldier. My prayers go with you."

"Thank you, sir, but being called a hero when the battle was lost is of little consolation."

After securing horses, William and Zachariah left for Bradley Manor and arrived at eleven that night. Zachariah took the horses to the barn while William rushed up the front steps. He found Ruth standing on the portico crying. He felt a tightness in his chest when he saw the terror in her eyes.

"Master William, I'm so glad you've come home," Ruth cried between halting sobs.

"How are my wife and children?" William said fearfully.

"Master Bradley, little Abner done gone from us just this morning. Miz Mary Alice is deathly sick with the fever," Ruth cried, sinking to her knees and burying her face in her hands.

"O' dear God," William cried. He ran through the front door and up the circular staircase. Upon entering the master bedroom, he found Dr. Steven, the family physician, seated beside Mary Alice's bed. The doctor looked at William and shook his head.

"It's typhoid fever, William. I'm terribly sorry I could not save your boy. Mary Alice is very ill, but I think she will make it. Besides your boy, two of your slaves died yesterday and others are sick. All we can do is pray until this plague runs its course."

William stood beside the bed and stared at Mary Alice's pale face covered with perspiration. Taking a towel from the night stand, he wiped her forehead and whispered in her ear, "Mary Alice dearest, I'm home. I'm here with you."

Mary Alice opened her eyes and smiled. She tried to speak but drifted back into a restless sleep as William continued whispering words of encouragement. An hour later Dr. Steven escorted William to Abner's room. He stood at the foot of the bed staring at the child's body. Shadows from candlelight flickered across his weary features when he leaned down and kissed the dead child's forehead. Ruth stood in the doorway, shocked to see that the hairs on William's temples had grayed over the past two months.

"I'm so sorry, Master William. Little Abner came down with the fever three days ago and I stayed with him day and night. He kept saying, 'I want my daddy.' But his little heart just gave out, and the angel of the Lord came and took him," she said between choking sobs.

"Where are Henry and Louise?" he asked, his face ashen and fearful.

"Miss Roberta took them away for a spell. Too many folk got the fever."

"And your son?" William asked, his voice barely audible.

"He got the fever just yesterday. I'm almost out of my mind. Hattie taking care of him while I stayed here with little Abner."

"I know you did your best," William said, placing his arm around her shoulders.

Big George tiptoed into the room. "Massa Bradley I got more bad news. When Hardy and Daniel come back, they say they going to join them Brits, 'cause they say the Brits gonna set 'em free."

"Fools! Don't they know the English will only use them? They'll end up being sold in some place like Barbados."

"Master Bradley, has the Lord left us alone in our misery?" Ruth asked.

William turned and stared into her eyes. "The Lord?" Turning away, he walked to the bed and placed his hand on his son's chest. "Right now I feel the Lord does not care that my son is lying here cold and dead. Damn you," William shouted, his voice echoing throughout the upper floors.

Ruth placed her hands over her mouth and backed away. She watched in horror as he turned and left the room.

When William reached the library, he poured himself a double whiskey, then stood before the huge oil portrait of his father, James Oliver. "Here's to you Papa. Your son, the conquering hero, has returned."

On his desk was a clipping from a newspaper someone had mailed to him. Placing his drink aside, he read: "Since war is the word, let us strain every nerve. To save our America, her glory increase; So, shoulder your firelock, your country preserve. For the hotter the war, boys, the quicker the peace."

William laughed bitterly, then crumpled the clipping and threw it into the fireplace. He continued drinking until he fell to the floor in a stupor. "My God, my God, why have you forsaken me."

Two days later William stood beside his son's grave. Due to the epidemic that still raged throughout the county, only a few close friends attended the graveside service. Mary Alice was too weak to attend. Reverend Paul J. Quincy, the eighty-year-old pastor of William's Methodist church, conducted the service.

After the closing prayer, Reverend Quincy approached the family members and whispered, "In this hour of grief it is not for us to question the will of God. We do not know why God, in his wisdom, willed that little Abner be taken from us."

William's face reddened. "Preacher, are you standing there telling me God willed the death of my son?"

The mourners all stared at William in disbelief. Roberta, who had returned home that morning, stood up and shouted at the pastor, "By all the gods and stinking fishes, please refrain from making stupid statements, Reverend."

"I... I didn't mean-," Reverend Quincy sputtered. He quickly muttered a closing prayer and rushed to his carriage.

Reverend Harris, his black face wet with tears, watched from the section reserved for the slaves. After the white mourners filed by the open grave, he made his way to William's side and bowed.

"Master Bradley, may I say a word?" he whispered. William simply nodded.

"I hear what your preacher had to say. All I gotta say is, the good Lord was in the same place when his son died, as he was when your son died."

William stared at Reverend Harris with astonishment. "You're the first person that's said anything that's made sense to me today."

On January 25, 1815, William received word that the United States and England had signed a peace treaty in Ghent, Belgium, the prior December 24. Unaware that the war was over, English troops had landed at New Orleans, but were defeated by American forces under the command of General Andrew Jackson. Jackson's force had been composed of three thousand farmers, free blacks, and a band of pirates. Together they defeated the pride of the British army. The treaty and the victory at New Orleans were bitter pills for William. He wished he had served with Jackson, not William Winder.

Newspapers from Washington City reported that the Maryland Senate had passed a resolution deploring the terms of the Treaty of Ghent as "ignominious and humiliating."

Throughout the spring and summer months it concerned Mary Alice that William's drinking had grown worse, and the financial situation at Bradley Manor had reached the crisis point. Mary Alice ordered Ruth to hide William's whiskey.

"He gonna find his whiskey anyway," Ruth said. "Hiding it will only makes him mad at you."

"I don't know what's come over him. My William wakes up at night calling to that young man that was killed before his very eyes," Mary Alice said, wringing her hands.

"Miz Mary Alice, may I ask you a personal question?"

"Of course you can, Ruth."

"Why Master William sleeping in the guest room by himself lately?" Ruth asked.

"Ruth, you know how sick I've been," Mary Alice said on the verge of tears. "And I have not recovered from little Abner's death."

"Excuse me for saying this. Your husband needs to be in bed with you," Ruth said boldly. "You best open your door and give him some loving."

"Ruth, return to your kitchen," Mary Alice said curtly. When Ruth left and closed the door she could hear Mary Alice crying.

On a warm September afternoon, William summoned Mary Alice and Roberta to the library. When they entered, he paced back and forth for several moments, then turned to face them.

"I have something tell you. I have been offered a large sum of money for one of our men and a hundred head of cattle. If I don't act now, we will not be able to pay our taxes, let alone feed ourselves and our people this winter."

Roberta stood motionless, while Mary Alice burst into tears. "You've always said you would never sell any of our people. How will you ever decide whom to sell?"

William placed both hands on Mary Alice's shoulders, forcing her to look into his eyes. "What I'm about to say will be extremely hard for all of us. I have sold Zachariah."

Mary Alice put her hand to her mouth and stared at him with disbelief. "Zachariah! Why Zachariah?" Mary Alice whispered. "Ruth will just die."

"Zachariah is a master bricklayer. With all those federal buildings destroyed in Washington City I have been offered a handsome price for him. He is worth more than ten unskilled slaves. If we sell him and the cattle, there will be enough money to keep our plantation solvent for one year. Mary Alice, my decision is final. I have signed the bill of sale."

"Brother, I would rather see you sell ten field slaves than Zachariah," Roberta said. "He and Ruth are almost a part of this family."

"You are right, but I have to consider the welfare of all my people," William said. "Skilled labor is needed in Washington City, and there were those willing to pay the price."

"You have made a hard-nosed business decision. Now sober yourself up and live with it," Roberta shouted bitterly.

William's hand shook while pouring another whiskey. "It will be done as quickly and quietly as possible. You are to inform Ruth only after Zachariah's gone. It's best we handle it this way."

"William, what has become of us?" Mary Alice cried.

"It's the cruel reality of life, Mary Alice," he replied, sipping the whiskey.

"You certainly won't find reality in that bottle," Roberta said sarcastically. She took Mary Alice's arm and left the room.

William pulled the cord to summon Jim. When he entered, William asked him to be seated. "Jim, you are aware my father made a pledge never to sell any of our people. However, this war and drought have forced me to break that pledge. It pains me to tell you that I have decided to sell Zachariah. The money I will receive from the sale will keep Bradley Manor operating until next year's crop comes in."

Jim listened quietly, showing no outward sign of emotion. "You are aware this may kill Ruth."

"Nonsense. She's a strong woman. In time, I'll see that she finds another husband," William said. He failed to see the disgust registered on Jim's face as he left the room.

William waited until the next afternoon to summon Zachariah. When he entered the library, Zachariah's smile faded when he saw two white men dressed in dusty riding clothes staring at him.

"Zachariah, I regret to have to tell you this. Bradley Manor plantation is my life and I need money to save it. I have no choice but to let you go. I have sold you to these men who will take you to Washington City. Once there, you will help rebuild all those government buildings that were burned."

Zachariah's eyes grew wide. Like a caged animal, he backed into a corner. He had come thinking he would be rewarded for his services. There had to be a mistake! "You done sold me, Massa?"

"Yes."

"What about Ruth and my son?" Zachariah shouted, his voice echoed off the walls, hurting William's eardrums. William suddenly found it hard to breathe as beads of sweat formed on his forehead. Unable to look into Zachariah's eyes, he turned aside and replied sharply, "Ruth remains here. I have no choice. Go with these men, *now*."

Zachariah moved along the wall, pleading in desperation, "Can't I just see my family before they takes me?"

"It will only make matters worse. Don't make trouble for yourself."

William waved his hand, motioning the men to take Zachariah. They moved quickly and placed chains on his hands and feet. Enraged, Zachariah began resisting when they dragged him toward the double doors leading to the rose garden.

"Massa, you said if I do a good job fo' you, you do something good for us. Please don't do this to me. Please, Massa Bradley, please. Sell Ruth and Anthony so we can all stay together?" Zachariah shouted, struggling to break the chains. "Why can't you just rent me out."

"Shut up nigger," the men shouted, striking Zachariah across his back. With great effort, they pulled him along the garden path, placed him in a wagon and drove away.

During the transaction, Mary Alice and Roberta remained in the parlor. Mary Alice covered her ears when she heard Zachariah's cries sounding through the library door. William finally opened the door, but could not bring himself to say the dreaded words. Both women were shocked when they saw the strain on his face. He nodded then closed the door.

Roberta took Mary Alice's hand and led her to the kitchen. Roberta motioned for Ruth to follow them to the parlor. Ruth tensed when she saw the worried expressions on their faces. She sensed something was seriously wrong and for a split second wondered if someone else was sick or dead.

"Why you got such long faces? Sun gonna shine tomorrow," she said, cheerfully.

Mary Alice held Ruth's hands. Unable to hold back tears, she whispered, "Ruth, it pains us to tell you this, but Master William had to sell Zachariah. Try to understand. He did it to save Bradley Manor for all of us."

Ruth blinked, looking first at Mary Alice then at Roberta. Surely what she heard was a mistake. "Miz Mary Alice, Miss Roberta, where my Zach?" she said, panic in her voice rising. Her throat constricted as she looked around wildly.

"I'm afraid they've taken him away, Ruth. Master William thought it best," Roberta said.

Ruth flung her arms upward, breaking Mary Alice's grip. "Where ya'll take my Zach?" Ruth screamed. The two women made no attempt to restrain her as she bolted from the room. Screaming hysterically, she ran to the kitchen where Hattie and Jim stood waiting. Jim had just informed Hattie what had transpired.

"Where my Zach?" she shouted, her eyes filled with terror. Jim stepped over and blocked the back door, as Hattie restrained her.

"Ruth honey, they done sold Zach. He's gone, sugar, and ain't nothing we can do about it," Hattie cried, shaking her head. Ruth pushed Hattie aside and attempted to leave by the kitchen door. When Jim blocked her, she slumped to the floor and fainted.

Ruth awoke with her body racked with fever. When the fever did not break after two days, William and Mary Alice had her moved from her cabin into an empty cottage next to the Manor house. Mary Alice instructed Hattie to stay with her day and night while she personally cared for Anthony. In desperation, Hattie went to William and Mary Alice and announced, "That po' child don't want to live and I's scared to death she gonna up and die."

"If it's God's will, so be it," William said sarcastically, nursing his third whiskey. Mary Alice broke into uncontrollable tears.

"Excuse me, Massa, but the Lord ain't got anything to do with what's ailing her. She got a broken heart that done split wide open, that's all."

They had never heard Hattie speak so bitterly. Without waiting for a response, Hattie left the room.

Hattie took Anthony to Ruth's bedside. "Look Ruth, little Anthony's all well. Girl, you gotta gets yo'self better for his sake." Ruth opened her swollen eyes and tried to smile.

"Get well mama, please," Anthony pleaded, placing his small hands in hers.

"Mama will get well for you," she whispered.

Two days later Ruth's fever finally broke. By the first week of October she felt well enough to move back into her cabin and return to work.

As November approached, William's drinking grew progressively worse. The loss of his son, the recurring nightmares, and the guilt over having to sell Zachariah, compounded his depression. Although the money from the sale of Zachariah and the cattle solved their financial problems, his relationship with Mary Alice and everyone in the house remained strained.

"I don't know what Miz Mary Alice gonna do about Massa William. Just last night I could hear her yelling at him. She be saying he drunk all the time and she getting sick and tired of it," Hattie said, while peeling potatoes at the kitchen table.

"Master William ain't ever gonna stop hurting over little Abner dying. And I'll always be hurting for my Zach, just like him. He don't spend much time with Henry or Louise," Ruth said. "I'm glad they off playing with your girls, Betty and Cathy. I wonder if God is punishing him?"

"God don't punish white folks, Ruth. They punish themselves."

"What's gonna become of us if Master William dies?" Ruth whispered, wringing her hands. "We might all end up being sold."

"I don't know. He sho' is acting strange and that scares me," Hattie confessed. "Girl, it's getting late. I'll keep Anthony with me tonight so you can get your rest."

Ruth worked past midnight, preserving strawberries in glass jars. Mary Alice had purchased some from a fruit wagon that passed through from Florida. After scrubbing the floor, she returned to her cabin, slipped into a flannel nightgown and stretched out on her bed. As tired as she was, she could not sleep for wondering what Zachariah was doing at that very moment. The sounds of crickets filled the night air. Now and then the soft cooing of a dove could be heard in the distance. Ruth sat up when she heard the cabin door open.

"Who coming in my cabin this time of the night without knocking?" The dark figure moved to the center of the room and struck a match. Ruth found herself starring into the unshaven face of William Bradley. From the glaze in his eyes, she knew he was drunk. She drew back when he sat beside her.

"Get dressed and come with me," he muttered.

"Master Bradley, what you want with me this time of night?" she said, recoiling from the smell of his breath.

"Just do as I say," he ordered, his words slurred. He turned his back while she dressed.

Ruth tried to run out the door, only to be blocked by William's huge frame. He grabbed her arm and dragged her the two hundred yards to the Manor house. Entering through the kitchen door, she saw Willie Johnson, one of the field hands seated at the kitchen table. The field worker rose, moved his cap and bowed.

William placed both hands on Ruth's shoulders, leaned forward only inches from her face.

"Ruth, you know why I had to sell Zach. You have got to accept that he is gone and will never come back. You are a single woman. It's not right for a fine woman like you not to have a man. Now Willie here is a good Christian and a hard worker. He will make you a fine husband."

Ruth stared at William with disbelief, then shoved his hands from her shoulders and backed away.

"What you say to me?" she cried, her voice strained.

"I'm offering you a new husband. In time you will learn to accept Willie." Through his drunken fog, William saw the rage in Ruth's eyes. "Willie, take Ruth into the pantry and be nice to her, you hear?"

Willie hesitated. "Miss Ruth, we gotta do like he say. We just talk when we gets in there, I promise." He reached for her arm, only to be slapped across his cheek.

"Don't touch me! I'm married and will be so for the rest of my life," Ruth screamed.

"I am the master of this house," William shouted. "You will obey me."

"You may be the master of this house, but you ain't God. You sold my husband, the only man I ever loved," Ruth shouted, walking to the kitchen table and picking up a butcher knife. "You force me to go into that pantry, come morning you will have one less cook in this kitchen."

Although drunk, William realized Ruth meant what she said. It frightened him when she turned the blade and placed its point to her chest. He carefully approached her and took the knife from her hand.

"Willie, return to your cabin," William said. Willie bowed twice while leaving by the back door.

Ruth gazed at William with mingled hate and pity as he stumbled out of the kitchen. She collapsed on a stool and remained for several moments. Taking deep breaths, she finally regained her composure. Reflecting on all that had happened, it frightened her to think she would have killed herself. It was not in her nature, but she realized, in that brief moment, she would have done it. Ruth walked out into the clear night air. With her head held high, she felt a new sense of pride in her black womanhood.

The next morning Ruth went to Hattie's cabin and fed Anthony before placing him in Cathy's care. There was a lightness in her step as she returned to the kitchen. An hour later she served William and Mary Alice their breakfast. William avoided making eye contact with her and read his newspaper in silence. At one-thirty in the afternoon, he summoned her to the library. He was standing at the window looking out at the rose garden when she entered. When he refused to face her, she walked to his right side, forcing him to look into her unrelenting gaze. He heaved a sigh as he turned and sat in his lounge chair.

"Ruth, I regret what happened last night. I had no right to force another man on you. I have asked the Lord to forgive me, and now I ask your forgiveness."

She stood waiting for him to make eye contact with her. He stared vacantly beyond her. "Well, if the good Lord forgives you, that will be enough forgiving for one day."

William flinched, but did not respond. Ruth turned and left the library with her head held high. He walked to the bookshelf and removed a pint of whiskey hidden behind several volumes of world history. His hands began shaking as he attempted to fill his glass. Standing before the portrait of James Oliver he lifted the glass then threw it and the bottle into the fireplace. "An angel of the Lord just spoke to me, papa," he said. From that day forward William's depression decreased and a semblance of order was finally restored to Bradley Manor.

CHAPTER 10

Summer 1822

Throughout Maryland, farmers worried about crop losses due to the prolonged drought. Relief came the last day of June when a thunderstorm swept through Prince Georges County. The winds and rain continued throughout the night, rattling windows and sending soft moans throughout the Manor house.

Ruth and Anthony were drenched by the time they arrived at the kitchen door to begin the morning's work. Sarah walked over and shook her finger in Anthony's face.

"Anthony, you in a heap of trouble with me," Sarah shouted.

"What did I do?"

"You knows what you done. My rain barrel's full of tadpoles and baby frogs and my Tony say you the one that put them in there. Well, what you got to say for yo'self?"

"Tadpoles eat wiggle-tails. We put them in there so they could eat them before they turn into mosquitoes," Anthony said, observing Ruth trying to restrain her laughter.

"Son, mosquitoes or not, you get them critters out of Sarah's barrel right now."

"But it's still pouring down rain outside."

"All the better. We use that rain water fo' washing dishes and clothes," Sarah said. "I don't want no critters in my water. So get moving."

"And don't take all day to do it," Ruth said, pushing Anthony out the kitchen door. "That boy is going to be the death of me yet. If it ain't tadpoles, it be baby birds, snakes and toads. You know he had the nerve to ask me to let him keep some baby rats that Moab found under our cabin floor."

When Anthony returned, he stood on the back porch and called out to Ruth. "Mama, come look at the clouds?" Anthony pointed to the sky that had now taken on a lavender-colored hue. Streamers of yellow light spread across the sky. "The sun's shining and it's still raining. The devil must be beating his wife."

Shielding her eyes with her hands, Ruth gazed at the cloud patterns. "Don't you go believing none of that silly talk those field hands are saying," she said.

"Look at that one, mama," Anthony said, pointing to a fast-moving cloud. "It looks just like a fish bone."

To Ruth's amazement, the cloud was shaped exactly like the bones from a well-eaten fish. There was the spine with dozens of thin clouds protruding from each side. It lasted only a few moments before breaking up. Ruth smiled, folded her arms around Anthony and pulled him into her tight embrace.

"I'm sure that is a sign from the Lord, Anthony." Her eyes shone with renewed hope.

"Why you say it's a sign from the Lord, Mama?"

"Preacher Harris say Jesus was a fisherman. That could be a sign our Zach is alive and well," Ruth replied, taking a deep breath.

It worried Anthony that if it was only the bones of the fish, maybe it was a sign his father had died. He kept the thought to himself. After returning to the kitchen, he took his ax and went to the woodpile to begin his first chores of the morning.

At noon Jim came to the kitchen and found Anthony peeling potatoes. "Anthony, I have received permission to take you to Annapolis with us tomorrow. Master Bradley, Alexander and I are taking a load of tobacco to the warehouse at daybreak."

"Me? I'm going with you?" Anthony shouted, having never been more then a few miles from the plantation.

"Yes. I thought it was time that you saw something besides this farm. You will ride in the wagon with Alexander while I drive the carriage for Master Bradley."

"You'll take good care of my boy, won't you?" Ruth said.

"He'll be just fine."

"Anthony, you stay close to Uncle Jim. You have never been in a big city before. I hear tell slave catchers be looking to steal boys like you, especially if you go wandering off somewhere by yourself."

"Ah, Mama, ain't nothing gonna happen to me. I can outrun any old slave catcher."

Jim slapped the top of Anthony's head. "You not listening, boy. You won't have to run from anybody if you stay close to Alexander. When we get to Annapolis, you will help Alexander unload the tobacco at the dock. Don't leave his side for one minute."

Anthony nodded, rubbing the top of his head. Jim had gotten his attention.

"I hear those towns got saloons and such. If you pass one of those places, turn your head. I don't want to have to wash your eyes out with water when you come home," Ruth said smiling.

"Ah, mama. Stop kidding me," Anthony said, grinning.

"Uncle Jim, why you driving Master William? That ain't you job," Ruth asked.

"Master William wants me to attend an auction with him. Since old Pete died last spring, he's been talking about buying one or two new men."

Ruth's smile faded. She had accepted the fact that Anthony would make the trip, but the last thing she wanted him to witness was a slave auction.

"You keep Anthony away from that place," Ruth said with indignation.

"Ruth, the boy will soon be thirteen. He's has to learn the truth about this world, no matter how ugly it is."

"Why do our children have to grow up so fast?" Ruth whispered under her breath.

At five-thirty in the morning, William kissed Mary Alice then boarded the carriage. Jim signaled for Alexander to follow with the heavily loaded tobacco wagon. Anthony sat beside Alexander.

"Can I drive this wagon part of the way?" Anthony said.

"Maybe when we come back. This road is muddy and tree limbs are down everywhere," Alexander said, watching the road nervously.

The carriage and wagon moved slowly past the barns, smoke houses, cabins and beyond the corn fields. Once beyond the Bradley Manor farmlands, Anthony saw shacks that were in far worse condition than any of the cabins in the Bradley Manor compound. A group of ragged white children could be seen sitting on the porch of an unpainted shack.

"Alex, look at those white children. I didn't know white folks lived like that?" Anthony asked, his mouth open with astonishment.

Alexander struggled with the reins to avoid the deep ruts. "Yeah, them farmer Mulholland's chillen."

"Their house looks like its about to fall down."

Alexander laughed. "Boy, you sure got lots to learn. All white folk ain't rich like Massa Bradley. Fo' we gets to Annapolis, you gonna see heaps of po' white folks like you see over yonder. There is more po' white folk in this state then there is colored folks."

"I thought all free people made lots of money. Moab, that free man who was here a spell back, he owns his own carriage and he's not poor."

"All I knows is what I sees, and I sees lots of po' folks that ain't got nothing but misery on top of misery."

Alexander slowed the wagon when William's carriage came to a sudden halt. Alexander stood up on the buckboard. "We got trouble. A tree done blown down across the road."

Anthony watched William step from the carriage. After surveying the field, he decided it was too muddy for the loaded wagon to drive around the fallen tree. The wagon's wheels would be knee-deep in mud.

"We have no choice but to remove this tree," William said. He took off his coat, selected an ax, and began working beside Jim and Alexander, chopping the limbs off the tree. "You boys didn't know I could swing an ax, did you?"

"No sir. Massa Bradley, you sho' swings a mean ax," Alexander said, laughing.

Anthony gathered the limbs and dragged them to the side of the road. He found himself staring into the face of a white boy who stood watching them. Anthony noticed his shirt and faded pants were torn and dirty. His oily brown hair looked as though it had not been washed in months.

"Hi, Mr. Bradley, I'm Joe, Andy Mulholland's son. Ya'll need any help," Joe asked.

"We could use another hand," William replied. Without hesitating, the boy worked beside Anthony without saying a word. When the last limb was removed, William reached in his pocket and handed the boy several coins.

"Thanks ah' heap, Mr. Bradley," Joe said. He turned to Anthony. "You the first nigger I ever work with."

William reached out and pulled Joe's ear, causing him to grimace. "The word nigger is a hateful word, son. Never say that in front of me again. Do you understand?"

"Yes sir. I didn't mean nothing wrong," the boy said, rubbing his ear.

"I know you didn't, son. Get on home and give my regards to your pa."

Anthony rode the next hour reflecting on William's rebuke of the white boy. The boy's remark had not upset him because field slaves used the hated word all the time. It was the terrible condition of the youth that upset him. He had equated freedom with freedom from poverty. As they passed other poor white families, freedom suddenly took on frightening dimensions.

The team pulled into Annapolis at seven that evening. William's carriage, followed closely by the tobacco wagon, slowly made its way through heavy traffic. The bumpy trip had been hard on Anthony's butt, but the strange sights and sounds soon made him forget his discomfort.

When they reached Circle Street in the center of town, Jim turned and pointed to a handsome brick building. "Anthony, that's the state capitol building," Jim shouted.

After circling the colonial style building, William ordered Jim to stop at the Maryland Inn. After Alexander handed William's bag to the porter and followed him into the inn, Jim walked over to the wagon.

"Anthony, the city of Annapolis was once the capital of these United States," Jim said, pointing to the building in the next block. "This Inn is where the United States government signed a treaty ending the first war with England. The locals use to refer to it as the 'Treaty Inn'."

"You sure are smart, Uncle Jim," Anthony said.

Jim had taken it upon himself to educate Anthony, but it was a well-kept secret. It was not enough that he taught Anthony to read and write. Jim's own knowledge had widened considerably due to his secret reading of the classics and other literature in his brother's library. It was there that he had hidden among the volumes of poetry the little book given to him by Betty Cox. There could be no better hiding place in Bradley Manor. Mary Alice confined her to reading books on gardening, while William's readings were confined to history and politics. After Anthony's birth, he treated him as his adopted son. Jim had never married. As a young man he had fallen in love with an attractive, eighteen-year-old-woman, but she rejected him when she learned from field slaves he was the son of James Oliver Bradley. Heartbroken, he decided never to marry, for he could never father children who would be subjected to the abuse and humiliation he endured.

William registered for his room then returned to the tobacco wagon. "I will see you boys first thing in the morning. Jim, make sure we get a good price for my tobacco."

"It's a good year for tobacco," Jim replied, turning to Alexander. "Alex, take Anthony and unload the tobacco. After you finish, we will go to Aunt Trudy's boarding house for tonight."

"Who is Aunt Trudy?" Anthony asked.

"She is a free woman who cleans white folk's kitchens and rents rooms to folks like us."

Anthony felt his excitement rising. He would soon meet the second person of his race that was free.

As the wagon rolled along the cobblestone streets to the docks, Anthony stared into the windows of the small shops. Never had he seen so many wonderful articles of clothing and tools. He wished he had money to buy one of the fancy hats for his mother. After reaching a warehouse, a baldheaded white man came over and took the slip of paper from Alexander. He walked to the back of the wagon, picked up a tobacco leaf and held it up to the fading sunlight.

"Looks like your master had a good crop. You boys unload your wagon and place that tobacco in the third stall over yonder in my warehouse."

The man stared at Anthony. "That's a mighty fine darky." He reached over and felt Anthony's arm. "Ya'll think your master might be willing to sell him?"

"No sir, our Massa don't sell none of his people," Alexander replied, picking up a bundle of leaves.

Anthony's throat constricted. He suddenly remembered Ruth telling him about the sale of his father, and now he felt extremely vulnerable.

"Come on Anthony, we got work to do. This ain't no time for dreaming."

They completed unloading the wagon just as Jim arrived. Still extremely upset, Anthony tried to conceal his feelings.

"You alright?" Jim asks.

"Nothing's wrong with me," Anthony said, avoiding eye contact with Jim. He was a man now, and had to act like one.

Alexander handed Jim the receipt for the tobacco. "Anthony's fine. That white trash wanted to know if Massa would sell him, that's all," Alexander whispered.

Jim placed his arm around Anthony's shoulders. "Be strong, Anthony," Jim said. "It's time for us to go the boarding house on Pine Street, just across that bridge. A dozen colored families live over there. Tomorrow morning Master William wants us to meet him back here not later than eight-thirty."

They boarded the wagon and drove into the traffic of carriages, wagons, and foot peddlers, all heading toward a narrow drawbridge. The bridge had just been raised to allow several small ships to pass through. Never in his life had Anthony observed such a beautiful sight as the ships anchored in the harbor. Thirty-five minutes later a horn blew, signaling that the bridge was finally lowering. After crossing the short span, Alexander turned left at the first street and drove several blocks to Pine Street. It was eight-forty that evening when they arrived at the address given them. A stout, black woman with graying hair was sitting in a rocker on the porch of an unpainted frame house, smoking a corn cob pipe.

"Howdy, I been keeping supper warm. I just knowed that old drawbridge was making ya' late. Come on in and make yourself at home. I'm Aunt Trudy," she drawled.

"We are pleased to meet you. I'm Jim Bradley, and this is Anthony and Alexander."

Anthony was so hungry he headed for the table, picked up a slice of cornbread and stuffed it in his mouth. "Anthony, where are your manners? We have trained you better than that," Jim scolded.

"Let that po' chile eat. He looks half starved. You folks don't have to put on no airs around me," Aunt Trudy said, patting Anthony's head.

They went out back to a pump and washed their hands and faces, then returned and took seats at the table. Aunt Trudy returned from the kitchen with a platter of corn and a pot of gumbo soup, rich with vegetables, crabs, and shrimp. After serving themselves, Jim bowed his head and said a short prayer.

"Good bread, good meat, good God, let's eat," Alexander cracked, reaching for an ear of golden corn.

Anthony stuffed himself then went to the cot prepared for him, and within minutes was asleep. It seemed only a short time had passed before he heard bells ringing in the distance. He squinted when Aunt Trudy pulled back her homemade curtains, allowing bright sunlight to fill the bedroom.

"I hope you got yo'self some good rest, little fellow. Go out back to the pump and wash up. By the time you gets back, I'll have breakfast ready," Aunt Trudy said, handing him a wash cloth.

After waking Jim and Alexander, who slept in the adjoining room, she served them cups of milk, scrambled eggs and thick slices of smoke-cured ham.

"I'm glad you woke us when you did. We need to be at the docks by eight-thirty," Jim said.

"The seven bell just rung. Ya'll got lots of time. Guess you be going to that auction?"

"Yes. How long will it take to walk to the dock from here? I don't want to be delayed by that drawbridge. Alexander's leaving now to take our wagon to a blacksmith to repair a wheel."

"I walks over every morning to sell my eggs. Just follow me and you'll gets there in time. Your Anthony can carry my breadbasket. I bakes bread and I takes my loaves and eggs to sell to the white folks."

"I will be glad to help," Anthony said.

"I hear a ship from Cuba coming in with a batch of folk from Africa. It suppose to be against the law to bring colored folks into this country, but these white folks do what they wants, law or no law," Aunt Trudy said.

"This is a lawless nation," Jim replied quietly.

After the hearty breakfast, Aunt Trudy led the way to the dock on foot. Jim was relieved to see the drawbridge open for traffic. Anthony paused briefly to observe black boys crabbing beneath the bridge. Using string, iron weights and raw chicken necks, they skillfully pulled the crabs to the surface of the water and caught them with their bare hands. One of the boys told Anthony that their crabs would be sold on the streets of Annapolis for two pennies each.

"Hurry along Anthony, you'll make us late," Jim called out.

"I sure would like to catch me some crabs," Anthony said wishfully.

After crossing the drawbridge, Anthony saw dockworkers loading and unloading merchandise. Suddenly he froze and stared at the black men, women and children walking down the gangplank of a ship, all chained together. He felt Jim's hand on his shoulder.

"Don't stare," Jim whispered.

Anthony followed Jim to where clusters of men stood near a wooden platform. The structure had been erected in front of a store. The sign over the door read: 'L. J. ROBINS & Son, Slaves for Sale.' Anthony's knees buckled after reading the sign.

They found William standing in the crowd, talking to a stranger. Seeing Alexander, William called out, "Ah, there you are. Did you boys have a good rest."

"We sure did, Massa Bradley," Alexander replied.

"Jim, you come with me. Alexander, go get the wagon and load the tools I just purchased this morning. They are outside that hardware store across the street. Anthony, you can wait for us under that shade tree." William pulled a paper from his pocket that listed the slaves that would be sold.

Anthony watched as a black man mounted the platform and stood with his half-naked body glistening in the sun. He appeared to be about thirty. His body was covered with palm oil so that his muscles would show well. The man looked frightened and bewildered, staring down at the sea of white faces.

"What do I hear for this prime darky from Africa? He's got all his teeth and is in good health, folks. He's strong as a bull." The bidding started at two hundred dollars. It continued until someone made a final bid of three hundred and twenty dollars.

"Sold," the auctioneer's coarse voice rang out as the bidder moved through the crowd. Anthony saw the smug satisfaction on the bidder's sunburned face when he led his captive to a wagon in chains.

William whispered to Jim, "I decided long ago to never buy Africans. They are too much trouble to break in. I have my eye on a boy they are holding in the pen. He's about Anthony's age. I had a chance to get a look at him and he appears to be strong and healthy. Looks like they're bringing him in now." William pointed to a youth being brought to the platform. As the auctioneer instructed him to mount the stairs, a woman's screams could be heard coming from the holding pen.

"Lord Jesus, don't take my chile. Please don't take my chile without me," she screamed.

"Keep that wench quiet," the auctioneer barked. One of the guards opened the gate, moved through thirty men, women and children and threatened the woman with his whip.

"Shut your mouth, wench, or I'll give you five lashes." No further sounds came from the pen.

"What we've got here is a fourteen-year-old darky from the MacHenry plantation. He's strong as an ox, has all his teeth and is in good health." The auctioneer instructed the youth to jump up and down and turn around several times. His dark brown skin glistened in the strong sunlight.

"Two Hundred," William shouted.

"Three hundred," shouted a bidder from the center of the crowd.

"Three-seventy-five," William countered.

"Who will make it four hundred? Do I hear four hundred, four hundred? Come on folks, do I hear four hundred." From his vantage point under the shade tree, Anthony held his breath. The auctioneer shouted, "Three hundred-seventy-five once, three hundred-seventy-five twice. Sold to William Bradley."

William handed the money to the auctioneer, then motioned to the boy. As the youth approached, William placed his hand on his chin and forced him to open his mouth. After inspecting his teeth, William turned to Jim, "I wanted to make sure that the auctioneer was telling the truth. All his teeth are sound," William said. "What's your name, boy?"

"Bubba, Massa."

"Is that your full name?"

"Only one I knows of, Massa." William felt his neck and arms, which were firm and hard. William smiled with satisfaction, knowing he had made a good purchase. He prided himself on being a good judge of flesh, both human and animal.

"Bubba will do for now. I will give you a suitable Christian name later. I want you to know I treat my people kindly if they obey me. I will treat you well if you do your work, stay out of trouble and don't try to run away. Do you understand?"

"Yes Massa," Bubba said, bowing twice.

"Are you a Christian?"

"No Massa."

"One of the first persons you meet will be preacher Harris. He will teach you about our Lord, Jesus Christ."

"Massa, can I go say goodbye to my mama before you takes me away?" he asked, pointing to the holding pen.

"Uncle Jim, take this boy over to his mother, but don't be too long."

Jim unlocked the chains from Bubba's hands and feet. "I'm trusting you not to run away, you hear?" As they approached the pen, Jim saw two extended brown arms waving frantically through the wooden fence. Bubba ran into the arms that pressed him tightly against the rough boards.

"Where they taking you, Bubba?" the mother sobbed hysterically.

"I don't know, Mama?" Bubba replied, without emotion.

Jim stepped beside Bubba. "Your son now belongs to Master Bradley, owner of the Bradley plantation in Prince Georges County. My master is a Christian gentleman, and if your son is a good worker, and behaves himself, it will be the last time he will ever be placed on an auction block."

"Thank you for them kind words. And thank you, Lord Jesus."

Jim allowed them to talk for five minutes. "We must be going now," he said.

The mother held onto her son who made no attempt to free himself. Jim waited patiently then pulled Bubba loose from her grip. The youth did not look back when she started wailing at the top of her voice. He did not see the overseer enter the pen and strike her across the back with his whip. He paused when he heard her final scream, but did not look back. Gritting his teeth, he followed Jim to where Anthony was waiting.

CHAPTER 11

On their return trip, William was relieved that the Maryland roads had dried under a brilliant sun. However, the heat and humidity made the bumpy ride to Bradley Manor uncomfortable for everyone except Alexander. As a field hand, heat never seemed to bother him. He often bragged, the hotter the days the better he liked it.

Anthony and Bubba sat beside each other in the back of the wagon. Anthony waited for this newcomer to speak, but he remained silent. Becoming impatient, Anthony turned to Bubba and smiled.

"Where you from?" Anthony asked. Bubba shrugged his shoulders and kept staring at the passing landscape. Anthony decided to wait him out. An hour later Bubba turned to Anthony.

"You ever poke a wench?" His baritone voice startled Anthony.

"What do you mean?" Anthony asked.

"Poke a wench. You ain't dumb, is you?" Bubba said, frowning. "I know you seen bulls poke heifers?" It finally dawned on Anthony what Bubba was crudely referring too. "Well, that's the way I poke my wenches. Ya'll got any good looking wenches where we be going?" Bubba said.

Anthony remembered how upset Ruth had been after overhearing two older boys talking about doing something nasty with a girl called Millie. She warned them that if she ever caught them messing with Millie, she would have Big George give them a whipping they would never forget. She explained to Anthony that when he was a little older he would learn about such things. Being a house boy, she felt certain he had not been influenced by the vulgar talk about sex so common among the sons of field workers.

"Why you call girls wenches? You better not call them that when we get to Bradley Manor." Anthony warned.

"Where I come from, I poked a wench named Carla. One day she say she gonna have my baby. Soon her belly swelled up like a watermelon. After she birthed my child, Massa sold both of them."

Anthony stared at Bubba who showed not the slightest sign of regret. He thought about his father and the pain it still caused his mother.

It was dark by the time the carriage and wagon rolled into the barn at Bradley Manor. Jim instructed Anthony to take Bubba to Ruth's cabin for the night.

When they entered, Anthony said, "Mama, this is the new boy Master William bought." Bubba walked around the cabin examining the table, chairs and dishes.

"I know you both must be hungry," Ruth said. "Sit yourselves at the table." She served them a bowl of chicken soup. When Bubba picked up the bowl and began drinking the soup, she restrained him and placed a wooden spoon in his hand. "First thing you gotta learn is to eat with a spoon and fork."

"It sure is nice here. I never slept in a cabin that had a floor," Bubba said, reaching down and touching the pine boards. "Where I come from, we put straw in our cabin. That be our floor and up to seven of us be sleeping in it. When it rained, the cabin leaked and sometimes the whole place be full of mud. When it be real cold, the winds blow through the cracks and it seem like we never gets warm. We mix mud and straw to fill the cracks, but it don't keep the cold out. In the summer time it be so hot, sometimes I go sleep out under a tree. Other times I sleep in the barn 'cause that's where I catch rats that be trying to eat Massa MacHenry's corn. After I skin them, my mama make the best rat soup you ever did taste."

Ruth shuddered and shook her head. "Bubba, let me tell you right now that we don't like rats and we don't eat them. Kill all the critters you want, but don't bring rats or critters in my cabin," Ruth said. Anthony tried hard to restrain himself from snickering.

"How the white folk treat you where you come from?" Anthony asked. His smile faded when Bubba lifted his shirt and showed them a brand shaped of the letter '*M*' located on his upper shoulder. The four-inch scar had formed a keloid scar that rose a quarter-inch above the surface of his skin.

"Does it hurt?" Anthony asked, cautiously touching the thickened tissue.

"Not now. When they put the iron on me, the old folks say they could hear me yelling clean over in the next county."

Ruth placed her hands to Bubba's cheek. "Folks don't get branded here," she said, sadly. "Now I know you boys are tired, so get to bed." Ruth took three blankets and placed them on the floor for Bubba.

The next morning Anthony felt someone shaking him. "Wake up. You gotta show me where the wenches be," Bubba whispered.

Anthony rubbed his eyes and sat on the edge of his bed. "I told you not to call girls by that name. You best go back to sleep until you hear the bell ring," Anthony whispered, relieved that Ruth was not in the cabin.

"I needs to poke a wench real bad."

"Is that all you think about?"

"Sho' is. Over where I come from, folks be poking wenches most every night. Sometimes the white boss come and takes the high yella gals fo' himself."

"What if they're married?"

"Married! Nobody married but Massa MacHenry, but that don't mean nothing to him. He keeps two wenches in the big house. A house nigger's say he pokes one in the morning, the other in the middle of the day and his wife at night," Bubba said, laughing. Anthony was startled when they saw Ruth staring down at them. Their conversation had been so interesting, they did not hear her enter the cabin.

"Bubba, I heard every word you said," Ruth shouted, tapping the top of his head with a wooden spoon.

"I's sorry, Miss Ruth," Bubba said.

"Anthony, go to the well and wash your ears out."

"Yes, mama."

After Anthony left, Ruth sat beside Bubba. "Son, you best forget all that nasty mess you see and heard where you come from. Don't you be filling my Anthony's head with that trashy talk, you hear me?"

"Yes'um, Miss Ruth. I don't mean no harm."

"Next time I catch you talking nasty, I'm gonna wash you mouth with lye soap. Now, you go wash your hands and face then come back for breakfast."

Ruth's anger finally subsided after feeding them grits, hot biscuits and fat back. When Alexander arrived, Ruth invited him to sit and have a biscuit with some of her homemade apple jelly.

"I come to fetch you, Bubba." Alexander said. "I's taking him to the barn where he gonna learn to be a stable boy."

Bubba grabbed two biscuits, stuffing one in his mouth and the other in his pocket before following Alexander out the door. He paused and called out to Ruth, "Miss Ruth, thank you fo' the food. It be the best I eat in my whole life."

Anthony reflected on his conversation with Bubba. He would not tell Ruth about it, for after all, it was man-talk. He had found himself feeling strangely excited when Bubba spoke about 'poking.' He would have to ask Uncle Jim, especially about the way it caused him to experience an erection. It was then he remembered his dream. He was at the auction, watching slaves being sold. Suddenly he saw his father, standing on the platform. When he called to him, a white overseer threatened to whip him. Then he saw Moab standing on a hillside, calling to him, "Remember Anthony, you gotta plan for freedom and take it to the Lord in prayer." The shifting tide of the resulting emotions, left him confused and frightened.

Three weeks later, Anthony went to the kitchen door and stopped suddenly when he saw the overseer, Joseph Hanks, sitting at the table, drinking coffee.

"I need your boy in the fields today, Ruth," Joseph said. "The bean crop needs extra hands." He turned to Anthony. "Get yourself over to the barn and join up with my crew. Big George will show you what needs doing, you hear?"

"Yes sir."

Ruth followed Anthony to the kitchen door. "Go get you straw hat. You ain't use to working in heat like this." She felt fearful, remembering the threat the overseer had made regarding Anthony.

"It's about time your boy learned what real work's all about. Sun's good for him. Makes all young bucks hot, don't it?" Joseph said, winking at her.

Joseph harbored a dislike for all of William's house-people, especially Ruth. The brick cottages most lived in, the finer clothes they wore, and the food they ate was on par with his. He could afford better, but spent most of his wages on gambling and cheap whiskey. Ruth had become an obsession with him since the night she stood up to him. When drunk, he admitted he found her far more attractive than his pale, anemic wife, Sue Ellen.

When Anthony arrived at the barn, he was pleased to know he would be working with his friends, Bubba, Peter, and John. None looked happy over the prospect of working in the sweltering heat on the hottest day of the year.

The overseer had left instructions for Big George to have his crew pick beans, hoe the weeds, and remove worms that were destroying the tender leaves. In the spring, the men had planted twenty-five rows of bush beans covering four acres in the south field. Many of the leaves on the foot tall plants were turning brown, a sure sign of insect infestation.

"Move out, mens," Big George shouted. Anthony picked up a burlap sack and followed the crew. When they reached the field, Bubba raised his hand. "I's in charge of you boys today. Ya'll gotta do what I say."

"You just come here. You ain't no boss over us," Peter shouted. "Big George in charge here, not the likes of you, fat head."

"Who you calling fat head, black boy?" Bubba croaked. "I'll take this African soup bone and hit you so hard you won't be able to see for a month of Sundays."

"Who you think you is?" John sneered, shaking his fist in Bubba's face.

Big George leaned his huge frame on his hoe and listened to the argument. He stepped in before the fight began. "Pete, what you boys yelling about?" Big George said.

"Bubba say he gonna boss us," Peter protested. "Him and his fat head."

"Now listen up. Where Bubba come from, he done lots of work in the fields. Now, I can't have you boys slacking off on me. I told Bubba that he would be in charge of you boys today." Big George turned to Bubba.

"Being in charge don't mean acting like white folk. Only one boss out here. That's me, you hear? Show these boys respect and how to pick these beans without pulling the whole damn plant out of the ground. If they gets to acting up, come tell me. Don't go hitting on em', you hear?"

"Yes sir," Bubba said. The friends smiled, picked up their sacks and positioned themselves along the bean rows.

Big George watched them with satisfaction. He was pleased that he had resolved the conflict so easily. Despite his great strength, he was a gentle man, known far and wide for his work songs and folk stories. As a natural leader, he often taught his workers songs he made up on the spot. Singing made a hard day's work go faster. He listened as Bubba motioned the boys to come closer.

"When ya'll pick these beans, just pinch 'em off at the stem like this with yo' fingernail. Don't go pulling on them." Bubba demonstrated by snapping off several of the tender beans. "If you see a bush with brown leaves, turn them over and see if any bugs or little white things be hiding under there. If you find them, mash em' with yo' fingers. If the men dig up any worms, put them in your jars and take 'em to the worm pit ya'll made after we through. We can use 'em for fishing later on."

Anthony glanced under a bush and removed a green worm. "I found the first one."

When the men began hoeing the weeds, the boys followed close behind, picking beans and searching the plants for insects. As the work progressed, Anthony noticed his fingers were being stained green.

"Big George, you gonna teach us a new song today?" Peter asked.

After removing his straw hat, he glanced at the sky and wiped the sweat from his face. "It's much too hot. Maybe this afternoon when it gets cooler."

By eleven that morning the temperature rose more than a hundred degrees. A dust devil twisted its way down the bean rows, blowing dirt into the worker's eyes. Anthony walked over to Big George.

"I feel sick."

Big George placed his hand on Anthony's shoulders to steady him. "I know you ain't never worked these fields, but you gotta gets use to it. We all gets to rest soon as the noon bell rings."

"Big George, I'm going to throw up."

"You better hold that food down. This heat will make a real man out of you," Big George said, handing Anthony his canteen. "Drink some of my water first."

After taking a drink, Anthony returned to his assigned position and dropped to his knees. When he reached for a cluster of beans he suddenly froze. He found himself staring at a copperhead snake, coiled and ready to strike. Terrified, he remained still. Suddenly, he heard a sharp crack, like the sound of a tree limb snapping. The snake, minus its head, became a massive rope knotting and twisting itself in a frightening dance of death. Big George stood beside him, his whip at his side.

Anthony crawled backward and tried to stand up. Gaining his feet on wobbly legs, it seemed as though the colors of the bean field were fading, and everything moved in circles around him. He watched Big George reach down and pick the snake up by its tail. He closed his eyes and tried to steady himself, then dropped to his knees.

"Stand up, boy. Ain't no time to get scared of no snake," Big George shouted. As he spoke the bell rang, signaling the rest period. "You boys get yo' self out of this heat and rest up." He tilted Anthony's head back and looked into his eyes, then took him to a grove of trees.

"I'm sick, Big George," Anthony said, collapsing beside a stump.

"You be feeling better after a bit. Here, take another drink of my water. When you come back you gotta slow down. I been watching you. You out there trying to do more than all them other boys put together. This nigger work. That overseer see you working that hard, he be 'specking us to do that much all the time."

Anthony nodded, not fully understanding what Big George was telling him. At Bradley Manor he took pride in doing his job assignments well and ahead of time.

"Don't you fall asleep, and you get back soon as that bell rings, you hear?"

Anthony closed his eyes and slept. He did not hear the bell and someone calling his name. He woke with a searing pain across his thighs, and found himself staring into the angry face of Joseph Hanks.

"Nigger, you here sleeping while others out there working?"

"I'm sorry Master Hanks, I'm truly sorry," Anthony screamed, rubbing his legs. When he tried to stand, the overseer struck his back with his whip, cutting through his shirt and flesh. From the smell of his breath, Anthony realized Hanks was drunk.

"You think you better than the other niggers, don't you. You and that uppity mama of yours. Get back to work and if I catch you here again I'll skin you alive." His gravel voice sounded to Anthony as though it came from the bowels of hell itself.

Anthony ran to the bean field and fell at Big George's feet. The field workers looked to see if Hanks was watching them. They showed no sympathy for Anthony who failed to return on time. Anthony knew it was useless to explain his tardiness. Who would believe that he was sick from the heat? Who would care?

"I hope you learnt your lesson, boy," Big George whispered.

When he saw the extent of the cuts across Anthony's thighs and back, Big George muttered, "One of these days that man is going to get his reward from the Lord, and if not from the Lord-" He paused, not daring to say what he was thinking.

"Anthony, you done for today. I's taking you back to Bradley Manor, You fellows mind yo' work. Don't stop a lick 'til I gets back," Big George said.

When they approached the house they met Roberta returning from the rose garden. "What's wrong with Anthony?"

When Big George showed her the cuts on Anthony, Roberta recoiled and dropped her basket of flowers. "By all the gods and stinking fishes, who did this to him?" she screamed, wringing her hands.

"Capt'n Hanks whipped him fo' being late fo' work, Miss Roberta."

She picked up her basket and handed it to Big George. "Take my flowers to the kitchen," Roberta said, pausing to regain her composure. "I'll care for Anthony."

She took him to the plantation infirmary and dressed his wounds. "This dressing will sting for awhile, but you are a brave boy. When I finish, go home and rest," she said.

After returning to the cabin, Anthony sat at the table and waited for Ruth. He knew Roberta would tell her about the whipping. He wiped his tears when Ruth ran into the cabin. After Anthony explained what happened, she made him rest on his stomach. He tried to sleep, but the throbbing in his legs and back made sleep impossible. It was dark when he heard Ruth praying, her voice unrestrained.

"Lord, the Bible teaches us that you are a loving and forgiving God. But you are also a God of vengeance when folk do evil and hate you," she said, pausing for breath. Her voice dropped to a lower register, like the sound of an angry lioness protecting its cub.

"What kind of God are you to let the likes of that white trash beat my boy. If you are a God of vengeance, speak to the devil down in hell. Ask him to prepare a special place for the likes of Joseph Hanks. Send him there soon, 'cause I got some ugly in my heart. I can't even say it out loud, Lord, but you know what I'm thinking."

Anthony pulled his blanket over his head. This was not the gentle mother he knew. What was happening to her?

Ruth paced back and forth like a caged animal. "Your son, Jesus, say forgive seven times, but I ain't got no forgiveness left in my heart. Your Bible say 'there be a time to hate.' Well, this my time of hating because I despise, I hate that evil man. With you as my witness, Lord, I will hate him 'til the day I die." Ruth picked up her carving knife and raised it over her head. Her words of defiance rippled through the cabin, echoing off pine-timbered walls. When her hand began trembling, she threw the knife into the far corner of the room and sank to her knees. "Lord, forgive me for what I'm thinking. My burden just got too heavy," she cried in muted tones.

She did not sleep that night. The cabin was still pitch black when she heard a knock at the door.

"Who that knocking this time of the morning?" Ruth cried out, fearful it might be of Joseph Hanks.

"It's me, Hattie. Open up." Ruth rose slowly, lit a candle and opened the door. Hattie's face was lit with excitement.

"Girl, I just had to come and tell you what's been happening," Hattie said breathlessly.

"Tell me what?" Ruth said, shutting the door and pulling down the latch.

"Well, I was working late in the sewing room. I had to finish Miz Mary Alice's new coat. That's when Massa Bradley and Miss Roberta sent for Massa Hanks. They close the door to the living room, but, chile, I got down on my knees and I could hear most every word they say through my grate. Don't miss one word 'cause they got to yelling so loud. Massa William say, 'Why you whip Anthony the way you did?' Capt'n Hanks say, 'That boy needs whipping, 'cause he lazy.' Massa William say, 'I told you never to whip my people unless you got good cause.' Capt'n Hanks say, 'I had good cause.' Miss Roberta, she say he ain't nothing but white trash.' Then Massa William say, 'You thought you had good cause when you whipped a slave to death in Virginia before I hired you. If I knew about it before I hired you, I would have never let you set foot on my land.' That's when Massa Bradley say he don't need nobody working for him that mistreats his people. He told Capt'n Hanks to pack his things and be gone by morning. That's what he say. Well, girl, my heart almost stopped when I hear that fool slam that door. I's so happy I thought I would bust."

Ruth grabbed Hattie's hands. "You telling me that Master William has run that snake off because he whipped my boy?"

"He sho' did."

Ruth sank to her knees. "My sweet Jesus. Thank you."

They sat at the table and talked for the next hour, then made their way through the fog toward the Manor kitchen. Ruth stopped abruptly and took Hattie's hand. A wagon rumbled on the road toward them. When it came into view, they saw Joseph Hanks seated next to his wife, Sue Ellen. The woman stared straight ahead, as though in a trance. The wagon was filled with their household possessions.

Joseph pulled the reins and stopped the wagon a few feet from them. "You bitch. Someday I'll see you and that nigger of yours in hell. You hear me?" Joseph shouted. In her final act of defiance, Ruth lifted her head and looked straight into his eyes. Both women watched as he whipped the mule. The animal lunged forward, causing Sue Ellen to almost fall into the back of the wagon. When the wagon vanished into the fog, Ruth and Hattie held hands and danced in a circle, laughing and crying. Ruth wiped tears from her face and began singing, "My Lord, what a morning. My Lord, what a morning, when the sun did finally shine." Just as they reached the Manor kitchen, the fog lifted and bright sunlight flowed through the window.

CHAPTER 12

December 1822

Ruth and Cathy Johnson returned to the kitchen from the hen house, each carrying two dozen eggs. Cathy sat at the kitchen table watching Sarah mix dough for the hot rolls that Mary Alice ordered for breakfast. Sarah leaned over and whispered, "I overheard Master William say he got a letter from Henry yesterday."

"Why you telling me?" Cathy replied sharply. "He don't mean nothing to me."

"Just thought you wanted to know."

Cathy began pouting. "What did it say?"

"Well, Henry wrote, saying he wants to come home for Christmas. Master Bradley told Miz Mary Alice that he did not want him in this house yet, and that he could spend Christmas week with his Uncle Calvert, down in Savannah. Master ain't forgiven him for what he done to you," Sarah whispered, looking over her shoulder to make sure the door was closed. "Lord, Miz Mary Alice had a fit. She started one of her crying spells, saying she wants Henry home for Christmas. Master had to give in to her."

"I don't care if I never see him again," Cathy replied bitterly. "I just want him to stay away from me."

"Now you listen to me, Cathy. What's been done is done," Ruth said, angrily breaking eggs into a bowl. "You might as well face it. Henry will be coming home soon and I don't want you walking around here with your head down. Keep your head high and walk with pride, you hear me?" Ruth said, shaking her finger at her. "I'm sure he's learned his lesson but if he so much as looks at you the wrong way, go straight to Master William and tell him. Don't make the same mistake twice."

"Yes um'. Thank you for them words, Miss Ruth. I'll do just that," Cathy said, wiping her tears on the corner of her apron. "I want you to know that Hale Sanders wants to marry me. Master Bradley put him up to it. I know, because Master Bradley told me that Hale is a Christian and he's hard-working and kind, but I don't love him."

Ruth patted Cathy's hand. "Look at it this way, Cathy. Kindness is like the bulbs we plant in our flower gardens. Those ugly bulbs aren't much to look at, but when they bloom in spring, we sure love them for their beauty. Hale's like a bulb right now, not much to look at. But his kindness gonna bloom, and when it does, you will know love, just like I did. Now it's

Christmas Eve, and I made us some eggnog and slipped a little brandy in it. We'll have ourselves a cup before you leave tonight."

Ruth loved everything about the Christmas season. As she lay in bed, reflecting on all that needed doing, her thoughts turned to the fun she and Anthony had on Christmas Eve helping the Bradley clan decorate the house. The morning began with William taking Anthony to the woods to find the right fir tree. It now stood in the living room, reaching to the ceiling and filling the ten-foot tall window. In the afternoon, she had sat with Mary Alice and Roberta cutting out decorations from colored paper. Ruth used a pink sheet to make a star on which she pasted an assortment of red and white beads from a discarded necklace. The result was so original, Mary Alice insisted it be placed at the top of the tree.

Anthony, Betty and Cathy spent the evening in the kitchen stringing popcorn and drinking hot chocolate that Roberta always provided them once a year. Hattie complained they ate more popcorn than they had strung.

After she finished dressing, Ruth stood over Anthony momentarily, looking at his peaceful face. On impulse, she kissed his forehead, then nudged him. She hated to wake him so early this morning, but they needed to be in the kitchen by five-thirty. The Bradley's son, Henry, had arrived from college, and his sister, Louise, her husband, John Tolliver, and their two children were expected by noon. Mary Alice had instructed her to come in early to prepare a special lunch. She placed one candle near the small tree Anthony had brought from the forest. They would light it when they returned home that night.

Anthony pulled the blanket over his head as she tugged to remove it, speaking softly in his ear, "Anthony, it's Christmas morning and time to get up. Hurry now and get dressed. I'll give you breakfast as soon we get to the kitchen."

Anthony sat up and rubbed his eyes. The temperature outside had dropped well below freezing during the night, and the water in the tin cup beside his bed was covered with a thin coat of ice. He dressed quickly, putting on the heavy coat Hattie had fashioned for him from the skins of several dozen rabbits. Ruth placed his cap on his head and beckoned him to follow her. Outside, he snuggled close to her for warmth. Mother and son looked up and marveled at the pattern of stars that shone brilliantly in the crystal predawn air.

"I wonder if the baby Jesus was born on a cold night like this?" Anthony said. "And if those wise men gave him warm clothes and a nice blanket for his manger, along with that gold and other stuff?"

Ruth smiled and tightened her arms around him, then hurried their pace until they reached the kitchen door. Anthony rubbed his hands briskly while turning the huge log in the fireplace that had been smoldering all night. He placed bundles of sticks and smaller logs beside it, and shortly a roaring fire threw off welcome heat throughout the kitchen.

Ruth smiled and hugged him. "You are a fine son. I've been thanking the good Lord, because you've been my Christmas gift for thirteen years. Eat this bread while I get breakfast ready," she said smiling.

"Good morning Ruth. Good morning, Anthony." The voice startled her. It was unusual for anyone in the house to be up so early. Turning, she saw young Henry Bradley standing in the doorway. "I need a strong cup of coffee," he said.

"Henry, you gave me a start. Come sit yourself right over here by the fire. My coffee be ready soon," Henry pushed the strands of blond hair from his face, strolled over and sat beside the fireplace.

"Anthony, you sure have grown recently. What's Ruth been feeding you?"

Anthony pointed to the bread and muttered 'lots of this' with his mouth full. Once finished, he took his ax and went outside to chop wood.

"How you like college?" Ruth asked, motioning for him to sit at the table.

"Don't ask. Father and mother will not be happy when I tell them I've flunked out."

Ruth placed her hand on her hip and studied him. "Why you not do good? You a smart boy, when you put your mind to it."

"That's just it, Ruth. I guess I was not ready for college and it certainly wasn't ready for me." As he brooded, he reflected on his predicament. He had arrived at St. Johns College in September, expecting to study the classics and law. It was understood that when he graduated he would return to help manage the plantation. His roommate, Kenneth Henderson from Frederick, Maryland, turned out to be a heavy drinker who treated college life as one big party. Under Kenneth's influence, he spent five months going to parties and drinking, which soon become their only curriculum. There was also the guilt associated with Cathy Johnson's pregnancy and the alienation it caused his family. Just before they left home for the Christmas holidays, the dean notified Henry and Kenneth they would not be returning to St. Johns.

"I think you best not tell your papa and mama until after Christmas day. It would ruin it for sure," she whispered. When she handed him the mug of coffee, she smelled liquor on his breath. His hands shook as he held the cup.

"As always, you're so right, Ruth."

"You gonna need more of my coffee. You best not let your papa find you in this condition," she said, shaking her head sadly. Ruth had helped Mary Alice raise Henry and Louise, and both children respected her for her wisdom and the love she had showered on them. Henry did not resent her scolding him. In fact, he sometimes thought of her as a second mother.

"How are Cathy and the baby doing?" he asked quietly.

Ruth placed her rolling pin aside. "They are doing just fine." When Anthony entered with a load of wood, she turned and called to him, "Go get some more wood for the stove."

"We don't need any more wood," Anthony protested.

One sharp look was enough to send Anthony on his way. She turned to Henry and whispered, "Henry, I sure hope you leave well enough alone. Your father wants Cathy to marry Hale Sanders."

"Hale Sanders! That ugly field darky?" Henry shouted. "Cathy will never be happy married to him."

"Happy! How can you say that word after what you done to her?" Ruth whispered with indignation. "She sure will be a lot happier married and giving that child a name he can be proud of. Besides, you don't know a thing about Hale."

"You're meddling, Ruth," Henry hissed, impulsively slamming the mug down, breaking it and splattering coffee on himself.

Ruth knew she had overstepped her bounds, but she didn't care. She calmly walked to the sink and returned with a cloth. She refused to look at him as she wiped the table, removed the broken mug, and handed him the towel.

"Everything happens in this house is my business."

"I'm sorry. I didn't mean to yell at you." Henry said. Her disarming honesty had unnerved him.

She pulled the stool and sat beside him. "Let Cathy be. It best for you, it best for her, and it sure best for that child you two made," she said, placing another cup of coffee in front of him. "Take this coffee to your room and sober up. Come have breakfast with your mother and father when the bell rings."

Henry sat on the edge of his bed reflecting on the events of the past year. He wished he could turn the clock back and undo the damage he had inflicted on his family. He began recalling with vivid clarity the events of that fateful November week when he and other students were sent home from the preparatory school his senior year. The dorm that housed the young men was being repaired, following a minor fire.

In late night bull sessions, Henry's classmates had bragged about losing their virginity with slave girls their parents owned. When Henry could not contribute any such stories, they guessed the truth and kidded him unmercifully. Their ribbing about his virginity had irritated him and he decided he had to do something about it. Upper class white girls were off limits as they were expected to be virgins on their wedding night. He had been warned to stay away from lower class girls that were referred to as 'poor white trash.' His classmates said that many were infected with the dreaded French disease.

When Henry arrived home, it was Cathy Johnson who served him breakfast. He quickly decided she was Bradley property and his for the taking, although mindful of the risk involved. He certainly did not want to father a child by a slave. When he spoke of his fears to Robert Scheer, his roommate, Robert had laughed disparagingly, "Pull your knob out before it blows, stupid."

When Henry learned that his parents and Aunt Roberta had been invited to the Presidential House for a reception and would be gone for two days, he found it hard to restrain himself. With three days left, the prospect of being alone with Cathy became unbearable. Early Sunday morning his parents boarded the carriage for Washington City. All the house servants, except Cathy, would be attending the afternoon church service at the old oak tree. Henry had instructed her the night before to remain and clean his parent's room after they left. When she entered the bedroom, he followed her and closed the door. As she prepared to change the bed sheets, he placed his arms around her waist and kissed her. The startled look on her face excited him.

"Why you kiss me?" Cathy asked, placing her finger to her lips.

"Because I like you. I've always liked you," Henry said feverishly.

"I like you, too, but Master Bradley beat both of us if he finds out you kissed me," Cathy said, visibly upset. She turned her head when he tried to kiss her a second time. "Take your hands off me."

Henry hesitated when he saw the terror in her eyes. He decided on a different tactic to calm her. "Remember how we used to play together as children? How we climbed trees together and waded in the stream? I've always liked you, Cathy. Trust me. I won't let anything bad happen." It thrilled him that she made only a feeble attempt to restrain him when he unbuttoned her blouse. She dug her fingers in his scalp when he kissed her breasts. After removing his swollen penis, he placed it in her hand.

"You scaring me, doing that," Cathy gasped, not daring to deny the son of her master.

Henry felt empowered. Now was the time to test the limits of its boundaries. "Cathy, take off your dress and sit beside me," he commanded, removing his shirt.

Cathy hesitated, then stood before him and began removing her skirt. "Please don't hurt me."

When she stood before him unclothed, the sight of her body left Henry momentarily breathless. As a boy, he knew she was beautiful, and growing up in the same house, there were times he thought of her as a second sister. Her body was far lovelier than the shapely goddesses he had discovered on the pages of his father's Greek classics. He felt a tinge of jealousy, wondering which of his father's field hands had taken her virginity. After removing his trousers, he pressed her on the bed. His first attempt at penetration proved extremely difficult. All of the advice his roommate had suggested did not prepare him for this. He finally succeeded, totally oblivious to her whimpering. Afterward, he collapsed beside her and rested. How could he have taken Robert's advice when he had ejaculated twice before achieving penetration?

"I best be going, Henry. Folks be coming back from church soon," Cathy whispered.

After she left, he discovered blood on the sheets. It shocked him to know that she, too, had been a virgin. He dressed and went to the library. When he opened the window, he saw Cathy sitting on a bench in the rose garden crying. Opening the French doors he walked over and sat beside her.

"Why did you do that to me?" she asked. "You know I can't ever be nothing to you."

"That's not true, Cathy. You are mine now and will always be. I have to return to school in three days. I want you to come to my room tonight when everybody is asleep."

"Yes, master," she replied shyly. She smiled when he kissed her lips.

Henry returned to the prep school and bragged to his classmate how he lost his virginity. A beer party was held to celebrate the event. In June, he graduated with honors and returned to Bradley Manor. When he found his first opportunity to be alone with Cathy, he noticed her breasts were larger. She remained unresponsive while he used her. Afterwards, she lay in his arms and began crying.

"What's wrong?"

"I'm scared to tell you."

"Tell me what?" His heart began racing as fear coursed through his veins.

"Soon after you left, I started getting sick most every morning. Mama say I'm gonna have a baby."

Henry pushed her away and sprang to his feet. "If it's true, you gotta say it's not mine, you hear."

"Why you say that? You know what we done," Cathy cried, "You said you loved me."

"I never said any such thing," Henry shouted, frantically pacing back and forth. When he said he liked her, did she mistake his words for love? Finally it dawned on him that the truth would soon be known. There was only one person he trusted to break the news to his parents, Ruth Bowen.

Two days later, Ruth spoke to Mary Alice while Henry sat beside her. "Miz Mary Alice, I hate to be the one to tell you. Cathy's gonna have a baby and Henry is the one that's responsible."

Henry looked on helplessly while Mary Alice sank into her chair and cried hysterically. His mother knew such things happened on other plantations, but she and William were confident no member of their family, certainly not her beloved son, would abuse any of their people. When William learned the truth, he became so outraged he packed Henry off to visit his Uncle Gerald in Savannah for the reminder of the summer, and from there, he entered St. Johns College in September.

After Cathy had given birth in August, Mary Alice confided to the women in her sewing circle that the father was their uncouth overseer, Joseph Hanks. "Mr. Bradley warned him that if he abused any of our people he would be fired. Mr. Hanks is no longer in our employment." The women nodded and smiled, but all knew the truth. News traveled quickly from plantation to plantation through the slave's communication network. House slaves enjoyed supplying their masters and mistresses with juicy gossip.

The bell at the entrance gate rang, signaling the arrival of guests. Mary Alice called to her husband excitedly, "Louise and the family are here."

Jim and Anthony rushed to take their assigned positions in the circular driveway. As the carriage arrived, Louise, her husband John Tolliver, and their children, Esther and Edward, waved and shouted greetings. They emerged from the carriage with arms filled with gifts.

John had driven the closed carriage from Alexandria, Virginia himself and was proud of his skills as a horseman. He handed the reins to Anthony and placed a silver coin in his hand. It was the first coin Anthony had ever received, but he sensed he was being accorded something more, even though he couldn't think what it was. Jim unloaded the baggage and followed the family into the house.

Soon the house was filled with joyful noise of children running up and down the stairs screaming and laughing. Louise, at twenty-four, was a stunning woman. Despite having borne two children, she could be laced into the same corsets she had worn before her first pregnancy. She was William's pride and joy, and his eyes glowed with a special pride when she hugged and kissed him.

"Papa, it's so good to be home. The last part of the trip was terrible, with all that wind and blowing snow, but John was just great. He drove us through it all without mishap," she said. Her smile melted his heart.

"Why John refused to allow me to give you one of our women to help you with my grandchildren I'll never understand," he whispered in her ear.

Tolliver had never discussed with William his anti-slavery feelings. His parents were Quakers who had moved to Virginia from Pennsylvania, and he shared their values.

"Papa, John and I don't need servants. I do have a sweet colored women who comes in three times a week to clean, but I enjoy taking care of our home and children." Louise had never told her parents how much she resented not having them around when she needed them as a child. William was always in the field attending to business. Mary Alice's priorities were her rose garden, the women's circle, and the social activities connected with the Methodist Church. Ruth had been her surrogate mother. Louise overcame her abiding sense of loss by being overly protective of her own children, which was one of the reasons she and her husband refused the gift of slaves when she married.

At five-thirty the family assembled in the festively decorated dining room for the traditional Christmas dinner. The noisy affair was highlighted by side chatter and laughter as everyone stuffed themselves on wild rice, turkey, peas, sweet potatoes and corn bread, and for dessert, Ruth's famous sweet potato pie, topped with crushed walnuts.

After dinner, Louise went to the kitchen to thank Ruth and Sarah for the meal. "Ruth, you and Sarah outdid yourselves," Louise said, giving Ruth a hug. "Papa wants all of you to join us in about an hour. He has gifts for all the house folk." As Louise left the kitchen, Ruth's smile faded. William had told her that Cathy would not be welcomed at the family festivities, and she should remain in the sewing room with her child.

At the appointed hour, the family gathered around the tree, now gaily decorated with strings of popcorn, red ribbons and carefully placed candles. The Yule log burned brightly, giving welcome heat to the living room on what had turned out to be a cold, blustery afternoon with blowing snow. After the family gifts were opened, William signaled Jim to assemble the house people. As they filed into the room, Henry noticed that Cathy was conspicuously absent.

William rose from his chair. "Merry Christmas. Mary Alice and I have gifts to express our appreciation to you all." William and Mary Alice alternated giving out the gifts. Hattie tore the paper and removed a handsome sewing box, Ruth's contained a floral table cloth, and Jim's a mahogany pipe. Sarah, Betty and Anthony each received boxes of imported candy.

Henry sat brooding, upset that Cathy had been excluded from the family festivities. He walked to the tree, picked up two packages and handed them to Hattie.

"Aunt Hattie, these gifts are for Cathy and her baby."

"Henry, go to the library and stay there." William shouted, his voice quivering.

William paced back and forth muttering to himself. Louise walked over to William and placed her hand to his cheek. The redness in his face subsided, but only briefly. He went to the cabinet, poured a double whisky and hurried to the library. The windows rattled when he slammed the door.

"Damn you, why in heavens' name would you pull a fool stunt like that in front of the family?" he shouted. "You have disgraced this home, and now you have the nerve to insult us in front of your sister's family by acknowledging that girl. I want you to pack your bags and return to college the first thing in the morning."

"I'm not returning to college, papa. I flunked out."

William stared at his son for a few moments then sank into his chair. He felt dizzy, and it took him a few moments to compose himself.

"Why do you continue to disgrace us after all we have done for you? You know your mother and I have always tried to conduct ourselves according to the principles of our faith. I warned you to never touch these girls. Since I was a young man, I have been deeply ashamed of the way some owners abused their people. I made a solemn pledge to always treat them with kindness, and I've tried to pass that value on to you. Now, I have to be reminded every day that a near-white child in this house has my blood in his veins. To make matters worse, you tell me you've failed in your studies."

Henry raised his hand. "Don't preach to me. I'm sick of the hypocrisy in this family," he shouted,

"Hypocrisy? What do you mean speaking to your father in that tone of voice?" William shouted, rising from his chair.

"Papa, you're not listening. I have known for years that Uncle Jim is your half brother and my uncle, and in all these years, you and mother have never spoken of it. All my life I have wondered how Uncle Jim feels as he moves about this house faithfully serving us. You own him, but he is a part of us. We have never acknowledged that he is a highly intelligent human being, a Bradley in the truest sense of the word. I've known for years that when you and mother are away he reads your books. He understands and loves the classics. Did you think when grandpa taught Jim to read and gave him special status above the other people here, it somehow atoned for his sins?" Henry took a deep breath, stood up and walked over to the fireplace. He gazed up at the huge oil painting of his grandfather, then walked to the table and poured himself a drink. He lifted his glass.

"Here's to you, grandpa. You old hypocrite." He took one sip, then smashed the glass against the hearth. Tears flowed down his face as he stood in front of William. "Papa, did you know Zachariah was my friend. While you were too damn busy running this plantation, he taught me to hunt and ride. When you sold him, I never got a chance to say goodbye or thank him. I used to cry at night because I missed him so much. Ruth's heart broke the day you sent him away, and she almost died. She has never looked at another man, not even the one you tried to force on her. So don't talk to me about the principles of your faith because it's all a lie."

William sank back into his chair. His mouth felt parched and for a moment he could not speak.

"I want you out of this house."

"I confess what I did was wrong. I have a son and he is now *your* property. I just want you and mother to treat Cathy and the baby with respect. You can do that by not forcing her to marry one of your field niggers."

"Never use that term in my house," William shouted.

Henry walked to the door. "I will be out of *your* house by morning."

CHAPTER 13

March 1823 - *We hold these truths to be self evident...*

The morning air was sweet and clear after an early shower. Anthony searched for yellow and purple crocuses and found several blooming in the last patches of snow on the thawing lawn. He made them into a bouquet for Ruth's twenty-ninth birthday.

Later that morning he watched as William, Mary Alice and Roberta boarded the carriage and left for Washington City. Mary Alice told Ruth they were taking Roberta to see a doctor because she had several fainting spells and was having trouble remembering where she put things. He returned to the woodpile and began chopping wood for the kitchen stove and fireplace.

Ruth called from the kitchen window, "Anthony, Uncle Jim wants to see you in the library. You can finish later."

Anthony placed the ax on a stump and sprinted through the rose garden, entering through the double doors. He found Jim sitting in the master's leather chair reading a book.

"Master Bradley sure would be mad if he saw you sitting in his chair," Anthony said grinning.

"Well, what he doesn't know won't hurt him, will it?" Jim said, placing the book on the coffee table. "Come with me. I have something for you." Anthony looked out the window, fearing the new overseer might be nearby.

"There is no one out there." Jim said. Anthony followed Jim to the bookshelf where he removed several books, then reached for the thin book hidden behind them. "Do you remember the visit by the Reverend and Mrs. Cox last year?"

"I surely do. Mrs. Cox was one of the nicest white ladies I ever did meet."

"Well, she wanted you to have this book of poetry. It was written by a young colored woman many years ago."

"Mrs. Cox gave me a book?" he stammered. "Why did you wait so long to give it to me?"

"Two reasons. Mrs. Mary Alice thought it best that you not have it. It is inconceivable to her that you would have the brains to appreciate it. I waited until I felt you were old enough to appreciate it."

"You say this is a book of poetry? What's poetry?" Anthony asked.

"What is poetry?" Jim reflected, repeating the words slowly. "I know you've heard Big George makes up work songs from time to time. The words in his songs are a kind of poetry. Think of the waves you have seen on the river when it's windy. Words in a poem flow like ripples of water on streams. Listen carefully."

Jim moved his hand in a wavelike motion. As he spoke, he paused between the phrases, "She took my hand...and walked beside me...down by the windy sea...And as we walked...we came upon... a twisted wind-blown tree." Jim whispered softly. "Did you hear the waves in the words?"

"I think so."

"Well, that's a simple way to describe a poem. It's a special way of bringing out the beauty in words. You will understand it better after you learn to read poems."

"I like the waves in Big George's poems. 'A bull frog jumped...in the frying pan. His soul is now...in the promise land,'" Anthony said, waving his hand and laughing.

Jim pointed to the book shelves with its hundreds of volumes. "Here in this room I come to explore the world, Anthony. I have been places you have never dreamed of; and the men who wrote these books take me there. John Keats, Thomas Gray, William Shakespeare and now a member of our own race, a woman named Phillis Wheatley. Though they are long dead, they are here in spirit. They can be your friends too, but you must improve your reading."

"I can read parts of the Bible really good."

"I know you can. That's why the time has come for you to read other books, and you will do so with my help. Before I share one of Miss Wheatley's poems, I want to read you a poem I wrote when I was your age." After returning to the lounge chair, he reached into his pocket and took out a scrap of paper. Anthony pulled the footstool beside him as Jim cleared his throat.

> "Though chains lock my hands and feet,
> here in this room I come to meet
> My poet friends from far and near.
> The words they wrote I hold now here
> Within my heart. They've set me free,
> To soar with gulls down to the sea."

For a few moments, only a catbird's call could be heard through the open window. "You wrote that?" Anthony asked with astonishment.

"Yes, and I have composed others, but I keep most in my heart. I'm not much of a poet, but I enjoy writing to express both my pain and joy," he said, handing the sheet to Anthony who read it silently.

"Uncle Jim, a moment ago you said the names of poets. Which poet do you like best?"

"Oh, I have several that I especially like. Of the British poets, John Keats and Robert Burns are my favorites, but it's the poems and plays of William Shakespeare that draw me here when Master Bradley and Mrs. Mary Alice are away." He paused and stretched himself. "The years I have been coming here have been lonely. I've watched you grow in mind and spirit and I felt the time has come for you to join me. But this must be our secret. Only your mother and Hattie know that I come here. Never, never speak with any of the field hands about this."

"What about the new overseer, Jack Davis? Aren't you scared he might walk in here and catch you one day?"

"Jack Davis is not Joseph Hanks. He never meddles in the affairs of this house and comes only once a week to meet with William Bradley."

"I still worry he might find us here."

"Hattie knows I'm here. She watches out for me. Now I will read lines from the book Mrs. Cox left you. First, let me tell you something about this remarkable woman named Phillis Wheatley. She was born in Africa. When she was only seven, slave catchers stole her from her village. White men put her on a ship and took her to Boston. She was sold to a tailor named John Wheatley. The Wheatley family soon realized she was a very bright little girl, just like you, Anthony. They taught her to read and write. Soon she was not only reading the Bible, but writing poems. When she grew to be a young lady, the Wheatley family set her free. She became a great poet and traveled to England where she met the Queen," Jim said, handing the book to Anthony.

Anthony ran his hand over the cover before handing it back. "It's beautiful."

Jim opened the book and motioned Anthony to come closer. "Phillis wrote these lines in a poem entitled, 'To the University of Cambridge, In New England.' In it she speaks of her passage to America. I will read only a part of it.

> 'Twas not long since I left my native shore,
> The land of errors and Egyptian gloom;
> Father of mercy! 'Twas thy gracious hand
> Brought me in safety from those dark abodes.'

"That's wonderful." Anthony said, reaching for the book and carefully turning its pages. "She sure uses beautiful words."

"In this, one of her early poems, she speaks of being transported to America as a slave. However, it is clear she had little knowledge of the history of Africa or her people, being only seven when she was kidnapped. Whites told her nothing of the glories of Egypt and Ethiopia. In another poem she speaks out against the tyranny of slavery in this nation," Jim said sadly.

"Don't be sad, Uncle Jim. We gonna be free one day. I've been thinking about it a lot."

"I am free, Anthony. Freedom begins in the mind," Jim said, touching Anthony's temple. "Learn to read and love these books and your soul will be as free as the wind, even if your body is not. No one can place chains on your mind or your heart if you educate yourself," he said. Regaining his composure, Jim rose from the chair and placed his poem and Anthony's book behind the Shakespeare volumes on the top shelf.

"Today's journey ends. Now go finish your work," Jim said.

When Anthony walked into the kitchen, he found Cathy and Ruth preparing to place chickens in the oven.

"Anthony, I'm glad you came when you did. I got something to tell you and your mama," Cathy said smiling. "Miss Ruth, Anthony, Hale asked me to marry him and I said I would."

Ruth threw up her hands and shouted, "Praise the Lord, I'm so happy for you. Hale's a good man and I know he's gonna do right by you and little Henry"

"When ya'll gonna get married?" Anthony asked.

"We want to get married real soon. Right after Master Bradley and Miss Mary Alice come back, we gonna tell them. Master William told Hale he would let us get married in his living room. Ain't that something?"

Ruth pointed to the back door. "You run along and help Bubba. He's outside whitewashing the chicken coop and he needs some help."

With Anthony out of hearing distance, Ruth patted Cathy's cheek. "Girl, I can't tell you how happy I am for both of you. Why did it take so long for you to make up your mind?"

"Well, you remember last Christmas? I never told nobody about this, but before Henry left he came to the sewing room looking for me."

"No he didn't!" Ruth replied, her mouth hanging open.

"He sure did. He told me he was going to Annapolis to find himself a job, then he gonna come back and take me and little Henry with him. I told him I don't want to hear no more of his lies, and to stay away from me and my child. That's when he say he never lied to me and that I was real special to him, even when we were children, playing together. I say, 'You still can't say you love a colored girl that's a slave.' He just stood there, looking at me.

That's when he grabbed me and kissed me. After that he say, 'Good bye, Cathy.'"

"Well, hush my mouth! Minute he gets his hands on you here come another baby, then another. Then he up and marry some white lady and when she learns the truth, you would be in for nothing but trouble," Ruth whispered under her breath.

"I waited this long because I loved Henry. I guess I always loved him from the times we played together. I gonna learn to love Hale that way."

"I'm sure you will, child. Henry ain't no different from his grand pappy and that's the truth. Well, I guess it won't hurt to tell you. Miz Mary Alice got a letter from Henry last month. She say he got a job working for a Jewish store owner in Annapolis, and the owner helped Henry get back in that college. He told her that he doesn't plan to come home anytime soon."

"That's good. I don't want to see his lying face."

Anthony found Bubba brushing the last coat of whitewash onto the wooden fence around the chicken coop. "I've come to help ya. Got another brush?"

Bubba pointed to a nearby pail. "Where you been?"

"Talking to Uncle Jim."

"What ya'll talk about?"

"Just stuff. He was telling me how plants grow and how to take care of the soil. That's why Master Bradley lets some of his fields rest for a year or two. If he doesn't, the crops won't do good the next time," Anthony said, recalling one of his past conversations with Jim.

Bubba scratched his head. "You and Uncle Jim good friends, ain't ya? Field niggers say he acts like white folk. Most don't like him."

"They don't know it, but he's their best friend," Anthony said, resisting the urge to tell Bubba to shut up. He picked up the brush and started painting, muttering under his breath, "The Rooster with the long red chin, chased the little spotted hen. Across the barnyard every day, she never has no time to play.' I just made that up. It's called a poem."

"Guess what?" Bubba whispered. "My little hen let me poke her last night and it sho' was good."

Anthony stood up and stared at Bubba. "You gonna get yourself into deep trouble, for sure. What's her name?"

Before Bubba could answer, Big George strolled over to the fence and gave it his critical inspection. "You boys done one fine job. I's gonna take you fishing as soon as you put yo' things away. Now go wash that mess off yourselves and meet me at my place."

125

Anthony and Bubba ran to the pump and washed themselves, then raced to Big George's cottage. Bubba arrived a step ahead of Anthony and knocked on the door. Big George's oldest daughter, Cora, opened the door and stepped outside. To Anthony's surprise, she playfully slapped Bubba's cheek.

"Pa coming with the fishing poles. He say for ya'll to wait here fo' him," Cora said, rolling her eyes at Bubba.

When she left, Bubba nudged Anthony. "She the one that I poked last night."

Anthony's jaw dropped open. "If Big George finds out, he will skin you alive," Anthony whispered.

When Big George arrived, he took them across the meadow to his favorite fishing spot. When they reached the stream, Anthony rolled over a stone and found several earthworms.

"There is a big catfish in this stream. I calls him Scooter 'cause he always scoots away with most of my worms. He sleeps over there in the deep part where that big tree is," Big George whispered, pointing to a shaded area on the opposite bank. Branches from a weeping willow hung close to the water. "He one smart catfish. He knows we after him, so we gotta keep low and be real quiet."

After baiting the hooks and throwing their lines into the water, they sat on the bank without speaking. Anthony grew impatient, pulled in his line and found the hook bare. Bubba and Big George pulled in their empty lines.

"How did he do that?" Anthony asked.

"Well, I told you he one smart fish. I can just see him down there swimming all around them worms and thinking to himself how he gonna get em' off our hooks without getting caught. That's when he use them whiskers on the side of that ugly face and tickles the worms." Reaching over he tickled Anthony, then Bubba. "Them worms gets to laughing and wiggling so hard they slide right off the hook and into that old catfish's big mouth."

Their laughter was cut short by the sound of dogs barking in the distance. The cadence of the long excited howls told Big George that bloodhounds had picked up the scent of some animal or human.

"You boys be real quiet," Big George whispered.

He stood up, shaded his eyes, and scanned the field. "Get under that bush and don't move 'till I calls ya." Anthony and Bubba grabbed their poles and hid under the thick cluster of bushes.

Big George saw a dark figure running in his direction. The howls of the hounds grew louder. Two white men on horseback followed the hounds. The man slipped and fell, face down in the mud. The three hounds tore at his clothes as he screamed and struggled to get to his feet. Big George watched the men dismount, and for several moments they made no move to stop the dogs from tormenting the victim. When they finally drove the dogs back, then beat him with whips as he continued screaming. The men pulled the man to his feet and tied his hands behind his back. When one spotted Big George, he mounted his horse and rode in his direction.

Big George's eyes widened when he recognized Joseph Hanks. He removed his cap and bowed.

"Well I'll be damn. Big George, how did you like the show?" Joseph asked, leaning over the saddle and grinned through tobacco stained teeth.

"Howdy, Capt'n Hanks," Big George replied.

"Got me a runaway. You tell your nigger-loving master I got myself a real job catching runaway niggers. Tell him I'm good at it."

"I hears you, sir," Big George said, fearing the boys might be spotted.

"You ever think about running off, Big George?" Joseph asked, grinning.

"No sir, never. Not me, Capt'n Hanks."

He leaned closer. "I wish you would. I wouldn't bring you back, 'cause I could get a heap of money for your black ass." He laughed as his expression turned to rage. "You tell that bitch, Ruth, I ain't forgot her. I got something special for her and that little nigger of hers. You make sure you tell her what I say, you hear?" he sneered, then turned his horse and rode back to his waiting partner.

The captive's hands were tied to a rope that now extended to one of the horse's saddle. Joseph struck the man in the back of the head with the butt of his whip, and yelled to him to move out. Big George waited until they were out of sight.

"Don't move 'til I calls ya," Big George said in a low voice, daring not look in their direction. He waited for twenty minutes then motioned for them to join him. Anthony and Bubba came out and stood beside him, both holding a fist full of stones.

"That was Captain Hanks, wasn't it?" Anthony said. "I know his voice anywhere."

"It be him, all right. That man's the devil that come all the way up from hell," Big George replied, scanning the horizon. As they stumbled across the muddy pasture, they did not pause to observe the rainbow that had suddenly appeared and arched itself above the lush fields of Bradley Manor.

CHAPTER 14

The Freedom Plan

Anthony tossed and turned most of the night after learning that William and Mary Alice would be leaving for Annapolis the next day. The prospect of a second visit to the library made sleep impossible. He got up at first light and spent most of the morning mulching and pulling weeds from the flowerbeds. Jim finally summoned him at four that afternoon.

When he arrived, Jim said, "Did you wash your hands?"

"Yes, my hands, arms and face," he said, extending both hands. Jim inspected his palms and fingernails then pointed to the bookshelves. After browsing for a few minutes, Anthony selected an American history book. On the first page was *The Declaration of Independence.* He read silently then turned to Jim and read aloud, "We hold these truths to be self-evident, that all men are created equal, that they are endowed by their Creator with certain un-."

"The word is unalienable. Unalienable rights," Jim said.

"They are endowed by their Creator with certain unalienable rights, that among these are life, liberty and the pursuit of happiness." Anthony paused. "What does 'unalienable' mean?"

"As it is used here, it means there are God-given rights that cannot be taken away. But it really means, *should not* be taken away."

"Uncle Jim, this says *all* men are created equal," Anthony insisted.

Jim wanted to read Shakespeare's *Othello,* and had not expected to become involved in an extended conversation, but sensing the question was a turning point for Anthony, he closed his book.

"One reason there are laws in Southern states that forbid slaves to be taught to read is that they fear smart colored boys like you will read it and start a revolution."

"All means everybody, doesn't it?" Anthony said impatiently.

"I know what it says, but the writers meant all *white* men are created equal, not black men, not Indians. But, in the sight of God, all men *are* created equal."

"But if God made all men equal, why do white people treat us the way they do?"

Jim picked up a water pitcher and a glass. He poured the water into the glass until it was full.

"This glass is full, isn't it?" Anthony nodded, watching when Jim walked to the window and poured some of the water into a potted plant. "Now this glass is two-thirds full, right?"

Anthony looked puzzled as Jim drank the remaining contents. "This is a crude way of making my point, but white folks see their glass filled to the brim. To justify slavery and their treatment of us, they tell themselves we are not fully human, that our glass is only two-thirds full. They have convinced themselves we lack higher qualities, and are not endowed with rational minds."

"Rational minds?"

"Yes, the ability to reason and think like you are doing right now. They train us to be little better than their work animals. Sadly, many of our people survive by playing the role of the jackass. Some are so successful at it, they now think like jackasses," he said bitterly.

Anthony recalled several of the early lessons Jim had taught him on how to behave in the presence of white folks, and how some of the field hands laughed and acted stupid when whites came around. He remembered finding the courage to speak to Mrs. Cox.

"White people were slaves once. Mrs. Cox told me that two years ago."

"Mrs. Cox is right. From my reading of history, many whites were slaves. Jesus lived in a nation that was held in bondage by the Romans. When the Jewish people fought to free themselves, the Romans destroyed their nation and made slaves of their leaders."

"Mrs. Cox promised me that she and Reverend Cox would work to set us free. Do you think they will?"

"I doubt if it will happen in my lifetime, but it's possible freedom will come in yours." Jim walked the bookshelves and returned with a book entitled, *The Institution of Slavery in America.* He removed a pamphlet from between its pages and handed it to Anthony.

Anthony read aloud, "*The Outrage of Slavery.* It says that Reverend Samuel Cox wrote this," Anthony said, excitedly.

"Indeed he did. I have often wondered why Master Bradley keeps it hidden in his book on slavery. I have no idea how or where he got it. But that's not important." He raised the pamphlet and shook it. "This is the most powerful statement I have ever read. It attacks slavery as a sin against God and all humanity."

There was a soft knock at the door. Ruth entered and whispered, "I know all this book learning is important, but Anthony, the wood pile is getting low again."

For the rest of the day Anthony felt as though he had a fever. That night he had difficulty sleeping as the words *unalienable rights* kept echoing in his head. Suddenly he sat up. His heart raced, wondering how long it would be before morning. Feeling his way to the table, he lit a candle. As the flickering light illuminated the room, he walked to Ruth's bed and gently shook her.

"Mama, I gotta talk to you. Please wake up," he pleaded.

Startled, Ruth lifted herself on one elbow. "Anthony, what wrong with you, child? You sick or something?" she asked, reaching out and feeling his forehead.

"Mama, I just gotta talk to you and it can't wait."

Ruth rubbed her eyes, straining to see him. By dim candlelight, the anguish in his face came into focus. She had spent the afternoon washing a week's supply of tablecloths, napkins and towels and desperately needed her rest. She was tempted to make him wait until daylight. From the urgency in his pleadings she realized his need to talk could not wait. She got up, went behind the curtain that served as a partition. After slipping on her kitchen work dress, she sat at the table beside him.

"Now son, what so important it can't wait till morning?" Ruth said, holding his hands.

"I got my plan, Mama. It came to me in a dream. I'm gonna ask Master Bradley to let me work in my free time to earn money for my freedom."

The force and vigor of his declaration did not surprise her. She patted his cheek, "Well, I sure wish you had waited till sunup to tell me that. Did you take your plan to the Lord in prayer?"

"Yes, Mama. When it came to me, I heard a voice whispering, 'I will be your help and your shield.' I went back to sleep for a spell, then I started dreaming about Jacob that's in the Bible. Mama, it was so real. He was talking to Rachel, and he told her he loved her so much he would work another seven years for her. That's when I sat up, wide awake. That's my plan, Mama. And when I'm a free man I'm gonna go to Washington City, get me a job and earn more money and buy your freedom."

The unwavering resolve she saw in his eyes frightened her momentarily. She clasped her hand in a prayerful manner before reaching out and hugging him.

"Well, Master Bradley and Miz Mary Alice be back Sunday. I'll be at your side when you go talk with them." She saw the uncertainty drain from his face, replaced with his infectious smile that she loved so much. "Rest now, son. Tomorrow needs doing, and we both gonna make it a good day," she said.

For the next two days Anthony rehearsed what he would say to William and Mary Alice. He tried to convince himself that he had nothing to fear, but if William refused, how would he cope with the disappointment? Each time he prayed, the words he heard in his dream gave him strength, *'I will be your help and your shield.'*

Sunday morning dawned cloudy when Ruth shook him, whispering, "Wake up, son. The day needs doing. Master William and Mrs. Mary Alice came home last night. I know in my heart this will be a specially good day."

Throughout the morning, a hard blowing rain soaked the fields. Anthony was pressed into service with other field hands, moving rolls of hay into the barns. At noon Ruth and Sarah brought food to the wooden table that had been set at the edge of the field.

Ruth sat beside Big George and whispered, "I gotta take Anthony to meet with Master Bradley and Miz Mary Alice."

"What for?"

"I'll tell you all about it later." Ruth took Anthony's hand and led him toward the Manor house. As they trudged across the rain-soaked field, Ruth slowed their pace when she saw Anthony trembling. She made him stop and look into her eyes.

"Though we walk through the valley of the shadow of death, we will fear no evil," Ruth whispered. Anthony straightened himself and walked with renewed determination. When they entered the library, William placed his cigar in the ashtray, stood up and faced them. Mary Alice continued knitting.

"Good afternoon, Ruth. Good afternoon Anthony," William said.

"Miz Mary Alice, Master Bradley, we are glad you had a safe journey," Ruth said.

"It's been months since we last saw Henry. You will be glad to know that he is doing well with his studies. He apologized to us for his disgraceful behavior last Christmas," Mary Alice said, placing her knitting aside.

William motioned for Anthony to step closer, "Anthony, your mother tells me you want to speak with us. What do you have to say for yourself."

The intimidating tone of his voice left Anthony speechless. He glanced at Ruth, but seeing the strength in her face, he turned and faced William.

"Master Bradley, all my life I have truly wanted to be free, and I want my mama to be free too," he said clearly and distinctively.

"Just when did you get this notion in your head, boy?" William said, staring directly into Anthony's eyes. It was his favorite tactic for keeping his people in line. It surprised him that Anthony did not lower his head as other slaves would have done under the circumstances.

"When that freeman, Moab, came here two years ago, he told me how he earned his freedom. Ever since I heard what he said, I been thinking about it," Anthony replied with growing confidence. He felt energy flowing to him when Ruth placed her hand on his shoulder.

"Have we not been good to you and your mother?" William asked.

"Yes sir."

"Have we not fed you, clothed you and even taught you to read and write?"

"Yes master, but all the same I want to be free," he said, taking a quick glance at Ruth for comfort. Ruth stood beside him, with her eyes trained on William.

"Master Bradley. I'm not asking you to set me free for nothing. I will continue to work hard for you like I always do. I'm asking, after I finish my work will you let me work at night to earn money? When I earn what you think I'm worth, I will buy my freedom. You set the price and tell me how much I'm worth and I'll earn it and pay you, no matter how long it takes."

William's explosive laughter caused Anthony to step back. "By God, boy, you've given me the best laugh I've had in years. Right now you are worth more than three hundred dollars, and when I train you at some useful trade you will be worth a lot more. You could work here for years and not make that much."

"Master, all I'm asking is to let me try," Anthony pleaded. He felt Ruth's fingers tightening on his shoulder.

Ruth stepped forward. "Master William, I got something to say."

"Certainly Ruth," William said, lighting his cigar.

"My grandmother, her family and me have served your family all these years. We've been loyal and hard working. But all the time I dreamed that one day my boy will be free."

Mary Alice interrupted, "Ruth, I never thought I would see the day you would say such a thing. We consider you a part of this family. How can you be so ungrateful after all we've done for you?"

Ruth pulled her shoulders' up. "Ungrateful? You call me ungrateful? Was I ungrateful when I nursed your son and mine from these breasts?" she cried, placing her hand to her breast. "Was I ungrateful when I left my own son and stayed with little Abner day and night when folks come down with the fever? And, did I turn my back on you after you sold my husband?" she cried defiantly.

Mary Alice stood up abruptly. "Ruth, you and Anthony are our favorites. Why, we allowed Anthony to be taught to read and write along with little Abner, rest his soul. You know why we had to sell Zachariah. The war and the drought that year was so bad we could have lost this farm, then where would we all have been?"

"Yes, you sold my husband and the cattle to save this place. I want my son to be free so he will never have to fear of being sold like a cow or hog. Can't you understand that?" Her pleas now came in halting sobs, as Anthony placed his arm around her.

"Master Bradley, you say it may take a long time to raise that amount of money. I'll work no matter how long it takes. Please sir."

William rose and waved them away. "Return to your stations. I must think on this."

Ruth took Anthony's hand and hurried out the back door. The sun had broken through the clouds and, despite the humidity, its warm rays comforted them. They did not stop until they reached the shade of the oak tree where Sunday services were held. Ruth dropped to her knees and looked to the sky.

"Lord, I know you in this place. I feel your breath in the wind. Please open Master William's heart. He ain't like Pharaoh, Lord. Deep down he has a kind and loving heart. You don't have to send no more plagues on this place."

The next morning, Ruth and Anthony returned to the kitchen where Hattie was waiting. "Ruth, what ya'll say to Massa William? I hear him talking so loud, I could hear him without having to put my ear to the grate."

"What did you hear?" Ruth asked nervously.

"Don't make no sense to me. Seems like they was talking about Anthony wanting to be free. You up to something I don't know about?"

"I asked Master Bradley if I could work at nights and on my free time to earn money for my freedom," Anthony replied. "That's after I finish my work for him."

"You ask him what? Is you crazy or something?" Hattie whispered.

"No, he ain't crazy. I was with him when he say it," Ruth replied.

Hattie sank down on the kitchen stool, shaking her head. "Well, ya'll both touched in the head, if you ask me. Ruth, why you not be telling me what you and Anthony up too? Ain't I yo' best friend?"

"I should have, Hattie. Just had too much on my mind thinking about it and I knew you would try to talk us out of it." Ruth heard Mary Alice's bell ringing from the dining room. She placed the plate of eggs, bacon and grits on a tray and handed them to Anthony. When he entered the dining room, Mary Alice spread her napkin across her lap and remained silent while Anthony served them. William quietly read his paper throughout the meal.

"Annapolis is a lovely town but the heat almost made me sick. I'm so happy that Henry is doing well with his studies and has gained some weight," Mary Alice said, while coffee was being served.

"He's no longer making a fool of himself by drinking too much. He's also been involved with students that are working to secure the vote for Jews in Maryland. The Jewish merchant who gave him the job that Christmas he stormed out of here, has been very kind to him. That's when he learned that Jews are required to sign a loyalty oath to Christ before they can vote," William said.

"Oh, why would he involve himself in such a controversial issue? Our friends at Washington Memorial Church will never understand."

"And what wouldn't they understand?" William asked.

"Well, Reverend Wigfall told our Bible class that Jews killed our Lord and Savior, Jesus Christ. He said they should never be allowed to vote unless they accept Christ. Those that don't will be lost."

William reflected for a few moments. "Mary Alice, may I suggest that you not bother yourself with politics. It will only tax that sweet brain of yours." Before she could protest, he motioned to Anthony.

"After you and your mother clean the kitchen, I want to see both of you in the library."

"Yes sir." Anthony said, barely able to restrain himself.

When Anthony and Ruth entered the library, William rose from his chair, walked over to the huge bay window and gazed out at the rose garden. Mary Alice continued knitting.

William finally spoke with his back to them. "Anthony, I have given considerable thought to that scheme of yours," he said, finally turning to face them. "Ruth, we are grateful to you for your loyalty all these years."

"Thank you kindly, sir."

William stepped closer and stood only inches from Anthony. "I believe slavery has benefited the colored race. White men brought your people out of a savage, heathen land and taught them about our Lord and Savior, Jesus Christ. All this talk about freedom is nonsense, Anthony. But since you've got freedom on your mind, and because your mother has been so loyal to us, I've decided to give you permission to try that fool scheme of yours. Therefore, you have my permission to work in your spare time, both here and at any farm that will hire you."

Anthony opened his mouth but was unable to speak until Ruth nudged him. "Thank you, thank you, Master Bradley," Anthony stammered, wiping tears from his cheeks.

"You will put in a full day's work for us, as you have always done. I will pay you for extra work completed during your off time. If other farmers hire you, I will set the price for your labor, and I will give you a letter that will allow you to travel during your off hours. However, if you slack up in your duties or in the quality of your work, I will keep all you have earned and the bargain is off. Is that understood?" William said sternly.

"Yes, Master Bradley. Sir, how much must I earn to buy my freedom?" Anthony replied, grinning broadly.

"In a few years you will be worth six or seven hundred dollars. Because of our respect for your mother, I'm setting your purchase price at four hundred and twenty-five dollars. That is my word."

"God bless you, Master William." Anthony said. Ruth placed her apron to her face and began sobbing.

"All right now, stop crying. Go back to work," William said. "Oh', by the way, Big George tells me that there is a section of fence in the west pasture that's in need of repairs. I intended to send a crew to repair it in the morning, but you can earn twenty cents if you get it done before daylight."

"Thank you Master Bradley," Anthony shouted.

After they left the room, Mary Alice rose from her chair and kissed him. "William Bradley, you are a soft-hearted, loving man. Maybe that is why I've loved you all these years."

William hugged Mary Alice and kissed her cheek. "You know, that boy just may raise that money. But he will have worked the best years of his life right here at Bradley Manor."

Big George found Anthony in the garden mulching the flowerbeds. He crept up behind him, put his boot against his butt and gave him a playful shove. "Massa Bradley wants to see you right away over at the cow barn."

"What for?" Anthony said, brushing the dirt from his hands.

"He didn't say. You best hurry along."

Anthony threw his tools into the shed and ran to the barn. He slowed when he saw William talking to Abel Baker, a farmer who owned a forty-acre farm that adjoined the Bradley Manor properties. Baker frequently visited to buy seeds and arrange stud service for his cows. Anthony had heard that the Bakers owned three slaves, two mules and five cows. The field hands referred to the Bakers as 'poor white trash.'

William placed his hand on Anthony's head. "This is my boy, Anthony. If you want to hire him, you can count on him to do a good job for you." Abel reached out and felt Anthony's right arm, then nodded.

"He seems strong enough. Right now I needs a boy like him to do some fixing in my house," Baker said, turning to spit tobacco juice. "That shiftless son of mine won't do a lick of work after dark. All he wants to do is drink liquor and lay up with his woman."

William took Anthony aside. "You will receive fifty cents for an evening's labor. It's far more then you would have gotten if you tried to bargain on your own. Go tell Ruth you will be going with Abel Baker this afternoon."

"Thank you, Master Bradley. That's mighty generous of you." Anthony said.

Anthony and Abel Baker arrived at the farm at seven-thirty that evening. There was still enough daylight for him to have a good look at the place. After feeding the cows, Abel took Anthony into the weather-beaten house and handed him a brush and two cans of paint. The interior walls of the house had not been painted in seven years.

"First things I want done is for you to paint this here room. Put that old tarp on the floor to catch the droppings. You do good, you hear?" Abel said, while lighting four lamps and placing two on the table and two on the floor at each end of the room.

After saying a prayer, Anthony hummed to himself while painting the walls and ceiling. It took three hours to finish painting the room, but he worried how the ceiling would look in the bright sunlight.

"You done real good." The voice startled him. Climbing down the ladder, Anthony saw a slender, dark-skinned girl dressed in a faded brown cotton dress standing in the doorway. "But you missed some spots on the ceiling. They gonna need more paint."

Anthony wiped his hands with a rag soaked with turpentine. "What's your name?" he asked.

"Catharine. Folks here call me Cat. What's yours?"

"I'm Anthony Bowen." By lamplight, her smooth, dark complexion reminded him of fine ground cinnamon. He looked into her doe-shaped eyes and guessed she was about fourteen years old.

"Bet you didn't know I been watching you," Catharine said. There was a soft shyness in her voice that sounded like music to him.

"When I got here this evening I didn't see you."

"I was working in the field, but I seen you. Ain't you gonna paint them spots you missed?"

Anthony felt his heart beating faster. He watched her as she moved the ladder and looked up at the ceiling. "I'll hold this lamp up so you can see better."

Anthony finally tore his eyes away from her, took his brush and climbed up the ladder. She stood close by, pointing to places that needed additional painting.

Several times Anthony took quick glances down at her. Paint from his brush dripped onto his hair and face. She laughed and pointed at his nose,

"You best look where you painting. You getting more paint on your face then on the wall."

After he finished and climbed down, she took a cloth and made him sit on a stool. "Now close your eyes. Don't you be looking at me. This stuff will sting real bad if it gets in your eyes," she said, carefully wiping the paint from his face and hair. The touch of her hands excited him beyond belief.

"Thank you for helping me."

"You be smelling all the way to your home if you don't clean yo'self. I'll take you outside to the well so you can wash your hands and face."

After he finished putting the brushes, tarp and paint cans away, he followed her to the well. She drew a bucket of water and poured it into a pan.

"Will you be coming back anytime soon?"

"I hope so," he said, splashing water on his face.

"Walk me to my cabin befo' you leave. I wants you to meet Aunt Mae and Uncle Joe. We all lives together."

"Ain't they sleeping by now?"

"No, this be the full moon. Aunt Mae always sits up on the full moon. She say that's when her spirits come and talk to her."

"Spirits?"

"Sho'. Don't you believe in spirits?" Catharine asked.

"I hear folks talking about spirits, but my mama say that's voodoo talk. I only believe in God and his son, Jesus Christ," Anthony said.

She led him across the field to a log cabin, opened the door and lit a candle. In the dim light, Anthony made out an old woman sitting in a rocker by the fireplace. Not a single wrinkle showed on her aged face, and her skin reminded him of well-tanned leather. He guessed she was in her late eighties. In the corner lay an old man on a bed of straw. He had difficulty sitting up.

"Cat, who you brung in here this time of night?" the woman said.

"Aunt Mae, Uncle Joe, this here is Anthony. He from the Bradley place, and he come here to work for a spell," Catharine said.

When Anthony shook the man's hand, he was surprised by the strength of his grip.

"My spirits be telling me a stranger coming," Aunt Mae said.

"I'm pleased to meet both of you. I wish I could sit a spell, but I gotta get home before sun up. Next time I come, will you tell me about your spirits?"

"They ain't all mine, son. Some be yo' folk's spirits. One of them told me you was here."

Anthony felt a momentary chill. Surely what she said was nonsense. Or was it?

"I walk you back to your mule," Catharine said, taking his hand.

"I hope I will see you the next time I come."

"I's sure you will. I ain't going no where," Catharine replied. She watched as he mounted the mule and guided it to a moonlit path. When he turned and looked back, she waved.

Although Anthony had worked for four hours that night, never in his life had he felt so awake and excited. He had read about love in the plays of Shakespeare and discussed them with Jim. He wondered if what he felt was love? When he arrived at the cabin at two-thirty that morning, he entered and managed to crawl into bed without waking Ruth. When he finally slept, Catharine filled his dreams.

CHAPTER 15

May 1824

Roberta's bedroom commanded a spectacular view of the Bradley Manor's cultivated fields and orchards. Two months after her return from Washington City she remained confined to her bed. The doctors attributed her memory loss to the onset of old age. William had not accepted their doctor's diagnosis, for Roberta had been physically active and alert until seven months ago. At age fifty-eight, she had been a picture of good health. Her condition first became noticeable when she failed to return from riding her favorite horse. She had lost her way, although still on Bradley property. Now she seemed totally unaware of her surroundings. Cathy was assigned to be with her while Hattie cared for her child.

As Cathy prepared her bath, she remembered Roberta's telling her that flowers were God's curtains on the windows of the world. She spent the night in a rocker beside Roberta's bed and by morning her back ached. Her sister was due to relieve her at seven-thirty. She rolled the ankle-length cotton nightgown up to Roberta's neck and gently removed it. When applying the washcloth to her chest, Roberta slapped at her hand.

"Come on now, Miss Roberta, you gonna like this nice warm bath," Cathy said, not daring to restrain her. After completing the sponge bath, she dusted her body with powder and put on a fresh gown. There was a gentle knock at the door.

"Is she decent?" William whispered.

"Yes, you can come in now, Master Bradley."

William walked over, sat on the edge of the bed and gently held Roberta's hand. For the first time he allowed himself to consider the possibility she would not survive. It was hard to face the fact that it was only matter of time before her life ended.

"Roberta, it's I," he whispered. Although awake, she did not move or look in his direction.

"She doesn't know us anymore," Cathy said sadly.

"Cathy, I fear my sister is not long for this world. We deeply appreciate the care you and Betty are giving her."

"I love Miss Roberta. She's been kind to me ever since I was a little girl," Cathy whispered.

William pulled a chair beside the bed and sat without speaking for the next quarter-hour. Of his two sisters, Roberta had been his closer companion. While stroking her hand, his thoughts drifted back to the tragic events that had tied her to Bradley Manor for the rest of her life.

When she was twenty-one she met high-spirited John Firestone at her birthday party. He was the son of a prominent Virginia planter. John had a reputation as a philanderer and heavy gambler. When she told the family that he had proposed, William warned her to stay away from him, but she ignored his advice. She was quite certain that she could tame and mold John to her liking.

A month later she surrendered her virginity under her blooming pear tree. John mailed her a letter several months later, explaining that he had gotten a Virginia girl in family way and was obligated to do the honorable thing and marry her. The humiliation and shame caused Roberta to retreat to her room, cutting off all contact with the family and the outside world. At one point the family feared for her life. She ate little, lost weight and cried incessantly.

William informed his father that he was taking it upon himself to avenge the family honor. While on a business trip to Alexandria, Virginia, he learned that John Firestone had lied about having to marry. As luck would have it, he stumbled into him playing draw poker at a tavern. He walked over to the table, removed his glove, slapped John across his face and challenged him to a duel. The next morning, as their seconds watched, William and John stood back to back, walked ten paces and turned. William's first shot drilled Firestone between his eyes. When he arrived home, he went directly to Roberta's room and informed her that he had shot John Firestone in a duel.

Roberta had stared at him for one silent minute, then said, "Tell mama and papa I will be down for dinner. Now, if you will excuse me, I wish to bathe and dress myself."

It saddened William that she never trusted another man. From that day she devoted herself to her books, garden and fruit trees. Until William married, she performed the duties of a social hostess at Bradley Manor.

Roberta's sudden movement broke his concentration. He leaned over and looked into her vacant eyes. "You and I have been through much together," he whispered. He turned to Cathy and patted her hand. "Keep up the good work," he said, then left the room. Cathy came weeping two hours later and told him that Roberta had died.

On Sunday, May 3, seventy-five guests arrived at Bradley Manor for the funeral service and burial. The carriages lumbered over the rutted road made worse by late spring rains. William stood on the porch and welcomed his friends while keeping an anxious eye on the road for Henry. The graveside service at the family burial plot was scheduled for three that afternoon. As the hour neared, his hopes faded.

With the living room, hallway and parlor filling with guests, William left the porch to greet his friends. Mary Alice, in her black silk dress, instructed Jim to place a chair by the front window. She continued to greet the late comers while keeping an eye on the road.

Mary Alice was about to join William when she spotted two riders on horseback coming up the driveway. She uttered a cry when she saw Henry. She rushed to the vestibule, lifted her skirt and petticoat before racing across the driveway into Henry's outstretched arms.

Hearing her shouts, William hurried to join her. When Henry approached, they smiled and embraced. Without speaking, both knew that the pain of that dreadful Christmas was finally behind them.

They had visited him at St. Johns College, but they knew the reconciliation would not be complete until he returned home.

"Papa, Mama, I want to introduce my friend, David Cohen. It was David's father who gave me part-time work while I'm completing my studies at St. Johns."

David Cohen shook William's hand. "Henry has told me so much about you folks, I feel I know you already."

"Welcome to Bradley Manor," William replied, placing his arms around both their shoulders while escorting them into the house.

"You'll be pleased to know I'm still doing well with my studies, Papa. However, I'm learning more about law and business from David's father than from all my classes."

"Your father's a lawyer?" William asked.

"He is a merchant, but was trained in the law in England before coming to this country," David replied.

As they approached the vestibule, Henry saw Anthony waiting on the stairs.

"Anthony, I believe you've grown a full head taller since I saw you last."

"It's sure good to see you, Master Henry. I'm fourteen now. May I take your horses?" Anthony said, smiling.

After William and Mary Alice took Henry and his guest into the house, Anthony walked the horses to the stable. Following the feeding and grooming, he went to the kitchen to help with the food preparation. He sighed when he saw the four headless chickens waiting to be cleaned and dressed.

"Them just for starters, Anthony," Hattie said. "We got lots of hungry folk to feed here."

Bubba entered the kitchen, pulled up a stool and began helping Anthony pluck feathers. Anthony wondered how long it would be before he brought up his favorite subject.

"Can you keep yo' mouth shut if I tell you something?" Bubba whispered.

"What you done now?" Anthony inquired.

Bubba glanced around to make sure Ruth and Sarah were not within hearing distance. "I told you Cora let me poke her," Bubba whispered. "Now she wants me to poke her every chance we gets. Last night we done it under Master Bradley's back porch."

"I'm telling you for the last time, you better stop it before both of you are in deep trouble," Anthony warned. "Big George's is sure to find out and when he does, he's gonna beat your butt."

"Can't help it. When you get to poking some fine gal, you'll understand why you can't quit. Cora got the best twat I ever had, and she loves my bone. You gotta let me find you a gal. Lots of them like you, but they say you stuck up."

Anthony placed the featherless chicken aside and stared at Bubba. "Well, if you and Cora make a baby, you won't be able to run or hide."

Ruth entered the kitchen from the dining room. "What you two whispering about? Bubba, you know what I told you. Both of you save your talking for later. The service for Miss Roberta will be at the graveside shortly, and those guests will be trooping back here to eat. So keep busy and stop all that talking. Anthony, you come out on the back porch with me."

Anthony washed his hand and followed Ruth the porch. "What you want, Mama?"

"You listen to me and listen carefully. That Bubba's been making trouble ever since he came here. I know the nasty stuff he been trying to put in your head. Well, he's in a heap of trouble but he doesn't know it yet. Did he tell you he has been messing with Big George's daughter, Cora?"

Anthony eyes widened, knowing he could not lie. "Yes'um."

"Well, Reverend Harris is going to marry them, come Sunday. That's because she's gonna have his baby."

The simple service at the family plot lasted only twenty-five minutes. Reverend Hiram R. Wigfall, the new pastor of Prince Georges County Washington Memorial Methodist Church, presided. He had held a personal dislike for Roberta. On his first visit to Bradley Manor he reminded her that he had not seen her at church since he arrived. She had spoken bluntly, saying sarcastically, "Reverend Wigfall, you won't be seeing me. I have no use for the tribal god you worship, so don't waste your time praying for my soul."

In shock he had responded, "Are you speaking of our Lord and Savior, Jesus Christ, madam?"

"No, only the son your god conceived out of wedlock, or was it by one of his holy ghost." From that moment, Reverend Wigfall was convinced Roberta would be barbecued in one of the Devil's special pits reserved for unrepentant sinners. With William being the largest contributor to his church, however, he knew he had to lie. The words almost choked in his throat when he closed by saying that Roberta was a fine Christian woman who truly loved 'our Lord and Savior, Jesus Christ.'

After the sermon, three young black girls walked beside the grave and began singing. *"Deep river, my home is over Jordan, Deep river I wanna cross over into camp ground."*

As the white guests dispersed, a retarded fifteen-year-old black girl walked to the edge of the open grave and began waving a torn rag. "I's gonna miss ya, Miss Roberta. We all loves ya.' Tell Jesus I say hello," she said, tossing a wild flower onto the coffin.

Until that moment Henry had sat passively holding his emotions in check. The girl's final farewell caused his tall frame to shake from his silent sobs.

Following the service, carriages transported the guests to the front lawn where picnic tables, filled with food and drink, awaited them. The somber mood now changed into a festive one, as several punch bowls of rum and fruit juice were quickly consumed.

Henry introduced David to the guests. David paused and nudged Henry. "Who is that remarkable creature?" Henry glanced at a group of young white women, dressed in bright organdy dresses.

"Which one?"

"Not those. That beautiful girl serving your guests?" David said, nodding in Cathy's direction.

Henry's face flushed. "She is one of our people," he stammered.

David failed to sense Henry's discomfort. "Your father owns her? My God man, how can you stand-?" David caught himself.

Henry turned away and walked to the punch bowl, struggling to maintain his composure. He motioned to Ruth. "Which one has the spirits?" Without smiling, she pointed to the bowl on the right.

"Henry, you go easy with that stuff, you hear?" Ruth cautioned. "Sip it real slow."

"Believe me Ruth, I will," Henry whispered. When he returned, he was relieved to find David talking with his sister, Louise, who had joined him in the serving line. As they moved slowly along the tables filled with barbecued chickens, pork ribs, baked beans and potato salad, they approached where Cathy was serving. Henry felt his heart racing. When he extended his plate, Cathy lowered her head and stepped back. Hale Sanders moved from behind her and scooped potato salad onto Henry's plate. For one brief moment, Henry and Hale stared at each other. Shaken, Henry led David to William's picnic table. Reverend Wigfall and his wife, Jo Ann, were already seated beside them. The preacher's plate was piled high with ribs, chicken and hot bread.

"Henry, it's good to see you home. How long has it been?" Reverend Wigfall asked.

"Almost two years, Reverend."

"Do you young men attend Church regularly? I hope you are not neglecting your spiritual life."

"I attend services on campus. As for David, I'll let him speak for himself."

"I attend a Synagogue," David responded. The broad grin on Reverend Wigfall's face turn into a frown.

Henry turned to William. "David's father was a lawyer in London, but he does not practice law in Maryland. In part, he is protesting how Jews are treated in our state. Members of the Jewish faith cannot vote unless they sign a loyalty oath to Jesus Christ."

"I am aware of the law. I opposed it when it was first introduced some years ago," William replied.

"Maryland was founded on the principles of religious freedom. I am appalled that we have such a law that denies members of any faith the right to vote. It places Jews just one step above free colored folk. David and I would like to discuss our effort to repeal the law before I leave." Henry said passionately.

Reverend Wigfall threw his napkin on the table. "How can any Christian support the repeal of the Jew bill? The good Christian people who founded this state never intended to give the vote to nonbelievers who reject our Lord, Jesus Christ." Reverend Wigfall blurted out.

William jabbed Reverend Wigfall in his side. "Reverend, do not speak of political issues at my table." Reverend Wigfall coughed violently, spraying food across the table as he attempted to nod. He rose and tried to get his breath. William stood up and pounded his back, then escorted him from the table.

"If this matter ever comes to a vote, your father will make a great ally," David whispered, brushing specks of food from his suit. "He has a persuasive way of making a point."

After the meal, Henry reflected on the events that reshaped his life. He had left home that Christmas night, bitter and disillusioned. The alienation from his family, and his inability to cope with his true feelings about Cathy and their child, had left him depressed. An act of kindness by the Jewish merchant who hired him the week he returned to Annapolis had piqued his curiosity. One evening he found his employer, Solomon Cohen, reading from the Torah. After a lengthy discussion on several Biblical passages, Solomon Cohen asked him, "Henry, what does the Lord require of us?" Henry was struck by the simple question, but had no answer. After Solomon helped get him reinstated in college, one evening he read a passage from the book of Micah by lamplight. *"He hath shown you, O man, what is good, and what doth the Lord require of you, but to do justly, and to love mercy and to walk humbly with your God."* Henry had wept that night, remembering his treatment of Cathy Johnson.

CHAPTER 16

Cathy stood in front of the five-foot mirror in the sewing room, while Hattie made final tucks in her wedding dress. She could not believe her eyes when she saw herself in the white dress made from a pattern Mary Alice had given her.

Hattie sat back on her stool, looking admiringly at her daughter. "Lord, chile, you look just like an angel. Here you is on your wedding day getting married to Hale Sanders. And Master Bradley letting you get married in his living room. That's something for sho'."

Cathy turned from side to side, as Hattie made the final adjustment to the sleeve. "Mama, you the best dressmaker in the whole world."

Betty shook her head in disgust. "Huh, Miss Mary Alice just glad Cathy getting married, that's all."

"Now you hush your mouth. This is a happy day and we don't need any smart talk out of you," Hattie scolded.

"Mama, pay no mind to Betty," Cathy said, admiring herself in the mirror. She knew Betty resented the attention she was receiving, but she didn't care. She was determined that nothing would spoil her special day.

"Ya'll excuse me. I'm going to the kitchen to help Ruth," Betty said, flinging the petticoat at Cathy. "I forgot to tell you, Cathy. Henry came home this morning."

The smile on Cathy's face faded. The last thing she wanted was to be reminded of Henry. Until that moment, she had been able to conceal her innermost feelings about him. She recalled him saying, *"You are mine now and will always be."* Although he had lied and abused her, she still worshiped him.

"Chile, you ain't got a thing to worry about. I thinks it nice that Massa Henry be home during your wedding," Hattie said. "I hear Miz Mary Alice say he done found himself a nice young lady and they getting themselves engaged."

Cathy bit her lip while staring into the mirror. Here she was, on her wedding day preoccupied with thoughts of Henry. She had suspected he loved her in his own way, but never allowed himself to admit it. Why did he come back now? "I just gotta stop thinking about Henry and think only about Hale. He's my man now," she whispered to herself.

Six months earlier, Hale had confessed that it was William who kept urging him to marry Cathy. William had made it clear that the decision would be up to her, however. He had spoken of all the fringe benefits that would accrue from such a marriage. Hale would become one of William's house people, and they would live in one of the brick cottages close to Bradley Manor.

The evening Hale proposed, he said, "I use to see you down by the chicken house and I be thinking to myself that you the most beautiful gal I ever seen. I never dreamed our master would even let me look at you. I don't want you to do nothing you don't want, but if you marry me I'll be a good husband, and I treat your son like he my very own."

At first she rejected him, angered that her master had suggested it. Several months later she accepted his invitation to take a walk. They sat beside a stream where he taught her some of the fun-loving ballads he knew. She found herself enjoying his company. Following their second walk together, he took her to his cabin where they sat by his fireplace and talked for hours. She was surprised when he spoke of his desire to be free one day. Although his kisses were pleasurable, she found herself comparing him of Henry. On her third visit, she reluctantly went to his bed. The touch of his callused hands and the sight of his dark muscular body had frightened her. He had been gentle and patient with her. All comparisons to Henry evaporated when he took her into his arms and loved her.

The chiming of the grandfather clock in the hall brought her back to reality. Concentrating on Hale had done the trick. Their lovemaking had been extremely pleasurable, not quick or painful. She removed the wedding dress and decided to go to the cottage to rest. In the rose garden, she paused to pick a yellow rose bud and placed it in her hair. She did not see Henry watching her through the rose arbor.

Henry walked from the rose garden to the library where William was entertaining his fellow planters, Charles Taylor and John Skinner. Both were successful, slave-owning farmers and members of the Maryland House of Delegates.

"Gentlemen, 1824 is going to go down as an important year in American politics. This business of caucus nominations for the presidency has finally been changed once and for all. While I supported John Adams for president, the allegations there was corruption in the last caucus has stained his administration. Delegates sold their votes," William said.

"We didn't need to change the caucus system," John Skinner replied. "This new system for electing delegates will place too much power within the reach of the common people. It has always been the ruling classes that have guided great societies. Our republican institutions are much too fragile to place within reach of the ignorant masses. I hear General Andrew Jackson is thinking about running for President in 1828. In my opinion, Jackson is a backwoods bumpkin, uncouth and lacking any of the social graces. Such a system will work to his advantage."

"Come now. I know Jackson and he would make a fine President. He has a deep distrust of big government," William replied.

Jim opened the door and announced, "Gentlemen, luncheon is ready to be served."

"All this political talk has made me hungry. Let's enjoy a good meal," William said, leading his guests to the dining room.

"Gentlemen, after lunch would you care to witness a special event? A wedding is about to take place within the hour. Two of my people will be married. It is my custom to allow those of my people I deem to be the most trustworthy, loyal, and hard working, to be joined in the bonds of matrimony in my home."

"This should be entertaining," John Skinner said with amusement. "A slave marriage in Bradley's living room."

"I don't think of my people as slaves. Yes, I own them, but I treat them as part of my extended family. I consider myself a good shepherd."

"But William, good shepherds keep the sheep and the goats in the barn, not in the sanctity of their living rooms," Skinner said, chuckling.

"Do you sell them?" Taylor asked.

The question struck a raw nerve. "I've had to face that unpleasant prospect only once. In 1814, I sold one of my men to save this farm after the British seized my crops. You all remember the drought that summer. It was the only way I could keep my farm going."

"Well, under the circumstances, it was the Christian thing to do," Skinner responded.

When the clock struck two, William escorted his guests into the living room where they were seated in a roped off section near the front window. A podium had been set up near the fireplace with vases on each side filled with white roses.

Twenty-five of William Bradley's prize workers filed into the room and took their seats. As they did so, Charles Taylor noted that most were dressed in clothes of finer quality than those of his white employees.

Reverend Harris entered from the dining room with Hale at his side. Charles Taylor and John Skinner watched with astonishment as Louise sat at the piano and began playing the wedding march. Cathy had served Louise all her life, and the music was her wedding gift.

Henry sat watching as Cathy entered from the hallway. Her white dress complemented her hourglass figure that showed no hint that she had borne a child. As she stood beside Hale and repeated her vows, Henry felt a strong compulsion to leave the room. He wondered what could be upsetting him so?

William slipped a fifty-cent piece into Reverend Harris's hand an hour earlier, and made it clear that the whole service must not last longer than fifteen minutes.

At that exact moment, Reverend Harris said, "I now pronounce you man and wife. Hale, kiss your bride right now and get on over to the barn." Hale looked into Cathy's eyes then kissed her lips to the loud applause and back slapping of the black guests. Following the service, the happy wedding party trooped to the barn where food and drink were waiting.

William turned to his planter friends and said proudly, "If we treat our people well, then we will not have to worry about abolitionists up North writing lies about us."

"Abolitionists be damned," Skinner retorted.

As William's guests made their way to the library, Skinner nudged Taylor's ribs. "That' s one good-looking wench. If I owned her, she be warming my bed, not that ugly black nigger's." Henry overheard the remark but tightened his jaw and remained silent.

Anthony felt his head swimming as he removed the chairs and cleaned the living room. What he managed to overhear about the sale of his father had upset him. Once finished, he raced across the field to the compound and knocked on the door of cabin number eight. After a few moments a woman's faint voice called out, "Who that?"

"It's me, Anthony. Is Bubba home?" The door opened and Anthony looked at a very pregnant Cora.

"Come on in. Bubba's putting on his work clothes to go to work," Cora said shyly. Bubba sat on his bed smiling as he pulled up his trousers.

"Aren't you going to the wedding party?" Anthony asked.

"We not invited. Master Bradley's still mad at us," Cora replied.

"Ain't half as mad as your pa, Big George," Bubba said. "I guess you heard how he kicked my butt, then dragged me and Cora over to Reverend Harris's cabin and made him marry us."

"Yeah, I heard. Well, I gotta go. I'll bring you something from the party if any thing's left." While walking to the barn, he thought that Bubba seemed happy now that he was married and had Cora to 'poke' every night. He slowed his pace, wondering what it would be like to do it. On nights he thought about it, he had experienced erections that made it hard to sleep. Jim never told him why it happened.

The wedding party lasted late into the evening. When the tables were moved aside, several of the field workers mounted a platform and began playing their fiddles. Anthony found himself surrounded by more than a dozen girls, all clamoring to dance with him. Earlier, he had overheard several boys making fun of a shy, unattractive girl named May. Her cheek has been disfigured in a fire when she was a baby. When the music began, she had remained in her seat, certain none of the boys would want to dance with her. Anthony left his admirers, walked over and asked May for the first dance. She placed her hand over her scarred cheek and shook her head. He smiled, reached out and gently removed her hand from her cheek.

"I'm not going to leave until you dance with me," Anthony said smiling. When May saw all the other girls watching them, she reluctantly followed him into the crowd of revelries. After dancing with her twice, only then did he dance with his other admirers.

At eleven-thirty Ruth called out to Anthony, "Son, I just remembered. The wood-rack in the kitchen is getting really low. I know you hate getting up before sunrise, so you better run along and fill it tonight."

Anthony pushed through the crowd of well-wishers to where Cathy and Hale were standing. "I want to wish you lots of happiness." After Cathy kissed Anthony's cheek and Hale hugged him, he made his way over to the table where not a scrap of food remained. He left and hurried toward the Manor kitchen. While passing the horse stable, a figure stepped out of the shadows.

"That you, Anthony?"

Anthony paused and stared at the stranger. "Who's that?"

"It's me, Moab Jackson," he whispered, motioning for Anthony to come closer.

CHAPTER 17

Anthony stood gawking at the stranger, not daring to believe that the person standing in the shadows was his hero, Moab Jackson. Had the man who inspired his quest for freedom really returned? He hesitated before taking cautious steps toward him.

"Moab, is that really you?" Anthony whispered.

"It's me all right, and I come to see you and your mama. How she doing?" he whispered, looking anxiously in all directions. Anthony threw his arms around Moab's waist. The pungent smell of sweat and grime went unnoticed as Anthony hugged him.

"Moab, I'm so glad to see you," Anthony shouted.

Moab clamped his hand over Anthony's mouth. "Hush, boy. You wanna wake up the dead? Where your mama?" he whispered.

"She's at the wedding party over in the barn."

"Wedding party? She ain't done gone and got herself married, has she?"

"No, mama ain't gonna marry nobody," Anthony laughed. "She's already married. Cathy Johnson and Hale Sanders got married today. Master Bradley let them get married in the living room at the big house, and the wedding party is over in the barn."

"Cathy! I remember her. Ain't she one of Hattie Johnson's gals? The one with that white baby?"

"Yeah, that's right."

Moab stared at Anthony, then whistled. "Boy, you done sprung up like a weed. Now listen up. I come here to see your mama 'cause I got something to tell both of ya'll. Where can we talk that be safe? I seen some bounty hunters near here, so I gotta be careful."

Anthony remembered hearing Foreman Davis telling William about a runaway slave having been seen in the area. He didn't hear all the details, but it reminded him of the man that was caught by Joseph Hanks and his bounty hunter.

"I'll take you to our cabin."

"You sho'? If I gets caught there, it might go hard on you and your mama."

"Don't worry about us," Anthony whispered, motioning for Moab to follow him. They moved cautiously through darkening shadow until they reached the cabin. Before entering, Moab glanced over his shoulder, then walked over and sat at the table.

"Boy, you don't know how good it feels to get off my feet. It's sho' nice to be back here."

"Why you come back?"

"Like I say, I got something to tell ya'll, but I wants to say it when your mama's here. Listen up. Go tell her I got to see her right now and bring me something to eat. My horse went lame, so I been walking for the past two days. Had to stay off the main roads to keep them hounds from picking up my tracks. I also needs some water."

Anthony went to the well and returned with a tin cup of water. "I remembered what you said about freedom. Guess what? I asked Master Bradley to let me work for my freedom and I've got more than thirty dollars saved up already, and I'm just getting started."

"God bless you boy, but if you don't get out of here and bring me some food, I be starved to death," he said shoving Anthony toward the door.

Anthony started running but stopped abruptly when he heard someone call his name. Looking behind him, he saw Henry carrying a package wrapped in silver paper.

"Anthony, where are you running to so fast?"

Henry's smile put him at ease. "Gotta get back to the barn and help mama."

"Do you know if Cathy and Hale are still there?"

"They were when I left," Anthony replied.

"Give them this gift from me," Henry said, placing the package in Anthony's hands.

Anthony watched as Henry walked back toward the Manor house. Remembering Moab, he ran to the barn where Cathy and Hale were just cutting their wedding cake. He waited until everyone had been served.

"Master Henry sent this gift to you," Anthony said, placing the package on the table. Hale picked up the package and handed it to Ruth.

"Miss Ruth, me and my wife don't need no gift from him," Hale said, highly agitated. Cathy lowered her head and remained silent. The guests whispered among themselves as all eyes trained on Hale.

"Hale, you talk with Cathy about this after this party," Ruth said, turning to face the guests. "Folks, keep on dancing. This is none of your business."

Anthony moved beside Ruth and whispered, "Mama, I gotta tell you something. It's important."

"Anthony, can't you see I'm busy. What you gotta say that's so important?" Ruth said, annoyed by the untimely interruption. She placed her finger under Anthony's chin and looked into his eyes. No words were exchanged, for she realized he urgently needed to talk with her. Taking his hand, she guided him outside the barn door.

"What's so important it can't wait?"

"Moab Jackson has come back all the way from Washington City. He says he came to tell us something really important. I took him to our cabin," Anthony whispered excitedly.

Ruth placed her hand over her mouth and whispered. "Are you telling me Moab Jackson, that freeman, is back here and in our cabin?"

"It's him all right. I took him there myself, but don't worry, mama, nobody saw us."

"Lord in heaven. I fear an ill wind is gonna blow no good," Ruth said, wringing her hands.

"He's hungry, Mama. He ain't had nothing to eat."

"If I remember, he was hungry the first time I seen him. You go back and tell him to stay put until I get there. Don't you say a word to a soul, especially that loud mouth Bubba, you hear?"

Anthony suddenly remembered his promise to Bubba, but decided not to press his luck by asking for additional food.

Ruth felt dizzy as she rushed inside. Minutes later she returned with a biscuit filled with ham-hock that she had saved for them. "Tell him this have to do until I get there. Master William wants this barn cleaned up tonight. All us women will be here for a spell."

Anthony took the biscuit and ran back to the cabin. Moab was asleep, with his head resting on the table. When the cabin door opened Moab sprang to his feet, startled by the sound. "Boy, you spooked me. I guess I was tired from my journey."

"Mama's got work to do. She said for you to eat this. When she comes, she will bring you some more."

Moab took the biscuit and bit it in half. "Wish your mama would hurry up, boy. How long you think it be before she gets here?" he mumbled with his mouth full.

"She'll be here by and by."

Moab began pacing the floor. "I don't want to run into that fellow ya'll call Uncle Jim. I don't trust him."

"What you got against Uncle Jim?"

"You just don't understand, boy. Them the kind that don't know if they white or black, and that spells trouble for sho'." Moab pulled his stool beside Anthony. "Let me tell you a story about how half white niggers betrayed our race. Couple years ago there was this freeman down in Charleston, South Carolina named Denmark Vesey. He was smart as a fox and he worked hard and bought his freedom, just like me. He was a carpenter, but he wanted to free all our people. Back in 1822, Vesey organized more than nine thousand free blacks and slaves. They were all prepared to start a war fo' they freedom. They was planning to burn down Charleston and every city they came to. Guess what happened?"

"What?" Anthony asked, aware that his heart was beating rapidly.

Moab leaned across the table, his dark features gleaming from swat pouring down his face. When he spoke, his high-pitched tones reminded Anthony of the hissing of snakes. "Some high yella niggers told their masters what was about to happen. The whites took Vesey and thirty-five other black men and hanged them. Folks say they burned Vesey alive, chopped him up and fed his body to the hogs. They took all the slaves who knew about the plan and sold them to plantation owners in a place called Cuba. Last time I was here, I told your mama I don't trust yella niggers and she got mad at me."

"Well, Uncle Jim's not like that. We read books together. I wish you could hear his poems about freedom."

When the cabin door opened an hour later, Moab sprang to his feet. Ruth entered carrying a tin plate with hard-boiled eggs, potato salad and baked chicken.

"Moab Jackson, I'm glad to see you again, but why are you risking your neck coming out here?"

Moab reached for the plate and smiled. She was as beautiful as he had remembered her. "Miss Ruth, I's sho' glad to see you and Anthony again. I come this way to bring you some news, and it ain't good. I knows what happened to your husband."

Ruth sank on her stool and gripped the edge of the table. "What you gotta tell me about my Zach?"

"Miss Ruth, Anthony," Moab said, after placing his callused hands over hers. "I learned several years ago that Zachariah Bowen been dead, going on five years."

Ruth sat rigidly with her hands folded. She closed her eyes and gritted her teeth, but made no outcry.

"How did my papa die?" Anthony asked, trying to sound brave for Ruth's sake.

"He and some men was working on the Capitol building. The one them Brit soldiers burned down. Well, they were high up on what they called scaffolding, laying bricks, and it broke. All them men fell and died right off."

Ruth lowered her head on the table and cried. Anthony put his arms around her.

"Don't cry, mama."

She shook her head rapidly from side to side. "The Lord told me long time ago that my Zach was home with him but I didn't want to believe it. So

I kept on hoping and I cried a river of tears all these years," Ruth said, squeezing Moab's hand. "I thank you for risking your freedom to tell me the truth."

"Like I say, I had to come out this way, so I come see you first. When I leave here I's going over to the Anderson place and help two families make it to freedom. That what I do, along with being a coachman in Washington City. White folks got a new name for what we do. They call it the *Underground Railroad.*"

"You help slaves escape to freedom?" Anthony asked excitedly.

"That's right, boy." Moab studied Ruth's reaction. He hoped she would consider leaving now that she knew her husband was dead. He marveled as he studied her face. Even in her agony she was far more beautiful than he had remembered. Feeling hunger pains, Moab began eating the food she prepared for him. As he ate, he wondered about the spell she cast over him. He had more than his share of women, but none were like Ruth. Could he convince her to leave with him?

Ruth stood up and looked into his eyes. To his surprise, she bent over and kissed his cheek, then stepped back and smiled. A sharp knock at the door startled them. Moab looked around for a place to hide.

"Who's that?" Ruth called out.

"It's I, Uncle Jim."

Moab's eyes widened as he frantically gestured for her not to open the door. She opened it anyway. Jim entered the dimly lit room and stared at Moab.

"Woman, why you do that?" Moab said, throwing his arms up in despair.

"You got no cause to be scared of Uncle Jim. He's our best friend," Ruth said.

Jim moved to the window and closed the wooden shutters. He faced Moab and whispered, "You are in grave danger. Bounty hunters tracked you here and are talking with my master, seeking permission to search the grounds."

Moab sneered, "Why you 'speck me to trust you?"

"Jim's here to help you. Can't you see that?" Ruth whispered, upset.

"How did you know I was here?" Moab said. Caught between his distrust of Jim and Ruth's anger, he felt trapped.

"Nothing happens here that Jim doesn't know. You have to trust him," Ruth said, sharply.

"Anthony, Big George informed me he saw you taking a stranger into this cabin. I had just overheard Master Bradley ordering Joseph Hanks off his property," Jim said.

Ruth put her hands to her mouth. "Joseph Hanks. He's come back here?"

"He's a bounty hunter, but he's gone now, so don't worry," Jim replied.

"I hope he ain't out there waiting for me," Moab mumbled half aloud.

"I risked my neck to warn you and to keep Ruth and Anthony out of trouble. For whatever reason you came back, I want you off this plantation now," Jim shouted.

"Moab came to tell me that my Zachariah's been dead, going on five years," Ruth said, wearily. She took Moab's hand. "Moab, you gotta trust Jim. He would never do anything to hurt you. Now listen to him, you hear me?"

Moab wiped the perspiration from his face. He had experienced danger many times, but this situation left him feeling trapped and helpless. The last thing he wanted to do was to trust the likes of Jim Bradley. He sank on the stool and spoke in a low whisper, "What you want me to do?"

"Anthony will take you to the barn. Big George will give you one of our mules to ride. It is important that you stay off the main roads. The trail begins over by the north pasture. It will take you through some deep woods. When you reach the main road, turn the mule loose. It will make its way home."

Despite misgivings, Moab decided he had no other alternative. He went to the window and opened the shutters. "Ain't no moon out tonight and fog's rolling in. How I gonna find the trail through the woods?" Moab asked.

Anthony stood up. "I'll guide you to it."

"You do no such thing." Ruth shouted.

"Ruth, Anthony's not a child. He knows every foot of this plantation," Jim said. "Anthony won't be in danger if he shows Moab the trail. Hanks knows better than to set foot on this land."

"I'll be back soon, don't worry," Anthony said.

Ruth slumped on her stool and waved for them to leave. "Just go before I change my mind." Alone in the cabin, she knelt beside the bed. "Lord, be with Moab and Anthony as they move through dangers seen and unseen. Leave no mark of your displeasure on them, only on that devil, Joseph Hanks that's hiding out there. Please send his wicked soul into the fiery furnace."

Moab waited beside the barn door while Anthony saddled a mule. "Boy, it's black as hell out here. I can't see nothing. You must have eyes like an owl."

"I know right where we are. I'm guiding you to where the trail begins. Take it until you come to a fork in the road. Keep to the left. If you need to rest, you will come to an old barn that's about a morning's ride from here. Big George took us boys hunting and we stayed there one night. The trail ends at the turnpike that leads to Washington City."

"If I gets to that turnpike I knows where I be," Moab replied, grudgingly admitting that Jim could be trusted after all.

After reaching a wooded area where the trail began, Moab removed the bedroll from the back of the mule and spread it on the ground. "I's gonna sleep here 'til first light."

Suddenly Moab touched Anthony's arm and whispered, "You hear that?" Both remained still, listening to the rustling of leaves. "Don't move, Anthony," Moab whispered.

The sounds grew closer. Through the fog they saw the yellow eyes of a bloodhound. The hound lifted its head and let out a curdling howl that echoed through the deep woods. Moab sprang to his feet and yelled, "Get home as fast as you can." Moab ran into the fog with the hound close on his heels. The sounds of more dogs barking told Anthony that the pack had picked up Moab's scent.

Anthony mounted the mule. He heard angry voices, followed by shots and screams. While guiding the mule toward Bradley Manor, a hound ran out of the woods and began nipping at the animal's hind legs. The mule kicked the dog in its head, killing it instantly. Anthony found himself catapulted into a thicket. By the time he emerged, the mule had disappeared into the fog bank. Anthony ran toward a nearby stream, feeling as though his lungs were on fire. He paused, bent over and took several breaths. The bugle cries of hounds told him it was only a matter of time before they picked up his trail. He waded into the shallow stream and continued running. The water reduced his speed as he splashed up stream, away from the Manor plantation. He knew if he could reach a certain place where he and his friends played, he might be able to elude them.

The high-pitched sound of hounds grew louder, just as he reached a point where the stream became deeper. With the dogs coming closer, he searched along the bank for dry reeds. When he found a cluster, he broke several off at their base and blew through them to make sure they were hollow. He reached his objective, a large sycamore tree that leaned precariously over the water. Half of the tree's roots extended into the stream and the other half into the bank. Part of the root system had been exposed by the rushing waters and looked like five bony white fingers dipped into the stream. Anthony placed a reed in his mouth and squeezed between the exposed roots of the tree. He had used this technique while playing hide and seek. He thought he heard barking, but was not sure. Panic seized him momentarily when water got up his nose. Suddenly he thought he heard a voice say, 'Be still, for I am with you.' He managed to calm himself. After remaining submerged for a half-hour, ever so carefully he surfaced, stuck his head between the roots and listened. The only sound was the gentle waters of the stream. The current seemed to have slowed somewhat, and the only movement on the water was a single yellow leaf floating by.

After waiting another half-hour Anthony squeezed between the roots and climbed the bank. He found both dog and hoof-prints at the base of the tree. Anthony took several deep breaths and began running back toward Bradley Manor.

CHAPTER 18

Ruth sat by the window, staring out for the first signs of light. She rubbed her hands to relieve a tingling sensation and took quick breaths when she felt palpitations in her chest. The thick drifting fog reminded her of the starch she ironed on shirts every Monday morning. Tears flowed along the thin worry lines that formed at the corners of her lips. Jim and Big George watched helplessly. They had sat with her all night after she reported that Anthony failed to return.

"Anthony should be back by now?" Ruth said, rubbing her hands nervously. "I feel deep down in my bones that something bad has happened to him.".

Jim struggled for consoling words, but found none. He regretted having sent Anthony to do a man's job. How could he live with himself if anything happened to Anthony? The thought made him sick, but he tried to keep a calm face for Ruth's sake.

"Why did that fool came out here in the first place," Jim said, pacing the floor.

"I told you why he came," Ruth said, shaking her head. "Lord. I just can't lose my son."

Jim rose from his seat. "If Anthony does not return soon, I will inform Master William. I don't think it's wise for us to keep the truth from him much longer."

"What you think he does if he finds out we helped that man?" Big George said.

"We can't worry about that," Jim said, turning to Ruth. "All that matters is Anthony's safety."

"He will help us find Anthony. If we tell him why Moab came, he'll understand," Ruth said.

"He say he's a Christian. I guess we gonna find out just how Christian he is," Big George replied.

"Let's go tell him right now," Ruth insisted.

"You're right. He rises early and is possibly in the library." Jim walked to the window. "I sure wish that boy would come walking through that door. He knows every inch of this farm. The fog could have slowed him."

Ruth flinched when she heard a knock at the door. "Who's there?"

"It's me, Betty. My mama say Uncle Jim came over here to see you. Is he still here?"

When Ruth opened the door, Betty rushed past her. "Uncle Jim, Reverend Harris comes to our cabin just now. He say to tell you that a mule just come running to the barn, but ain't nobody riding him." Ruth uttered a cry and slumped to the floor.

William rose early, bathed and shaved, then went to the dining room where Sarah brought him a cup of coffee. Taking the cup to the library, he began working on the first draft of a speech. He had been invited to address a committee of Congress concerning the construction of the Chesapeake and Ohio Canal. Although there were cost overruns, he planned to speak in favor of it. When the door to the rose garden opened, William was surprised to see Jim, Ruth and Big George entering. From the somber expressions on their faces, he knew something was seriously wrong.

"What on earth are the three of you doing here this time of the morning?"

Jim stepped forward. "Master, I have news that involves all of us."

"Well, don't just stand there. What is it?"

Ruth stepped forward, wringing her hands, "Master, you remember three years ago when Senator Calvert came out here as your guest?"

"Of course I remember. What about it?" William asked impatiently.

"Well, his coachman was that free man named Moab Jackson."

"Ah, yes. That fellow who took a fancy to you. Don't tell me he sneaked out here to see you."

"He did come here yesterday, but to tell me about my husband."

"Your husband? What does he know about Zachariah?" William said, rising from his chair.

"He told me that my Zach was killed in a fall five years ago," Ruth said, determined not to cry.

Despite himself, William remembered Zachariah's screams of protest when he was placed in chains and dragged from that very room. He sighed as he walked over to her.

"I'm truly sorry, Ruth" he asked quietly. "Where is this Moab now?"

Jim stepped forward, "When Big George saw him hiding near the barn, he told me. I found him in Ruth's cabin and ordered him to leave. Anthony escorted him to the north trail, but we have not heard from Anthony since then. The mule they rode returned to the barn riderless this morning. We fear bounty hunters may have captured both of them."

Blood rushed to William's face as he recalled his conversation the night before with his former overseer, Joseph Hanks. Joseph and his two bounty hunters had arrived, requesting permission to search his property for a black man they were tracking. *"We got reason to believe that nigger knows something about the so-called Underground Railroad that's now operating out of Washington City and Maryland." Joseph had said.* William ordered him and his men to leave without further discussion. The very sight of the man had sickened him.

William turned to Big George. "Quick, saddle three horses. Jim, take the keys to the gun cabinet and load two guns. Both of you will ride with me. Ruth, go to the kitchen and wait until we return."

"Yes, master," she replied, her despair giving way to hope.

William rushed upstairs and hurriedly dressed in his riding habit. Mary Alice awoke, looked at her husband, and then glanced out the window.

"Where on earth are you going this time of the morning? Why, that fog outside is as thick as pea soup. You might break your neck if you go gallivanting around out there."

"Mary Alice, I will explain later." He completed dressing, ran down the stairs and out to the barn. Jim was waiting with the hunting rifles. After William handed Jim a rifle, they mounted the horses and rode through the fog. After riding a short distance, William spotted a figure running toward them.

"It's Anthony," Big George shouted. "Thank the good Lord that boy's safe."

Anthony reached them, gasping for breath. They could tell from the scratches on his face and arms that he had been through a harrowing ordeal.

"Are you all right? What happened to Moab?" Jim asked.

"I'm not hurt but I think Joseph Hanks caught him. I heard him yelling after shots were fired. He told me to hide and I ran and hid under some roots of a tree down by the stream."

William rode closer to Anthony, reached down and shook his hand. "I'm proud of you, Anthony. You used your head."

"Massa, can't we go a little further and see if we can help that po' man?" Big George pleaded.

"If what Anthony tells us is true, he is either dead or well on his way to some slave pen," William said, not particularly anxious to rescue a man who defied him.

"Please Master Bradley, we can't just leave him. They can't get too far in this fog," Anthony pleaded. As they waited for a response, William noticed that the fog was beginning to lift. He wondered how long it would be before it cleared.

Moab felt a sharp pain in the back of his thigh. He tried to recall what had happened, then he remembered he had been shot. He tried to move, but found himself securely tied to a tree. In the fog he could see three sleeping figures in bedrolls a short distance away. Smoke rose from the smoldering ashes of a fire the men had made the night before. Four blood hounds lay sleeping around the fire pit. Moab tested the ropes that held him. Slowly he twisted the rope and finally freed his left hand. The pain from the gunshot wound became almost unbearable. When he moved his leg, the dogs rose up and began barking.

Joseph sprang to his feet and walked to his prize prisoner. "Well, the nigger almost got himself free," Joseph said, standing and stretching himself. "Jack, you and Twigg get up. We gotta start moving as soon as this here fog lifts. We may still be on Bradley's land."

Joseph retied Moab's arms so tight that soon he felt a numbness in his limbs. "Well nigger, you're *mine* now. I know all about you and them nigger loving whites that help slaves run off. You gonna tell me all about it, ain't ya?"

Moab stared at Joseph, but remained silent. "Well, what we got here? A nigger that don't respect a white man when he speaks. Now, I ain't gonna ask you again. Who the nigger-loving white folks that been helping you?"

Despite the knot of fear tightening in his chest, Moab still refused to speak.

"Jack, I'm gonna brand this nigger. Get the iron's hot" Joseph yelled, slapping Moab's face.

"Don't kill him. He's big and healthy. He'll fetch us some real money down south," Jack said.

"Don't worry? One way or the other, he's gonna tell me want we want to know."

Moab resigned himself that he would soon be dead. He prayed silently, asking that his lips remain sealed. As a key member in the Underground Railroad, he knew the location of all the safe houses where slaves were hidden, as well as the white leaders who owned them.

After Twigg placed the branding irons in the fire, Joseph knelt beside Moab. "Why you come out here, nigger?"

"I come to see somebody," Moab responded, staring at the irons in the fire.

"Want to tell me about it?"

"I come to tell Ruth Bowen that her husband, Zachariah been dead, going on five years."

Joseph's eyes lit up. "Now I remember. I caught you messing with Bradley's wench." Twigg handed Joseph one of a branding irons. Joseph stood over Moab, reached down and tore off his shirt. "Nigger, listen carefully. This here's my special branding iron. Ain't it pretty? Now are you going to talk?"

Moab pressed his head against the trunk of the tree as Joseph waved the glowing iron close to his face. His eyes bulged when he felt the searing heat, yet he made no outcry.

"Last chance, nigger." Joseph shouted, pressing the branding iron below Moab's navel. Sounds, like the frying of bacon in a hot skillet, filled the air. Moab's piercing screams shattered the fog's thick mantle, echoing throughout the forest. Joseph stood back and examined his handy work, while adjusting his crotch.

"This is better than a lynching party. Hand me another iron," Joseph said in guttural tones.

Jack hesitated, "Joe, we already shot him up bad. The more burns we put on him the less money we get. Too many burns will tell folks this nigger's trouble. Nobody pays top dollar for trouble."

"God damn it, don't argue with me. This nigger's got information that can make us rich, and I'm gonna get it out of him even if I have to skin and roast him alive."

Reluctantly, Jack went to the fire pit and pulled out another iron. Joseph snatched it from his hand and walked back to Moab. "You ready to talk now?" Moab stared at the iron while shaking his head from side to side.

"Well, this time I'm gonna burn that black rope you used on that bitch, Ruth. It won't be no use to you after I burn it off," Joseph sneered, reaching down and tearing opening Moab's trousers. Moab's eyes widened as he tried to jerk his legs to avoid the hot iron. Despite himself, Moab heard himself screaming, "Please don't burn me no more. Please don't burn me."

"Talk, nigger. God damn, it, talk!" Joseph yelled, lowering the iron closer to his captive's exposed groins. Moab's screams drowned out the rifle shot that suddenly split the morning air. He glanced up at Joseph, prepared to make a final plea, but his tormentor's face was now a splattered mask of blood and torn skin that fell away from him. Amid the confusion, Moab was certain he was dying. The branding iron fell on his trousers, but someone quickly removed it and cut the burning trousers from his skin. Moab stared unbelieving into the eyes of Jim Bradley. Was it Anthony who was loosening the ropes that held his feet and arms? They were speaking, but a cloud in his brain thickened like a drifting fog. Was he dreaming that he saw William Bradley standing over the body of Joseph Hanks? His pain subsided as a merciful darkness engulfed him.

When Moab opened his eyes, the fog was still there. He groaned from the searing pain in his leg and stomach. He saw the silhouette of someone standing over him. When he attempted to sit up, gentle hands restrained him.

"You need your rest, Moab," Ruth whispered.

He reached out, took her hand and pressed it to his lips. "This must be heaven," Moab said. He could see Ruth now, smiling down at him.

"No Moab, it's not heaven. You are here with us," Ruth whispered.

"How long I been here?"

"Two days. We were scared you were going to die. I been taking care of you days and nights and the Lord answered my prayers. Master Bradley say you can stay here with Anthony and me until you are better. But he say when you get well, he wants to talk with you. Until then, I'll take care of you." There was a trace of girlish glee in Ruth's voice.

CHAPTER 19

Ruth hurried to her cabin with a tray of orange juice, toast and two hard-boiled eggs. Upon entering, the squeaking door hinge woke Moab who tried to sit up. The pain from his wounds forced him to remain on the edge of the bed. She removed the shells from the eggs and set the tray on his lap.

"Look like that sleep done you good," Ruth said, sitting in a chair beside him. After he ate, she carefully removed the bandages and cleaned his wounds. "Looks to me like you getting better."

Despite the discomfort, Moab enjoyed having her close to him. "Wish it would take a little longer. I can't believe I's here and you taking care of me."

"With that kind of talk, I know you getting better. Master Bradley asked me how you coming along. I told him I thought you will be on your feet, come tomorrow. He asked me if you are behaving yourself."

"Why he say that?"

"'Cause you are a man," Ruth said, grinning. "As soon as you on your feet, he wants to talk with you." Ruth opened a package and placed a pair of cotton trousers and a work shirt on the chair beside the bed. "You put these on in the morning."

"Those some mighty fine work clothes. You don't reckon he gonna try to make me one of his slaves, do you?"

"No, he wouldn't do anything like that. I think he wants to see if you well enough to travel."

"Miss Ruth, I gotta tell you something. But you gotta promise you won't tell nobody."

"If it be all that important, maybe you best not say it," she said, patting him lightly on the back of his hand. "But you know you can trust me."

"Miss Ruth, for the better part of three years I be working in what folks call the *Underground Railroad*. I been helping our folks run away to freedom."

"*Underground Railroad*! What's that?"

Leaning forward, Moab whispered, "That's just a name some folks starting to call what we do. There ain't no real railroad, like the ones that takes them little coal cars down in the coal mine, or those city carriages that runs on rails. Folks that hide slaves in their home, we call them homes, *stations*. I guide our folks from station to station. We help them escape up north to free states. I got white friends that call themselves Quakers. They the ones that been helping us. They opens their homes along the roads we take at night."

"Any of those stations near here?"

"Closest one over in Montgomery County. These Quaker folks believe it is a sin for white people to make slaves of us colored folks. This farmer, he and his son built a special room under his house. It's got a trap door that looks just like the floor. A person could walk in that room and be standing on that door, not knowing folks hiding down in that cellar.

"Is that why you came this way?" Ruth asked.

"That's right. After I learned your husband died in that fall, I decided to stop by here first," Moab replied earnestly. "If I get out of here, someday I'll come back for you and Anthony, if you want me to?"

Ruth lowered her head and did not respond. William had given Anthony permission to work for his freedom. She knew Anthony had an obligation to keep his part of the bargain. "My Lord spoke to me in a dream and he told me my son gonna be free someday, thanks to you. But he would never steal himself. He will work and pay for his freedom, just like you did. So I gotta stay with him. I hope you understand."

"You ever hear our people sing, 'Steal away to Jesus?" That's a freedom song. That boy of yours gonna be working for your master 'til he done burned himself out." When she placed her hands over her ears, he knew that her answer was final. But there was tomorrow, and he would try again.

The next morning dawned cloudy and cool. Moab sat on the edge of the bed and painfully dressed himself. Anthony brought him biscuits, layered with fried eggs and a thick slice of fatback.

"Miss Ruth told me you working over at a white folks farm in your spare time? How much you gets?" Moab asked.

"Sometimes fifty cents. I've only been there twice now. I hope to be going back again real soon. The Bakers have only three slaves and one's a girl named Catharine."

Moab reached over and tapped Anthony's head. "You like that gal?"

"Well, we just met once. She's real nice and very pretty," Anthony said, remembering that the second time he worked there, he had not seen her.

"Watch yourself, Anthony. You got your plan for freedom and women can mess it up real quick."

"Don't worry about me. Nothing gonna get in the way of my plans," Anthony said. "Finish eating, 'cause mama say it's time for you to go meet Master Bradley."

After Moab finished eating, Anthony handed him a cane and walked beside him to the library. When they entered, William rose from his chair. He realized Moab was in pain.

"Anthony, bring this boy a stool from the kitchen." When Anthony returned with a stool, Moab was grateful for being allowed to sit.

"Ruth tells me you came here to tell her that her husband died in a fall several years ago."

"Yes sir," Moab said, bowing meekly.

"What other reasons did you have for coming out here?"

Moab met William's stern gaze and refused to be intimidated. "Ain't gonna lie to you, sir. I wanted to see Miss Ruth again. That be after I learned her husband died."

"And you would risk your freedom to see her?"

"You might say that, sir. She's a mighty fine woman."

William recalled the night he tried to force Ruth to accept another man. Despite the fact that he had been drunk, he remembered, with vivid clarity, the rage in her eyes when she defied him.

"Moab, you drove your carriage for my cousin, Senator Calvert, during the years he served in Congress. Are you still a coachman?"

"Yes sir. I drive mostly for white families in Washington City," Moab replied.

"I know you've heard talk about the so-called *The Underground Railroad*, have you not?"

Moab felt tension, but the mask he wore did not betray him. "The Underground what?"

"The *Underground Railroad*. Surely you've heard the word spoken among your people in Washington City."

"No sir. Only tracks I seen going underground is the ones going down in the coal mines. You 'speck that be what they talking about?"

William laughed, thinking to himself this black was either stupid or smart like a fox. "Well, I'm sure you have heard about slaves running away?"

"I hears that now and then, sir, but I worked fifteen years for my freedom. Ever since I be free, I works hard to feed my face. Ain't got no time to think about tracks that runs underground or folks running off," Moab said, aware that William was not amused.

William reached for his father's walking cane that he kept in a stand beside his chair. He rapped it on the floor three times.

"Moab, I'm nobody's fool. Did you hear the sound of this cane?"

"Yes sir. I hears it."

"Well, you don't want to ever hear it again, do you?"

"No sir, I sure don't, sir." Moab said, bowing twice.

"You may stay one more day, then I want you out of here. If I ever catch you on my property, or if you try to encourage my people to run away, I will hunt you down and put my own brand on your black hide. Have I made myself clear?"

"Yes sir. I won't be coming anywhere near here, sir" Moab stammered. "But if you ever in Washington City and needs a carriage, just call on me. I's always down at one of the hotels."

"You may leave by the back door," William instructed, pointing the cane toward the double doors leading to the rose garden. Painfully, Moab limped across the room. He turned and faced William. "Sir, I wants to thank you for saving my life."

At the garden path, Moab searched for a familiar face, but seeing none, made his way back to the cabin. Opening the door he limped to the bed. Before he could sit down he heard a knock at the door.

"Who that be?" he said. A tall brown-skinned man opened the door and stuck his head in.

"Howdy, I'm Hale Sanders," Hale whispered, walking over and shaking his hand. "I hear what happened to you. I come to ask you a question. Is it true what folks be saying, that you help our folks get to freedom land?"

Moab stared at the stranger suspiciously. After all that he had been through, how could he trust this stranger. He could be one of William Bradley's house niggers sent to spy on him.

"Who told you that?"

"Ain't much that happens in these parts that us field folks don't know about, sooner or later."

Ruth entered the open cabin door. "I been looking for you. Why did you walk back here by yourself? I was expecting you to come to the kitchen and fetch me?"

"Miss Ruth, after what your master say, I would have walked straight back to Washington City, if I could. He say if I come back here, he puts his brand on me. Now, here comes this fellow wanting to know if I help folks run way. Who is he anyway?"

Ruth stared at Hale, astonished that he was in her cabin that time of the morning. "Hale is the young man that just got married," she said, turning to Hale. "Hale, what you doing here?"

"I just wanted to know if it true he helps colored folk go north to freedom."

Ruth frowned. "Why you want to know that for? You and Cathy just got married."

Hale lowered his head and refused to answer. Moab rose from his cot and dragged himself over to the table. Common sense told him to keep his mouth shut and get as far away from Bradley Manor as he could. But reflecting on his mission, his instincts told him that Hale was a man that could be trusted.

"If you wants to talk before I leave, bring your woman with you," Moab whispered.

Ruth threw up her hands. "Moab, you almost got yourself killed coming out here. Master Bradley saved your life and now you gonna repay him by putting mess in Hale's head?"

"Freedom's got a price, Miss Ruth, and that price be trouble itself," Moab replied calmly.

At a little past midnight, Hale knocked on Ruth's door. When she opened it, he brought Cathy inside. Moab saw the unhappy expression on Cathy's face when they sat at the table.

"I told Cathy I just wanted to talk to you," Hale whispered, placing his arm around Cathy's shoulder. "I wants her to hear what you got to say about freedom."

Moab felt uncomfortable the moment he saw Cathy. Her light complexion and sullen attitude made her all the more suspicious, in his eyes.

"Look here, Miz. Cathy. If you don't want to hear what I gotta say, you best speak your mind now," Moab said.

Cathy turned to Hale. "Why you bring me here in the middle of the night?"

"I told you I wanted you to hear what he gotta say. You told me before we got married how much you wanted all of us to be free."

"That's right. But I ain't gonna run away with him. What if we get caught? Where would we be then? Just look what happened to him," she said, pointing to Moab. "Hale, we just got married and Master Bradley's doing good by us. Why are you talking like this just days after we married."

Hale slammed his fist on the table. "Because I's just a nigger living here. Cathy, I needs my freedom like I needs air to breathe and I wants it for you and our son," he shouted passionately.

"I think it best you take your woman home," Moab whispered. Cathy had confirmed his worst fears about not trusting mulattos.

Ruth walked over and hugged Cathy. "Child, Hale's not gonna make you do nothing you don't want to do."

"Cathy, you know how much I loves you, but woman, you gotta understand. I also loves freedom. I just want you to hear what he has to say," Hale said, wiping sweat from his face.

Cathy pulled up her skirt, stalked out the door and slammed it in Hale's face. He followed her outside but turned back. "Moab, before you leave, I wants to hear it from your lips."

CHAPTER 20

Anthony was beside himself with joy when he received word that Abel Baker needed him to help plow a four-acre field. During the first Saturday of every month, William gave his house people a half-day's rest. Anthony used the time to travel to the Baker farm. By working several daylight hours, it meant extra wages to be applied to his freedom fund. This would be his third job at the Baker farm. The second had lasted only an hour and he did not have an opportunity to see Catharine.

Abel's thirty year old son, John, led him to the field where they plowed the rich bottom land located near a shallow stream. John paused and pointed to a large sycamore tree. "We gonna rest for a spell over yonder. You can take a piss in them tall weeds." As they stood urinating, John laughed. "Hell nigger, your pecker ain't as long as mine." Once seated, John removed a flask from his overalls, emptied it and began bragging about how he made the best good corn whiskey in Prince Georges County.

From the smell of his breath, Anthony was sure John consumed as much as he sold. He noticed that half of the little finger on John's left hand was missing.

"I see you looking at this here finger. A god damn bear bit it off after I shot it. I thought the son-of-a-bitch was dead, but it jumped up and bit my finger. I took out my knife and finished him off," John said boastfully.

"I've never seen a bear, only in a book my master owns," Anthony said.

"By God, nigger, you sure knows how to plow," John drawled, slapping Anthony's back. "We thought you was a house boy. I was told house niggers ain't worth shit when it comes to doing field work."

Anthony disguised the disgust he felt. "I've made it my business to learn lots of things. I paint, plow, and I'm learning to make furniture."

"I seen some of them fine nigger wenches Bradley owns. You gets your pick of them, don't ya? How many you busted?"

"I don't do that, sir," Anthony replied, trying to put John's crude remarks out of his mind, knowing it would not be the last time he would have to listen to such filth from John Baker's lips. It only strengthened his resolve to work harder for his freedom.

"Nigger, you know you lying," John said laughing. "My pa said he sure would like to buy one or two of ya'll."

"My master does not sell any of his people," Anthony replied, struggling to maintain his composure. "Not these days, anyway."

"How you like Cat?" John asked, grinning.

"Cat?" Anthony replied, tense from the knot tightening in his stomach.

"That pretty wench we own. I know you seen her. Bet you want some of that twat, don't ya?"

Anthony stared at John with disbelief. How could he possibly respond to such a question?

John punched him in the ribs. "Foods ah' coming," he said, pointing to Catharine walking toward them, holding a basket. "You get your chance to meet her."

For the first time Anthony saw Catharine in daylight. She looked thin and undernourished, but her attractive face reflected a rich blend of African and Indian features, the African being dominant. The ragged gray dress she wore hung loosely from her shoulders. She wore her hair in two plaits that hung to her waist. Her full lips, high cheekbones and unblemished complexion, the color of almonds, left him speechless.

"Ya'll hungry?" Catharine said, placing the basket at Anthony's feet.

"Yeah. You late," John said, patting the ground. "Sit for a spell."

Catharine hesitated, then sat between them. John snatched the basket and took what he wanted. Catharine handed the basket to Anthony. He selected a fried chicken leg, boiled potato, and a slice of dark bread.

"How you like this nigger, Cat? He's sweet on you," John mumbled. She smiled nervously, sprang to her feet and started toward the farmhouse. "There goes one fine wench. I'll see that you get some of that while you here." John turned and winked at him.

Anthony managed a weak smile, wondering why John would make such a offer?

The workday extended into the late evening hours. When they returned to the barn, John pointed to the loft. "Sleep up there. Use them feed sacks to bed down on. I'll get you something better next time you come. Guess you be gone by the time I get up, so I'll see you next time pa sends for you."

Anthony waited until John left, then climbed the ladder and was asleep as soon after his head hit the feed sacks. He awoke when someone shook him.

"Good morning Anthony." Catharine's musical greeting caused him to sit up abruptly. He found her in a kneeling position beside him, holding a plate of scrambled eggs, grits and fried fatback.

Anthony sat up and rubbed his eyes. "Thanks for waking me."

"You glad to see me?"

"Yeah, real glad," he said smiling. "Where were you the last time I was here. I got to thinking they might have sold you and I was too scared to ask."

"Sell me!" she said laughing. "I do most of the work around here. They ain't about to sell me. I just had lots to do, that's all. I's glad Master Abel brought you here after John say his leg was hurting. John don't like working much. After he marry Miss Clara and brought her here last year, all he do is get drunk and lay up in bed with her every night and half the morning. It makes Master Baker real mad."

Her close presence made Anthony forget his hunger. "Gotta be leaving soon."

"Finish eating them eggs and come help me catch a mess of frogs," she said, standing and brushing the straw from her skirt.

After Anthony finished eating, they climbed down the ladder and walked outside into the crisp morning air. "I love it when morning take its first full breath," Anthony said, stretching his arms. He saw the surprised look on her face.

"You talk real pretty," Catharine said, taking Anthony's hand. "We gotta hurry, 'cause I gotta get back before everybody wake up." She guided him across the meadow to a small stream. As they approached the bank, she dropped on her hands and knees and whispered, "Get down." He knelt and crawled beside her through the tall weeds that lined the bank of the shallow stream.

"What you gonna do?" Anthony whispered.

She placed her finger to her lips. After removing her straw hat, she carefully pulled the weeds aside, and with one quick motion, slammed the hat into the muddy water. Anthony watched with amazement when she reached under the hat and held up by its legs the largest bullfrog he had ever seen. After handing it to Anthony, she cautioned him to remain quiet while she continued the hunt. Before long, Anthony was holding tightly to the legs of four slippery frogs.

"These gonna make a fine dinner for the old folks," Catharine said, removing a knife from her belt. She skinned and gutted the frog with such speed, their muscles continued switching after she placed them in her pouch.

Anthony could not believe that he had witnessed such skill. "Where did you learn to do that?"

"My mother taught me."

He held her hand while returning to the barn. "Tell me about yourself."

"Ain't much to tell. My father was a slave who ran away and lived with Indians. They was the Cherokee tribe that lived in Tennessee," she said proudly. "They liked papa 'cause he fought with them when white men tried to steal they land. After he saved the chief's life, the chief say he could marry my mama. When I was born, she named me Morning Star. That's 'cause a bright star was first thing mama seen in the sky the morning I was born. My pa's name is Noah. He's the one that gave me my Christian name, Catharine. When I be eleven, white men come and burned our village. My mama and most of our people were killed, but me and papa got captured and sold. The Bakers bought me when I was sick with the fever. They got me cheap, 'cause the man who owned me thought I was gonna die. After they brung me here, I got well."

"What happened to your papa?"

"Guess they sold him. I ain't ever seen him, never no more," Catharine said bitterly. "I dreams about him and mama most every night. He used to carry me on his shoulders, singing lots of songs and telling me stories. Now tell me about you."

"A few years ago my mama showed me a cloud that looked just like a fish bone." Anthony said reflectively. "My master sold my father when I was four years old, and I wondered if it meant that he had died. Well, I learned not long ago he had been killed after falling off a building."

"I dream my pa died too. I guess they both in heaven with Jesus," Catharine said. "What you do when you not working?"

"I read books. My master allowed his sister, Roberta, and my Uncle Jim, to teach me to read and write," Anthony said, with a mixture of pride and embarrassment.

"You got book-learning?" she asked, excitedly. "I wish I could read. Massa Baker reads a little, but his wife and his son don't. He say John too lazy to get any book-learning. I know some words from the Bible, like the Lord's prayer. The Bakers take us to their Church. We slaves sit in the back rows."

"Catharine, I wish I could stay longer, but I gotta be going."

"Will you teach me some words, that be if we can find time?"

"We'll find a way to make the time," Anthony replied, surprised that he made a promise that he possibly could not keep. Catharine threw her arms around his waist, hugged him then ran toward the Baker house. He stood motionless for a few moments, reflecting on how the warmth of her embrace had excited him. As he prepared to mount his horse, John stepped from behind a post, grinning at him.

"I seen you hugging her. You got some of that twat last night, didn't ya'?" John asked. "Was she good?" The stupid grim on his face left Anthony shaken.

"I have to be going now," Anthony replied, adjusting the horse's harness.

John stepped between Anthony and the horse. "Hell, nigger, answer me when I speak to you. Did you get in her twat or not?"

"No sir," Anthony stammered.

"She got uppity on you, didn't she?" John asked, rubbing the scarred nub of his finger as though it pained him. "Well, you keep trying, you hear? I'll see that she gives it up next time you come."

"I hear you, sir," Anthony whispered, alarmed by the suggestion.

"Before I bring my wife here, she come getting uppity with me, a white man," John said, "Trouble was, the little bitch had never been busted. You ever seen folks break in wild horses?"

"Yes sir," Anthony stammered, dreading what would spill from John's lips. He could smell the liquor on John's breath when he pulled his stool closer. The sadistic grin on his face terrified Anthony.

"I'll tell you how I done it. First, I gave her a taste of my corn. After I got her liquored up, I fed her some of my wild oats. Then I rode her sweet bucking ass 'til I busted her," John bragged, slapping his crotch. He leered while leaning closer to Anthony's face. "That sassy tongue of hers ain't uppity no more. That's 'cause she got a better use for it. Nothing better than busting wenches and wild ponies."

Overwhelmed with rage, Anthony resisted the compulsion to grab a pitchfork and use it on John. For the first time he almost lost control of himself. The surge of anger frightened him. After holding his breath, Anthony mounted his horse and rode out of the barn. While returning home, he felt totally devastated. Never in his life had he felt so degraded and useless. John's description of how he raped Catharine left frightening images that he could not erase. Was he abusing Catharine at that very moment? What could he do to protect her? He had made the decision not to become sexually active until he was free and married. It dawned on him how much he desired Catharine. Confused and bewildered, he finally reached the safety of his cabin. Upon entering, he took a scrap of paper and pencil and began writing. Suddenly remembering that the wood rack was low, he placed the sheet aside, ran to the back yard and chopped wood for the fireplace.

"I'm glad you got back safely," Ruth said, when Anthony entered the kitchen. "We got exciting news." When he showed no interest, Ruth became concerned. "You feeling alright?"

Hattie placed a bowl of chicken soup in front of him. "This po' boy's all tuckered out. Eat this soup and you be fit real soon. Your ma and me excited 'cause Henry done found himself a fine young lady. She and her mama gonna be visiting us next week."

"I'm happy for them," Anthony said, stirring the soup with his spoon. He thought of Hale, knowing he would be pleased. He had overheard Betty saying that Hale was worried that Henry might still want Cathy and he wasn't even sure of his wife's true feeling. Cathy had become upset after

174

Hale rejected Henry's gift without asking her. As for his fears about Catharine, he decided to seek Uncle Jim's advice. Uncle Jim had never steered him wrong.

CHAPTER 21

Ruth dumped bed sheets and tablecloths in a waist-high iron cauldron located in the outdoor washing area. After boiling the articles for thirty minutes, Betty helped her lift them into the rinse tubs, using long poles. Ruth paused to rest after all the articles were hung on long clotheslines to dry. She went to a shaded area and wiped the perspiration from her face.

"Betty, I don't know what's ailing me. I've been feeling poorly lately. I must be getting old, or worry's been settling in my bones."

"Miss Ruth, you not old. What you worrying about?"

"Anthony's keeping me awake at night. That boy ain't been himself since he come home night before last. I ask him what's wrong, but he don't say nothing. He just mopes around like a sick cat. It's not like him. I wonder if he's coming down with something."

"Come to think about it, he has be acting strange."

"Something happened over at that Baker place, I'm sure of it. I best have a talk with Uncle Jim."

"You be worried about Anthony, and mama's all worried about Cathy," Betty said, keeping a careful eye on a wasp that kept flying around her head. Using her apron, she drove it off.

"Cathy! What's ailing her?"

"She been complaining ever since Moab left here. She say all Hale wants to talk about is getting their freedom. You can hear them fussing some nights clean over at our place. It got worse after they hear Master Henry gonna get married and bring his lady to live here."

"She married to Hale now. Henry's not going to cause them problems. I know that boy."

"It's not him they worried about. What gonna happen when that lady finds out that he's the father of her baby," Betty said, shaking her head. "Hale say that's another reason he wants them to run away."

"Lord, there gonna be a mess around here for sure," Ruth said, gazing at the sky, "I see storm clouds coming and I don't mean the kind that bring rain."

When they returned to the kitchen, Jim was sitting at the table drinking coffee with Hattie and Hale. Ruth placed her basket in the pantry, then joined them. "Uncle Jim, I just said to Betty that I wanted to talk with you about Anthony."

"What about? I just had a long talk with him this morning."

"He ain't been the same ever since he came back from the Baker farm Sunday morning. He won't tell me what's ailing him," Ruth said.

Jim reached over and patted Ruth's hands. "Don't worry about Anthony. He's just growing up and learning the facts of life."

"What kind of facts of life?" Ruth asked with alarm.

"He's not sick, Ruth. He thinks he's in love," Jim said, grinning.

Ruth sat up with a start, as Hattie and Betty giggled. "Love! What my Anthony know about love at his age?" Ruth said angrily.

"He's almost sixteen, Ruth," Jim said.

Betty broke into laughter. "Anthony in love. Ain't that sweet. Who's the girl?

"Nothing funny about this, Betty" Ruth said, shaking her finger in her face. "Uncle Jim, if he so much in love, what's ailing him?"

Jim hesitated, then reached over and held Ruth's hand. "Now I do not want to upset you. It boils down to the fact that the Bakers' son, John, has been encouraging Anthony. How should I say this? He wants Anthony to bed down a girl they own. In other words, they want to use him for stud service."

"Lord, sweet Jesus," Ruth cried, throwing up her arms.

Jim placed his hand on her shoulder. "Now, now, Ruth, look at the bright side of it. The Bakers pay our master a stud fee to breed their horses and cows," he said, managing to keep a straight face. "I suggest we ask Master William to demand a stud fee for Anthony's services which, in turn, he could apply to his freedom fund." He covered his ears to drown out Betty and Hattie's burst of laughter.

"Uh- whee! Uncle Jim you in a heap of trouble," Betty said, wiping tears from her eyes.

Ruth's eyes narrowed, "None of this funny to me. I don't want Anthony messing with no girls, especially none that the Bakers own. Before you know it, she got her belly full and my grandbabies will be owned by white trash. All they gonna do is sell the child soon as it's able to work."

Jim turned to Ruth. "We discussed that possibility. You must accept the fact that your son has a good head on his shoulders. Trust him to do the right thing. I gave him some sound advice."

"It's not his head I'm worried about. It's what's between his legs. And just where is my son now?"

"He left for the Baker farm an hour ago. Abel sent word that they need him to help finish the plowing, and Master William gave him a full day off. He said not to worry if he does not come home tonight."

"Lord, what am I gonna do?" Ruth whispered. She picked up a large onion from the table, placed it on the chopping board and began slicing it with quick strokes.

177

"Careful," Jim said as he wiped his eyes. "You don't want to lose a finger."

Hale stood up, scowling. "Excuse me, I don't want to hear no more what you talking 'bout." All eyes trained on Hale as he hurried out of the kitchen door.

Mary Alice entered from the dining room, smiling and gesturing with her hands. "Oh, I'm so excited. Henry, his young lady and her mother will be here in the morning. He wrote and told me all about her. She sounds like an angel." She paused for breath. "Now Ruth, I want you to prepare a special meal. Cook that pork roast the special way William likes, medium rare. Serve it with new potatoes and sweet peas, and make brown gravy with those mushrooms Big George brought in yesterday. Bake two of your famous potato pies. And of course, we will use our best china. Now Betty, go help your mother with my new dress. She's making it from a lovely pattern that just arrived from Washington City. It's from one of those fashion houses in Paris. It must be ready before they arrive," Mary Alice said. She took a deep breath, threw up her hands and hurried from the kitchen. After the door closed, everyone paused, then burst into laughter.

While riding the mule to the Baker farm, Anthony reflected on the advice Uncle Jim had given him. At the end of their conversation, he had left confused and downhearted. Surely there had to be a way to rescue Catharine from such a cruel situation. All Jim had given him was a warning.

"Anthony, the best advice I can give you is to stay away from that girl. You don't want to jeopardize your chance for freedom. I know you think you love her, but the excitement you are feeling right now is not love. When you have gained your freedom, you will meet many fine young women, and possibly marry the one you love. As for this Catharine, from all you've told me, John has made her his personal property. It is painful for me to say this, but you need to hear it. John Baker uses her to satisfy his lust. There is only one reason he is offering her to you. He wants you to do what he can't do. He wants to breed her like they breed their cows. You are not someone's prize bull," Jim said.

After entering the barn, Anthony unsaddled the mule. He paused when he heard John hammering out a horseshoe.

"Glad you could make it, boy," John said, placing his hammer aside. "It's gonna be tough plowing in this heat, but we got a full moon after it's gets dark. I got the mules already hitched up and ready to go."

Anthony followed John into the field, and for several hours they plowed without speaking or resting. Anthony wondered if Catharine would bring them food during the rest period. At dust swarms of mosquitoes from a nearby swamp descended upon them.

John rubbed his face and arms. "These damn varmints suck your blood. They leaving tracks from my head to my butt."

Anthony continued plowing, miserable from countless stings on his exposed head and arms. John offered him a plug of chewing tobacco.

"Here, take a chaw. Spit some out and rub it on your arms and face. 'Skeeters don't like tobacco juice," he said laughing. Anthony took the tobacco plug, bit off a chunk and began chewing. He spit the juice in his hand and rubbed the substance on his face and arms. Shortly, he began vomiting.

"You ain't never had a chaw before, have ya?" John said, slapping his back.

"No sir," Anthony replied, trying to catch his breath.

"Well, nigger, I like you. You can have a chaw off my plug any time you want. Let's get the hell out of here. We done enough for one night."

"When are we gonna eat?" Anthony asked.

"My woman and me eating dinner with Pa and Ma. We'll send you some vittles."

After John left, Anthony stood at the barn door, his stomach growling from hunger. He felt relieved that John had made no mention of Catharine. It was as though their conversation of the past week had never taken place. Two hours passed and he feared he might not get to see her. Just as he prepared to climb up the loft, the barn door opened and Catharine entered, holding a candle and a plate of food.

"I brought your dinner, Anthony."

His heart began racing when he heard her voice. They stood close, staring into each other's eyes and smiling shyly. She raised the candle and placed her hand on the mass of welts that covered his face.

"You look awful. Them critters try to eat you alive, didn't they? What you put on your face?"

"Tobacco juice."

Catharine turned up her nose. "John Baker chews tobacco all the time. Don't you start using that stuff. It'll make your teeth ugly and fall out, just like most of his. And it will make your breath stink."

Anthony took the plate, but suddenly lost his appetite. He couldn't take his eyes off her.

"You can't eat and look at me. I cooked these vittles special for you, so eat every bit of it." She sat beside him and watched while he ate the fried chicken, boiled potatoes, green peas and corn bread.

"This taste just like my mama's cooking."

"You just saying that," she said, pulling a stool closer to him. "You miss me?"

"Yes, but I've been worried about you," Anthony said.

"Why you worrying about me?" Catharine asked, smiling. "I can take care of myself."

"Can't help it. I hate this place and how they treat you."

"You sweet to say that." She placed her hand to his cheek.

Anthony rose up and backed away from her, certain he hear Jim whispering, *'Stay away from that girl. You don't want to jeopardize your change for freedom.'*

"What's wrong? I thought you like me," Catharine said, stunned by his rejection.

Anthony looked around, staring into the dark corners of the barn. Was John Baker hiding somewhere, watching them? He felt remorseful when he saw tears in her eyes. Determined to overcome his fears, he reached out and hugged her. They stared each other, laughing nervously. Timidly, he kissed her lips. She was the first girl he had ever kissed. Her arms tightened around his neck when she returned his kiss. The taste of her lips and the awareness of her full breast pressing against his chest overwhelmed him. Stepping back, he tried to clear his head.

"Want to know a secret, Anthony?" she said, breathing rapidly.

"What kind of secret?"

"You the very first boy I ever let kiss me."

"You've never been kissed before?" Anthony asked, hopefully.

She hesitated, then whispered, "I said, you the very first boy I *let* kiss me."

His head cleared. "I best be getting up in the loft to rest. Will I see you before I leave?"

"You want me to stay with you tonight?" Catharine whispered. She seemed as frightened as he was.

In the semi-darkness, Anthony felt a sensation coursing through his loins. He wanted to run from her, but all he could do was stare into her sparkling eyes, highlighted by candlelight.

"You scared of me, Anthony?" she whispered.

His pride would not let him answer truthfully. "I'm not scared of you. It's John Baker that scare me. For all I know he might be hiding some place, watching us," he whispered, taking quick glances into the dark corners of the barn.

"He rode off after dinner. I hear him say he was going to sell some whiskey."

Despite himself, Anthony took her hand and led her up the ladder. In the loft, he stretched out on his cot and listened to the beating of his heart. Catharine knelt beside him, lit a candle and placed it on the bench. She loosened the plaits of her hair, leaned over him and kissed his cheek. He thought he heard John whisper, *"I'll see to it that she gives it up next time you come."*

"Catharine, I gotta asks you a question," Anthony said, rising up on one elbow. Did John tell you to come be with me tonight?" When she covered her face with her hands, he regretted asking the question. "You don't have to answer if you don't want to."

"What he say about me?" Catharine said in muffled tones, too ashamed to face him.

John said he would make you come be with me," Anthony said, moving closer to her. Gently, he removed her hands from her tear-filled face and placed them in her lap.

She gritted her teeth, fearing their short-lived relationship was now in jeopardy. "He say you wanted to do me. I know he lied, but that's not why I come. I's here because you the first friend I ever had," Catharine whispered, wiping her eyes. "I never give myself freely to him or nobody, but if that's what you want, I'll do it for you."

Anthony felt torn, desperately hoping what she said was true. John's lurid description of raping her burned in his brain like hot coals. If she was his personal property, and he was still using her, what possible chance would they have together? He had to know the truth. "Does John hurt you?"

Catharine lowered her eyes and turned away. "I don't want to talk about him."

"He told me what he did to you," Anthony replied.

"What else he say about me?"

"Just how he hurt you, that's all. Does he still hurt you that way?"

Catharine sat on the edge of his cot and turned her back to him. She should have known John would brag to Anthony about using her. Once, she overheard him telling a white man how he 'stuck bone' to her every night. At the time it angered her, but what could a twelve-year-old slave girl do about it. Masters and overseers used black girls and women all the time. If she was honest with Anthony, would he still want her? Could he love her, knowing the things she was forced to do to satisfy John's sadistic cravings? She had known him only a short time, and in that time he had given her hope and happiness. Could she find the courage to even speak of it? She suddenly realized she had no choice but to put her trust in their short friendship, for the sooner Anthony knew, the better. She took a deep breath, reached back and held his hand. "When I was twelve, John started messing with me. Every time his pa and ma ain't around, he be grabbing and feeling on me. When I saw him coming, I would run and hide. Most times, he don't stop 'til he fine me."

Her words felt like sharp spikes driven into Anthony's ears. "Don't say any more," he pleaded, hating that he had insisted she speak of it.

"I gonna say it now, 'cause you needs to hear it," Catharine said, wringing her hands. "One Saturday night our cabin got so hot, I slept out under a tree. John come home drunk. When he seen me, he dragged me in the barn and sat me on his bunk. I yelled and scratched his face, but he beat me 'til I stopped crying. He say, 'Little nigger gal, we gonna party.' He made me drink apple juice that had whiskey in it. I say I don't want no mo', but he kept filling the cup. I couldn't sit up. He pushed my face down on his lap and opened his pants." Catharine shuddered, shaking her head vigorously while squeezing Anthony's hand. "I couldn't breath 'cause of what he done. I got to choking and puked in his lap. He slapped my face and say if I ever do that again he gonna break my neck. When he pushed me on the floor, I tried to crawl away. But he come behind me, pulled up my dress and started doing me. He hurt me real bad. When I woke, he was sleeping on top of me. I tried to push him off, but he was too heavy. He opened them red eyes of his and say, 'party ain't over yet'. He kept me in his bunk all Sunday morning. She collapsed into Anthony's arms with her slender body trembling uncontrollably.

"Forgive me for asking you about it," Anthony pleaded, frantically wiping tears from her cheeks with his finger. He felt the uncontrolled rage surfacing again, and envisioned dropping a bundle of hay from the loft on John's head. It frightened him to think he wanted to kill another human being, no matter how evil he was. To calm himself, he whispered, "'Vengeance is mine,' saith the Lord."

"Anthony, I ain't finished yet. After what he done to me in the barn, all that summer he come fo' me most every night. If I don't do what he say, he burned me with his cigar," Catharine said, pointing to the burn scars on her arm. "I can't take being burned no more, so I done it. I drank his apple juice and whiskey so I don't puke when he put his thing in my mouth." She turned her head when Anthony moved closer and tried to kiss her. "You sure you want to kiss me? You ain't just trying to be nice?"

Patiently, he placed his finger under her chin, turned her face to his and kissed her lips. "Nothing he made you do could spoil these beautiful lips," Anthony whispered.

She wept with her head resting on his chest. "Did John ever tell you a bear bit off his finger?"

"Yes, but what's that got to do with you?" he said, on the verge of tears.

"When I turned thirteen, I say to myself I ain't gonna let him use me no more, even if he kills me. One hot night he comes busting in my cabin with an ugly white man. They was both drunk and they got to laughing when they seen me sleeping with nothing on. John say for me to get down on my knees 'cause they both gonna bone me. I grabbed his whiskey bottle and hit him over the head. When he grabbed me, I bit his finger so hard, it broke. I grabbed my poker from the fireplace and hit the other man in his head. I got to yelling and kicking and scratching and they up and run off. Guess they thought I done gone plum crazy. Come to think about it, I guess I was for a spell," Catharine said, laughing hysterically. She paused to calm herself. "About five days after that, a doctor comes and cut off a piece of John's finger. The doctor told John if he don't, he would have to cut off his whole hand, sooner or later. The next time he come trying to mess with me, I say, 'that ain't all I's gonna bite if you don't leave me alone.' He beat me for saying that, but from that day he don't mess with me no mo'," Catharine said, her eyes blazing with pride. "Now that I told you, I hope you don't start hating me."

"Hating you? I love you all the more for your courage," Anthony said, astonished by all she had said. He took her in his arms and kissed the tears from her cheeks, hoping to calm her. They clung to each other without speaking, for how long he did not know. He finally realized she had fallen into a peaceful sleep. He held her in his arms for over an hour, not daring to move for fear of waking her. Of one thing he was now certain, he loved her. It was not just her beauty, but her tender spirit and courage in the face of the most horrible brutality. When the candle burned out, he carefully freed himself from her embrace. After removing the short butt of a pencil from his boot, he stood by the loft's window and, by the light of the full moon, scribbled lines on the back of his travel documents. He returned, laid down beside her but could not sleep. Only when he saw the first rays of morning light did he close his eyes.

Anthony sat up abruptly. He found Catharine sitting beside him smiling.

"You look so sweet when you sleeping," she said.

Anthony laughed, feeling relieved that all traces of the pain she spoke of had vanished. Her cheerfulness astonished him.

"You hungry? Let's go catch us a mess of frogs," she said gleefully.

"Yeah, but before we go I want to read something I wrote last night just for you," he said, reaching into his pocket and remove the crumpled sheet of paper.

"You wrote something for me?" she asked excitedly, clasping her hands.

"It's called a poem. I started thinking about it the last time I was here and I finished it while you were sleeping. I've named it 'Catharine.'" He held the paper to the light and cleared his throat,

> "I stood there helpless in the rain.
> Hearing how you've lived in pain.
> And in my dreams, there in the sky
> I saw dark clouds floating by.
> They flew away without a trace
> Of tears collected from you face
> Last night. So with this pledge
> I make to thee,
> A solemn pledge, we will be free.
> And on that day this terrible stain
> Will wash away with all your pain.

She uttered a cry, threw her arms around his neck and kissed his lips and cheeks. "Them the sweetest words I ever did hear." She took his hand and led him to the ladder. They climbed down and stepped out into the humid morning air. Catharine looked up and pointed to two thin clouds swiftly floating by.

"Look Anthony, are those the clouds you wrote about?"

Anthony gazed up and smiled. "Yes, those are the clouds in my poem."

She swiveled on her toes with her arms flaying the air. "They like you and me. I know in my heart we will be free someday, Anthony." They kissed, then clung to each other, two survivors struggling to reach some unknown distant shore as yet unseen.

CHAPTER 22

Mary Alice scurried about the house inspecting every aspect of the work she had ordered done. She insisted on overseeing it herself, right down to the dusting of books in the library. Jim had removed his poems and Anthony's book and placed them to his cottage. Anthony helped the work crews paste new wallpaper on the living room walls. Under Big George's supervision, Bubba planted more azaleas in the flowerbeds, and mulched those that were in full bloom.

William watched the work with amusement, and finally admitted that he was just as excited about the visit of Henry and his prospective bride as Mary Alice. The arrival of Louise and her children added to their joy. With her third child expected within the month, Louise convinced her husband to bring her home so the child could be born in the room of her birth and in her beloved Maryland. It seemed to William that the good Lord was smiling down on his family at last.

William found Louise reading on the front porch. "Daughter, your mother is beside herself. I have not seen her this excited since your wedding day."

"I'm so happy for our family. You and mother have waited a long time for Henry to settle down and it's wonderful, knowing how he has matured. But may I ask you a delicate question, father?"

William put his book aside. "Delicate? You have always spoken freely with me."

"I'm concerned about Cathy. Is she happy, being married to Hale Sanders?"

"As far as I can tell, she seems to be quite content. Why do you ask?"

"Well, since I arrived, she seems to be, how shall I say it, rather withdrawn."

"Has she been sulking around you?" William asked irritably. "I told her not bring her child into this house while Henry and his guests are here."

"But father, don't you think Henry is mature enough to handle his own affairs? If he intends to marry her, the truth about the child will come out, sooner or later. If his lady is all that Henry says she is, they will work it out."

"Louise, trust your father in such matters. I've lived long enough to know there are some things that should not be shared between husband and wife. He would be insane to admit that he fathered that child."

"Are you and mother more concerned about how this may reflect on our family?" she asked quietly.

"I suggest we change the subject," William replied. He was relieved when Louise smiled, walked over and kissed his forehead.

When the carriage arrived in the early afternoon, Anthony and Jim rushed from the veranda to help with the luggage. A dozen children stood on the side of the house waiting to get a glimpse of the guests. Henry smiled as he stepped from the carriage, shook hands with Jim and patted Anthony's back.

"Welcome home, Master Henry," Anthony said.

"You're still growing, I see," Henry said, brushing dust from his jacket. He extended his hand to a young woman and assisted her from the carriage. When she removed her straw hat and shook it, the sun highlighted her brilliant red hair. She smiled at Anthony.

"You must be Anthony. Henry has told me all about you. My name is Abigail Schroeder.

Anthony observed her freckled face, thinking that Catharine's complexion was far more beautiful. "Welcome to Bradley Manor, Miss Schroeder."

Henry assisted her mother, Elizabeth, from the carriage. Mary Alice and William came out to greet them. After pleasantries, William escorted them into the house.

Jim and Anthony carried six pieces of luggage to the guestroom where Betty and Cathy waited to assist the women.

"With all this luggage, you would think those two women were coming to stay all year," Jim said, placing the luggage at the foot of the bed.

"Henry's girl sure is beautiful," Anthony said. He failed to notice that Cathy seemed upset.

"Come Anthony, we have work to do," Jim said. They passed Mary Alice and her guests on the stairway.

"Thank you for helping us," Abigail said cheerfully.

Abigail and Elizabeth Schroeder followed Mary Alice up the stairs and into the guest room. When they entered, Mary Alice motioned for Cathy and Betty to step forward.

"These are my servants, Betty and Cathy. If you need anything, they will provide it for you. Just pull this cord. If you would like something to eat, ring once. If you need towels or hot water, ring twice. There are chamber pots in the closet, but if you need to go to the Necessity House, the girls will show you where it is located. It is outside but there is a covered walkway to it," Mary Alice said.

Abigail Schroeder could not take her eyes off Cathy. Before she agreed to become engaged to Henry, he had confessed that, as a teenager, he fathered a child by one of his parent's servants. He had told her their relationship could not begin with a lie of such magnitude. Having grown up in a liberal home environment, she replied that she loved him all the more for his truthfulness. Now she found herself face to face with that truth, and felt shaken. This girl was stunningly beautiful and showed no signs of having given birth to a child. It had never dawned on her that she would meet the mother or the child on this visit. Why had she been so naive?

At seven that evening, William and Mary Alice led their guests into the dining room. All had gone according to plan and Mary Alice was thoroughly delighted. She had taken Abigail and Elizabeth on a tour of her rose garden and proudly shown them her place ribbons and other prizes. Henry anxiously waited in the parlor for Abigail's return, but felt contented, knowing his mother needed time to get acquainted with her future daughter-in-law.

Ruth's roast was cooked just as Mary Alice had ordered. "I know you ladies must be worn out from your journey. When we finish, we'll go to the parlor for dessert and coffee. You may retire early if you wish," Mary Alice suggested.

"I'm too excited to think of sleeping. I have never seen such a beautiful home," Abigail said.

"I'm glad you like it. My great-grandfather purchased this land, but this home was built by my father, James Oliver Bradley in 1783," William said, lighting his cigar. "If I may change the subject, Henry, I read that the amendment repealing that law that required Jews to sign a loyalty oath to Christ has been removed as a requirement for voting. I'm glad the Maryland House of Delegates acted as they did and I'm pleased that you were one of the leaders who fought for that change."

"Thank you, papa. But the real hero is Thomas Kennedy of Williamsport, Maryland. He worked for seven years to get rid of that hated oath. Some day there will be a monument to that man for his courage and determination. It was at a rally calling for the change that Abigail and I met," Henry said proudly.

"That's just one of the reasons I fell in love with him," Abigail said.

"My former employer, Solomon Cohen, is now a candidate for the City Council in Annapolis. He's receiving good support from local merchants. However, a few local ministers are asking their congregations not to vote for him," Henry said.

"If there is anything I can do, let me know."

After dinner everyone retired to the parlor where Mary Alice, Louise and Elizabeth renewed their discussion of roses and gardening. Henry motioned for Abigail to follow him to the front vestibule where they sat in the wicker rocking chairs.

"Tell me how you are feeling?" Henry asked, noticing how she fidgeted with her handkerchief.

"I'm excited. There is so much to see and understand."

"Say more."

"Henry, until this moment I never realized our worlds are so different. I guess I was blinded by our love. I grew up in the academic world of St. Johns College," Abigail said, reaching for his hand. "Yours has been a life of privilege and wealth. Your father owns slaves and one day you will too."

"But we discussed all that, did we not?" Henry said with concern. "I told you how I hated my father for selling my friend, Zachariah. And how I despised myself for taking advantage of one of our women and fathering a child. You said our love could overcome all obstacles."

"Yes, I know I said those things, but today I met Cathy," Abigail said quietly. "She's beautiful. You must have loved her, Henry."

"Loved her? I never knew what love was until I met you. You must believe me," he said earnestly.

Abigail placed her gloved hand to his cheek. "Now that I'm here, I will truly try to understand your way of life. You have been honest, shared your mistakes, and I believe you are truly repentant. I thought I was being noble by accepting it. I guess I need to learn more about myself. Until now, I never fully understood why my parents are so adamantly opposed to slavery."

"Are you telling me you do not wish to marry me? That you no longer love me?"

"Nothing will change my love for you, but do you remember the night we went to the concert and heard Haydn's Symphony in D for the first time. I saw tears in your eyes."

"Yes, it was the Clock Symphony, the Andante movement."

"You told me you felt the spirit of life in Haydn's music. That night I knew I loved you," she said, squeezing his hand. "Your parents have been very gracious to us, but I'm feeling anxious. I need time to reflect. Please be patient with me."

"Abigail, when I came to Annapolis four years ago, I was cut me off from my family. You gave me reason to hope again. I believe we will fashion a new world here that we both can be proud of."

She reached over and took Henry's hand. "I think I will go rest now," she whispered.

*　　　*　　　*

Hale Carter sat watching Cathy rocking their baby. The child had been asleep for the past hour, yet she refused to put him in his crib. Hale became impatient and forcefully removed the child from her arms.

"Why you take my child from me?" she protested.

"'Cause I'm tired of the way you acting, woman. Ever since Massa Henry brought his woman here, you don't want me touching you. I's your husband," Hale shouted.

Cathy stared at him. She had never seen him upset before. "I been sad 'cause Master William say he don't want me to bring our son in his house as long as those women are here."

"Don't you see what's happening. That be all the more reason we needs to leave this place"

"Don't be saying that. This my home where I was born."

"Cathy, no matter how good you think Master Bradley treats us, we always be niggers if we ain't free. This not our home, it's a cage. Last Sunday in church we be all singing 'Steal Away to Jesus.' While folks singing, I looks up in the sky and I see this eagle circling high over our heads. All the time we be singing, that old bird be flying round and round." Hale spread his arms and waved them slowly up and down. "That eagle come flying straight on down and sits himself on a branch in the old prayer tree. All the time Preacher Harris praying, I be looking at that bird and he be looking at me. I knowed he be trying to tell me something, so I closed my eyes and asked the Lord for a sign. When I opened my eyes, that bird had his tail pointed south and his head pointed north. Don't you see, Cathy, that was a sign from the Lord Almighty and he be saying for us to steal ourselves away from here."

Cathy placed her arms around Hale waist and kissed his lips. "Hale, you know I love you. You the sweetest man in the whole world, but I can't up and leave my mama and sister and never see them again."

"Soon that white woman gonna marry Massa Henry. How you think she gonna treat you after she finds out Massa Henry's his real pappy? I done made up my mind. One day soon we heading North for freedom land. Like the words of the old song say, 'I ain't got long to stay here.'"

CHAPTER 23

Abigail sat by the bedroom window meditating on a passage from her Bible. From the book of Amos, she read aloud, 'Let justice roll down like waters, and righteousness like a mighty stream.' She had met and fallen in love with Henry during the student effort to remove the so-called Christian oath that Jews were required to sign if they wanted to vote in Maryland. Now she pondered the question of justice for slaves. Her parents were appalled when they learned she wanted to marry Henry. It was her father who suggested that she visit Bradley Manor and see for herself how William Bradley treats his people. She pulled the cord twice. Betty responded in less than a minute.

"You ring, Miss Abigail?"

"Yes. I wish to take a bath. Will you please bring water for the tub."

"Yes ma'am. I'll be back shortly with lots of hot water," Betty said, scurrying from the room.

Betty and Cathy returned fifteen minutes later, each carrying two buckets of hot water. They went into the adjoining bathroom and poured the water into a iron tub that sat on legs shaped like lion paws.

"Good morning, Cathy" Abigail said, studying the girl carefully. "I would like you to remain and assist me with my bath."

Cathy avoided making eye contact. "I'll be glad to help you, Miss Abigail," she replied quietly.

After testing the water with her elbow, Abigail pinned up her hair, undressed and stepped into the tub. She hated herself for feeling a tinge of jealousy. She had prided herself in being open-minded when Henry first confessed his inexcusable behavior. The thought of this beautiful creature in Henry's arms was very unsettling.

Cathy stood beside the tub, holding a towel and wash cloths. "You like me to wash your back?" Cathy asked, timidly.

"I would love it, but I don't want to be a bother to you."

"What you say, Miss Abigail?"

"I don't want to trouble you with extra work."

"Miss Abigail, washing your back's not work." Cathy pulled a stool next to the tub and waited as Abigail rubbed scented soap over her body. "My sister and I wash each others backs all the time."

"I have a sister, but she would never think of helping me during my bath."

"You and Master Henry gonna get married soon?"

"We hope so. However, we want to know each other better. That's why I'm here."

"You love him a lot, don't you."

"Yes, I do," Abigail said, wondering how Cathy felt about Henry. "Henry tells me you're are married to a fine young man."

The warmth of her smile put Cathy at ease. "I been married, going on one year now. His name is Hale and he's real good to me and my little boy."

Abigail stiffened at the mention of the child. Did she detect a certain pride in Cathy's voice or was it her imagination? "How long have you and your sister lived here?"

"We born right here. Master Bradley's pappy bought our mama and bring her here. She married our papa downstairs in Master Bradley's living room," Cathy said proudly. "Soon after that, me and Betty was born. Our papa got sick and died of the fever when we were little girls. We take flowers to his grave every Sunday, that's when we find them blooming."

"He must have been a wonderful man. I've seen your mother. Is she always so happy?"

"Mama's happy most all the time. She does the sewing and ironing here at Bradley Manor. She so good, white ladies come and she makes dresses for them too."

"Does she get paid for her services? That is, when she sews for white ladies."

Cathy looked puzzled. "No ma'am. Miz Mary Alice gets the money. But she gives mama nice things from time to time. We gets to wear her clothes when she don't want them no more. Mama makes them over for us. Miz Mary Alice don't like to wear the same dress more then two, maybe three times, at most."

"Are you and your sister close friends?

"We gets along fine, now that I'm married."

"You may wash my back now," Abigail said, handing the cloth and soap to Cathy. "I do hope we will have a chance to talk again." After the bath, Cathy collected the towels and hurried from the room.

Abigail dressed then sat before her mirror reflecting on her feeling about the girl. She found Cathy to be charming. If she is married, why did she feel threatened by her? She tried to dismiss the thought and walked to the parlor where she found her mother and Mary Alice drinking tea.

"Did you rest well, dear?" Elizabeth inquired.

"Yes. I had a marvelous bath."

"Will you join us," Mary Alice said, patting the seat next to her. "We will be having breakfast shortly."

"No, I think I will just wander outside. There is a lovely breeze." When she reached the hallway she changed her mind and walked to the kitchen where she found Ruth sitting at the table peeling potatoes.

"Welcome to my kitchen, Miss Abigail. You wanna sit for a spell and have a cup of coffee?"

"That would be delightful. Coffee is just what I need right now, Mrs. Bowen."

"Miss Abigail, just call me Ruth." Ruth poured coffee into a mug thinking that Abigail would soon learn not to address slaves in the same manner she addresses white folks.

"All of you are making our visit most enjoyable," Abigail said.

"Have you and Master Henry set a day for your wedding?"

"Not yet."

"Life's too short. If you truly love him, don't go messing around too long, you hear?" Ruth said, reaching over and patting her hand.

"Henry told me how your husband, Zachariah, taught him to fish and hunt. Ruth, I hope you don't mind my mentioning his name. There is no way I can even begin to understand the pain you must have felt when he was sold."

"You mean the pain I feels right now, don't you?" Ruth said without emotion.

"I...I'm sorry if I offended you."

Ruth smiled. "Miss Abigail, you ain't hurt my feelings one bit. It's just a fact. I ain't gonna ever stop hurting for my Zach 'til the day I die. I know one day I be seeing him in heaven."

"Have you found it in your heart to forgive Mr. Bradley?"

Ruth reflected for a moment. "In a way I do and in a way I don't." Ruth said, placing one hand on her hip. "I use to hate him. Funny thing about love and hate. When they gets in your heart at the same time, love wins if you let Jesus tip your scales."

"What a wonderful thought."

"What has Henry told you about Uncle Jim?" Ruth asked out of curiosity.

"He told me his grandfather is Uncle Jim's father. It's very hard for me to understand relationships in this family," she said, sadly.

Ruth hesitated, then said quietly, "That's the truth for sure."

"Henry loves and respects Uncle Jim. When he was small, he was playing in the library and fell asleep behind the sofa. His father and mother were away at the time. When he awoke, he saw Uncle Jim reading his father's book. He crawled out unnoticed and never mentioned it until he was grown."

Ruth's mouth dropped open. "You sitting there telling me Master William has known all these years that Uncle Jim been reading his books?"

"Well, since 1822, the winter Henry came back to Annapolis."

Ruth shook her head. "You sure telling me something I don't know, and there ain't much I don't know about this family, that's for sure."

"Ruth, what are your hopes and dreams for Anthony? I know he is allowed to earn money toward his freedom."

Ruth stiffened as her eyes narrowed. "He's working for his freedom all right, but I'm worried about him. He thinks he is in love with a girl over at the Baker farm not far from here. I can't tell him nothing, he's so hardheaded. I don't want him messing with her."

"But if they're in love, why would you object?"

"The Bakers want my son to bed her so she can have babies. I don't want none of my grandbabies born to that gal, 'cause they will sell them as soon as they old enough to work the fields," Ruth said, twisting the corner of her apron.

Abigail placed her hands over her mouth. "Surely something can be done to help them."

"Miss Abigail, them Bakers ain't nothing but the worse kind of white trash," she said, hitting her fist on the table. "They own her and ain't nothing none of us can do about it."

Abigail felt lightheaded, having no appetite for the cookie Ruth placed on her coffee plate. She turned when Anthony entered the kitchen through the back door. "Good morning Anthony," Abigail said, struggling to control her emotions.

"Good morning Miss Abigail. Mama, you got anything else for me to do?" Anthony said.

"Go to the chicken yard and bring me a dozen eggs. Be careful not to break any."

"Anthony, I would like to go with you," Abigail said. Anthony grinned and nodded affirmatively.

"Don't go inside that yard where the chickens are. You don't want to get your shoes and dress all dirty," Ruth said.

"I'll be careful." Abigail put on her sunbonnet and followed Anthony across the field to the fenced in chicken yard.

"Mama's gonna use the eggs to bake one of her Lady Baltimore cakes," Anthony said proudly.

"Lady Baltimore cake! I love it."

"My mama is the best cook in the whole world," he said, picking up a pole. When he opened the gate, the red rooster charged in his direction.

"Mr Rooster, I don't want to hit you with this stick, but you come any closer, you just might land up in mama's pot." The rooster circled Anthony with its head lowered and its neck feathers raised. The bird retreated after Anthony stuck the pole in its feathered chest. When he entered the chicken coop, the hens protested loudly while leaving their nests. The rooster circled them for protection, crowing loudly. Anthony emerged minutes later, his pail filled with eggs.

"Henry has told me about you, Anthony. Now tell me something about yourself."

"What you wanna know?"

"I already know you are allowed to work to earn money toward your freedom, and I know there is a special girl that you like. Why don't you start by telling me about her."

"Mama told you about Catharine?" Anthony said, clearly upset. "What she say."

"Your mother is worried about you. She doesn't want you to get in trouble."

"She needn't be," Anthony said, certain he could never speak of the horrible abuse that Catharine had suffered. "Her name is Catharine Miles, and she lives over at the Baker farm about five miles from here. When Master Bradley sent me to work for the Bakers, that's when I first met her."

"Tell me more about her."

"She's the most wonderful girl I've ever met. When I'm free I'm gonna go to Washington City, get me a job and save my money. Then I'm gonna come back and buy her freedom."

Abigail bit her lower lip. "How long do you think all this will take?"

"I don't know," he said, shaking his head. "Maybe it will take seven years or even longer. You know, like the story of Jacob and Rachel in the Bible?"

"I love that story."

"Well, Jacob worked for fourteen years before Rachel's papa would let him marry her. I told Catharine I hope I don't have to work fourteen years, but if it takes that long I'll do it."

"And she will wait that long?" Abigail replied, struggling to hold back her tears.

"She said she will wait no matter how long it takes, that's if the Bakers don't sell her," he said, looking dejected. "That's what scares me the most."

Abigail felt sick at her stomach. From behind them, they heard the laughter of children. To her surprise, seven children had been following them. When she smiled, they screamed with delight and ran away. One of the girls, holding a small child's hand, tripped and fell. The child stood over her crying. Abigail rushed to the girl and helped her to her feet. After brushing the dirt from her dress, she turned to console the boy. She found herself staring at the tear-streaked face of a four-year-old white child. Brushing his blond hair from his face, she gave him a hug.

"There, there, don't cry. My, what a fine little boy you are. What's your name?"

The girl smiled and blurted out, "He Cathy's boy and his name is Henry."

Abigail cringed, trying desperately to catch her breath. She knew there was the possibility that she would see the child some day, but not this way. The girl took the boy's hand and ran to catch up with the other children.

Abigail sat at breakfast picking at her food. As the women chatted, she remained silent.

Henry became concerned over her moodiness. After breakfast she agreed to go on a buggy ride. Henry stopped by a pond where a flock of Canadian geese was swimming. They held hands and watched the geese and goslings for several minutes. Finally he turned and kissed her cheek. "Abigail, how are you feeling? You hardly spoke one word at breakfast."

She bit her lower lip, determined not to let her emotions turn to tears. She sighed and spoke quietly, "I've met some of your people this morning. They are truly remarkable. Ruth spoke of her husband. She harbors no ill will toward your father for selling him, but she still carries the pain of their separation in her heart after all these years. She's also fearful that Anthony will do something foolish. He's in love with a slave girl who lives on another farm under terrible conditions. Anthony spoke of freeing her some day, even if it takes many years. Henry darling, isn't there something you can do to help them?"

Henry felt devastated when he saw the pain in her eyes. He placed her arms around her. "I know our way of life seems strange to you just now, but please understand, I'm not in position to take on the personal burdens of the one hundred and sixty souls who live here."

"But darling, they are your burden. You and your family own them, including your own son," she replied, pointedly. "I accidentally met him this morning. He's beautiful, like his father."

"It saddens me that you met him under these circumstances," Henry said, visibly shaken. "My parents are responsible for our people's general welfare. They are better off than most poor whites in Maryland," he said, parroting words he had heard William say many times.

"That is true," Abigail said, struggling to control her emotions. "Do you remember our discussing the plight of poor whites in Maryland? They are also the victims of slavery. They cannot compete with this horrid system. By accident of birth, you are part of a privileged aristocracy that builds its wealth on the back of colored labor," Abigail said.

Her words stunned him. He knew she and her family held strong anti-slavery sentiments, but he hoped by visiting Bradley Manor, she would learn how tolerant his family was.

"One day I will be Master of Bradley Manor. There is one certainty I feel at this moment. It will difficult to assume this burden without you at my side," he said, his voice strained. "You and I can make life better, not just for ourselves, but for all of these people. It can be a model for others."

"Would you consider freeing your people some day?" she asked.

"I am not prepared to answer that question just yet. How can I think of freeing others, when I, myself, am in bondage. Bondage to self-doubt that almost destroyed me. Bondage to false pride," he replied soberly. "Marry me so that I will be truly free."

Abigail rested her head on his chest. She knew he loved Bradley Manor, with all the power and status that went with it. To the members of her family, power and status were the twin evils that destroyed men and nations. "Henry, I will not survive in your world without dignity and self respect. Please understand, I'm going to need time to reflect on all that I have seen."

Henry kissed her, then took the reins and drove back to Bradley Manor.

CHAPTER 24

Anthony rode his mule across the wet landscape to the Baker farm. A thunderstorm had left a lavender glow across the western sky, but he failed to notice it. His brief talks with Abigail Schroeder had lifted his spirits. She had brought back memories of Betty Cox, the wonderful lady who had given him the book of poetry. If she married Henry, would she help him find a way to free Catharine from the dreadful Baker farm? Just the possibility excited him. Before he left that afternoon, Ruth shook her finger in his face and told him to stay away from Catharine. When he lowered his head and refused to speak, she told him he was giving her the miseries. At first he thought she was playing on his sympathy, then he remembered hearing her complaining of shortness of breath. Was he the cause of it?

When he reached a bend in the road, he saw three men on horseback riding in his direction. His stomach churned when they stopped beside him and grabbed the reins from his hands.

"Looks like we got ourselves a runaway," said a heavyset bearded man wearing a tweed jacket. He pointed his gun at Anthony's head and ordered him to dismount. Anthony jumped off the mule and raised his arms that felt like iron weights. The riders dismounted and closed around him.

"Where you from, nigger?" the bearded man asked, unbuttoning Anthony's shirt.

"I'm from the Bradley Manor plantation, sir. I'm on my way to the Baker farm," Anthony replied. He felt certain the bearded man was the leader of a group of bounty hunters.

"Didn't ask you where you going, boy. You got any papers on you?" he drawled.

"Yes sir, in my left pocket, sir," Anthony replied, looking down at the pocket of his shirt while keeping his arms raised.

"Take off your shirt and drop them pants," the bearded man ordered. Anthony stared at the man while complying with his order. Standing in the middle of them naked, he grimaced as they felt his arms, jabbed fingers in his side and squeezed his buttocks.

"This sure is one fine nigger. Grease him down and he'll show well at any market. He talks good, too."

"Nigger talk ain't worth a crop of shit," the bearded man said, picking up the shirt and removing the paper from the pocket.

Anthony's heart pounded as his body trembled. The thought that they might steal him made his legs wobble. Would he end up in some slave pen far worse than the Baker farm? He suddenly knew the terror his father had felt the day he was sold. The bearded man motioned for him to lower his arms.

"This paper says this nigger's the property of William Bradley, owner of the Bradley Manor plantation here in Prince Georges County. He has permission to work at the Baker farm, and to travel on Peach Orchard Road to the Baker spread."

A third man, with the deep scar on his cheek, took the letter and looked at it. From the way he held it, Anthony guessed he couldn't read. "We could say we found him on another road."

The bearded man shook his head. "If we do, we just asking for trouble, and trouble ain't what we need just now. William Bradley shot and killed two bounty hunters he caught messing with his niggers. If we sell him, he'll find out and then we got hell to pay. Besides, we gotta keep tracking that nigger we spotted yesterday. I'm sure he's the one that's been helping slaves escape north. There's a big reward if we catch him. This one's a small fish."

"I say we keep him and keep after the other one too. That Bradley fellow don't scare me none," the second man said, boastfully.

"Bradley is one of the most important men in these parts. I don't want to cross him or any of his kin. We gonna let this one go," the bearded man said. "Nigger, get dressed and get out of here before I change my mind." He picked up the shirt and pants and tossed them into Anthony's face.

"Thank you, sir," Anthony said, hurriedly dressing. Relieved but terrified, he mounted the mule and rode toward the Baker farm. It was pitch dark when he arrived. Emotionally drained, he wondered how he would ever find the strength to work. He stumbled over to John who was pitching hay to the cows.

John stared at him. "What's with you, boy? You look like you seen a ghost."

"Bounty hunters stopped me on the road. I thought for sure they were going to take me with them," he said hoarsely.

"Them the same fellows stopped by here awhile back to water their horses. That was one mean looking bunch. They say they were tracking a nigger that been helping slaves run off. After two of them seen Cat, they offered me six dollars to bone her. Their boss says they ain't got time and off they go. I wish to hell I could catch that nigger and collect that reward for myself," John said, biting of a plug of tobacco. "Well, don't stand there looking stupid. Get started digging them postholes around the hog yard. When you gets 'em dug, call me. I'll help you put in the post and hang the gate."

Anthony walked to the hog pen, trying to control his emotions. What if the bounty hunters had raped Catharine? Just the thought of it sickened him.

It was near midnight before they completed fencing in the yard. After returning to the barn, they washed their hands in the horse trough.

"I'll see you next time, Anthony. My woman's waiting up for me," John said.

Anthony watched him jog toward the Baker's house. Big George had told him to be back by sunup because he was needed on one of the work crews. Frightened by the prospect of encountering the bounty hunters again, he decided to wait until daybreak and return on a little used trail through the back woods. Anthony climbed up the ladder, spread feed sacks in his cot and stretched out on his back. The day had been unusually hot, and the barn was humid. Although totally exhausted, he could not sleep. He removed his shirt and pants, and rested, wearing only his under shorts. With every night sound he flinched, imagining he saw the grinning faces of the bounty hunters standing over him. Every breeze through the loft's window reminded him of the stench of their breath. He touched the painful places where they pinched and jabbed fingers in his flesh as though his limbs were ripe melons. In desperation, he tried to put the thought out of his mind, but the scene keep resurfacing. Until that dreadful experience, he had maintained his pride, now he felt totally degraded. How could he save Catharine if he could not save himself? Tears flowed down his cheeks as he closed his eyes and drifted into a trouble sleep. Suddenly, he awoke to a treasure of kisses on his neck, his face, forehead and lips. Overjoyed, he attempted to sit up, but hands on his chest restrained him. His eyes adjusted to the faint moonlight shining through the barn window. Catharine was seated beside him with her chest pressed to his.

"Anthony, them tears on your face?" she whispered, gently touching his cheeks.

"Yes, because you are safe and here with me. Bounty hunters stopped me on the road," he said, catching his breath. "I was sure they were gonna steal me, but they let me go."

"They scared me too," Catharine whispered. She hugged him while eagerly kissing his lips. She saw the wonder in his eyes as her probing tongue exploring the roof and sides of his mouth. When her warm hand reached down and stroked his erect penis, he restrained her. Despite the intense pleasure, Jim's warning haunted him, *"He wants to breed her like they breed their cows."*

"What's wrong?" Catharine asked, startled at him. "Don't you want me?"

"Yes, I want you. I want so much it hurts, but not here, not now. I can't do that until you are free of this place and we are married," Anthony said, frightened by the sensation that was overpowering him.

After brief silence, she sat up with her back turned to him. "Fo' you come tonight I was hanging clothes on the line. Them bounty hunters seen me. Two of them grabbed me and started squeezing my breast and poking their finger between my legs. They asked John if they could take me in the barn and do me. John says they could, if they give him two dollars each. The big man say he wish they have time, but they had to keep tracking a nigger, and off they go. John would have took their money if they had stayed. Now I's scared they coming back fo' me," Catharine said, her voice quivering. "That's why I needs you. Just once, I want the taste of you on my lips. Just once, I wants to feel your glory inside me. Then, if they come and do me, I just close my eyes, put it out of my head and think of you."

The implications of her words stunned Anthony. He reached out and held her in his arms until her trembling ceased. Could he deny her when her need matched his own? Suddenly the moment was all that mattered. They held each other, listening to the beating of their hearts. He timidly kissed her while sliding his hand along the curve of her waist to the rising slope of her hips. When he found the warmth of her inner thighs, he hesitated. "You will know glory, and it's not going take seven years," he whispered.

She searched his eyes for reassurance, knowing if their union proceeded, it would be his first time. He laughed nervously as she pressed him back on his cot. While staring into his eyes, she unloosened her twin braids, unbuttoned her dress and pulled it over her head. After folding it carefully, she placed it under his head. She held her breath when he rose up and kissed the nipples of her breasts.

Anthony felt the pleasurable warmth of her slender legs straddling him. She looked so incredibly beautiful sitting upright in the middle of his abdomen. Reason took flight when she rose up and guided the fullness of him inside her. Slowly, her hips moved to the rhythm of an ancient drum that pounded in his brain. In the explosive pleasure that followed, Anthony knew his manhood had been fully restored.

Afterwards, they lay spent in each other arms. Never in Anthony's young life had he felt so complete as a man. But remembering the forbidden fruit from the Garden of Eden, he began reflecting on the possible consequences of his 'transgression.' Despite his growing apprehension, he smiled. It wasn't Eve who bit the apple and tempted Adam. Eve *was* the apple. As soon as he reached home, he would seek out Reverend Harris and confess his 'sins.' Catharine stirred, whispered his name and pressed closer to him. Soon thereafter, reason took flight again.

Ruth sat on the examining table in the plantation infirmary with Mary Alice, Elizabeth Schroeder and Louise standing beside her.

"I don't like it when you tell me you are having trouble breathing," Mary Alice whispered.

"It's just my worrying about Anthony, nothing more. Don't be fussing over me," Ruth said.

Elizabeth took Mary Alice aside. "You should have your doctor see her right away. It could be nothing more than anxiety or it might be her heart."

Mary Alice placed her hand over her mouth. For the first time she realized how much Ruth meant to her. She couldn't remember when she stopped thinking of Ruth as slave property. As the women walked along the brick pathway from the infirmary, Mary Alice wrung her hands and whispered, "If anything happens to Ruth, I don't know what I shall do."

"Mother, you must not allow yourself to get upset before we know what it is," Louise said.

"If it will put your minds to rest, my grandmother had a heart attack," Elizabeth said. "She lived another twenty-two years and insisted on carrying on all her duties until three weeks before she died."

After Mary Alice informed William of her suspicions, he sent for their family doctor to come immediately. He found Ruth in the kitchen making plans for the evening dinner.

"Why are you not resting?" William asked.

Ruth saw the worried look on his face. "I feel fine just now. Now stop worrying about me because I'm gonna get well. I've got to for Anthony's sake."

"Ruth, your faith has been an inspiration to us all these years. Our doctor will be here to examine you first thing in the morning. I hope you know how much you mean to us?"

"I know. Anthony and me truly love this family. The good Lord don't want me just now. He gonna let me live long enough to see my Anthony a free man," she said, wringing her hands. "But I worry about him. Anthony's sure he loves that Baker's girl and I don't want him anywhere near her."

"Henry and I know all about the two of them. Uncle Jim spoke to us about what's going on over there. I don't want you to worry about Anthony. He's going to be fine. If it will make you feel better, I am looking into the situation," William said, reaching over and patted Ruth's hand.

"Praise the Lord. Thank you, thank you, Master William."

"Now go to your cabin and rest," William said, taking her hand and escorting her to the kitchen door.

Abigail and Henry sat in the rocking chairs on the front porch enjoying glasses of lemonade and fresh picked strawberries.

"These three days seemed to have flown so fast. I wish you and your mother could stay longer."

Abigail turned to him and smiled. "In one of Jesus' sayings there is a passage that reads, 'Where your treasure is, there will your heart be also.' You are my treasure, Henry, and entwined in that treasure is our mutual love of freedom and justice," she said as the front door opened.

"Master Henry, Miss Abigail, dinner is served," Jim said.

After all were seated, the conversation remained festive during the first course. Henry and William debated what implications the proposed Baltimore and Ohio railroad might have on the Chesapeake and Ohio canal project now under construction. Louise, Mary Alice and Elizabeth discussed flower arrangements as Abigail listened quietly without comment. Suddenly, screams could be heard in the vestibule.

"What the hell was that?" William shouted, rising to his feet.

"Father, I'll see what's happening," Henry said, leaving the table. He followed Jim into the vestibule where they found Cathy on her knees crying hysterically. She grabbed Henry's dinner jacket sleeve.

"Hale done run off with my baby," she cried. Just as Henry lifted Cathy to her feet, William came into the hallway.

"What in God's name is going on here?" William said. Seeing Cathy in Henry's arms, he angrily pushed him aside and sat Cathy into a chair.

"Papa, Cathy just told me that Hale has left and has taken her son with him."

William blinked with disbelief. Jim quickly shut the dining room door while William took Cathy into the library and placed her into one of his leather chairs. Henry stood by watching helplessly.

"Master Bradley, Hale tried to force me to go with him, but I didn't want to run away. He took little Henry with him," Cathy said. William clamped his hand over her mouth when she started screaming.

William turned to Jim, "Keep her quiet and don't let her out of your sight. Henry, come with me." Henry followed William into the parlor. "For your sake and that of your young lady, let me handle this." William whispered.

Unable to think clearly, Henry nodded. He returned to the table and took his seat. Abigail touched his hand, sensing something serious had happened.

"What on earth is going on?" Mary Alice asked.

Henry calmly took a sip of wine and placed his napkin in his lap. "I guess you will know sooner or later. Hale Sanders has run away and taken his son with him. His wife refused to go."

"Oh, heavens, where is my fan?" Mary Alice cried.

"He took the child and the mother remained here?" Abigail asked, suddenly concerned that there was more to Cathy's relationship with Henry than she had been told.

"I'm afraid he did. It was Cathy you heard screaming," Henry said, highly agitated. All sat in stony silence while finishing their meal.

William sat watching Cathy, reflecting that only two of his slaves had ever run off. "Cathy, it pleases me that you have told the truth about what happened to your son. Now, if you want him back, tell me all you know about Hale's plans. He must have talked with you about it, didn't he?"

"Yes, Master."

"Did Moab Jackson come back and help him?" William asked. When Cathy nodded, he struggled to maintain his calm. "Did they tell you where they were going first?"

"Hale said something about stopping at a Quaker folk's farm for the night, that's all I know."

William knew a dozen Quaker farmers in Maryland and was certain he knew the one that possibly was hiding them. It angered him to think that he saved Moab's life. To be repaid in this manner by an ungrateful black was more than he could stomach. He would deal with Moab in due time. But for now, he had to think this through very carefully. What manner of slave would run away with a child he did not conceive? Could this crisis could be turned into an opportunity? William pushed his chair back from Cathy and pondered his options. He lit a cigar, blew smoke rings in the air and smiled.

CHAPTER 25

The old gray barn with its weather-beaten boards, was barely visible from the dirt road. For years it had stood vacant in the middle of a field overgrown with tall weeds and young trees. One end of the barn had partially caved in. It once was part of a productive farm that was abandoned after the soil eroded. Three men, two women and five children, ranging in ages from seven to twelve, huddled together in one corner of the barn. The tall black man wearing a waist-length, cowhide jacket kept watch outside the barn door. He nervously fingered the pistol in his holster, straining to hear over the incessant chatter of crickets in the thick fog. The occasional hoot of an owl nesting in the rafters frightened one of the children. He called to the mother and told her to place her hand over the child's mouth.

"Hush, baby. Mama's here," the mother whispered. "Joe, go tell Moab our chillen getting hungry."

Joe was one of the ten runaway slaves Moab had recruited from the nearby Anderson farm. He called out to Moab, "How long we be here? My boy's ain't had nothing to eat all day."

"I told you we don't eat 'til we gets to the first rest stop. Folks from the Bradley place should be here by now. I hope nothing gone wrong. We waits a little longer. If they ain't here soon, we be on our way," Moab whispered, suddenly alert to nearby sounds. "You hear that?" Both men heard what sounded like the cry of a lamb, only the sounds came in one short and two long bleating calls. Moab put his hands to his mouth and repeated the call, using the same short and long sound patterns. As the two men watched, a figure emerged from the fog holding a child. Moab stepped out to meet them.

"Where's your woman?" Moab whispered. "You lose her in this fog?"

"She runs off. Nothing I say could make her change her mind."

Moab stood with his mouth hanging open. Hale brushed past him, strolled over to the women and placed the sleeping child beside them. Moab, visibly shaken, pulled Hale around by his collar.

"What you done, man? Is you crazy, leaving yo' woman behind and bringing her chile out here?" Moab hissed in a low voice.

Hale backed away and sat beside his sleeping son. The child opened his eyes, crawled onto his lap and began sucking his thumb. Moab paced back and forth, cursing himself for returning to Bradley Manor. He was certain that Cathy was betraying them at that moment. He knelt beside Hale and spoke in a low voice. "I trusted you. Now you come out here with that boy you knows ain't yours. Your wife gonna go running to your master and telling him all she knows, then where we be? I risk my neck for your freedom. You sho' is one stupid nigger."

Hale bristled and rose to his feet. He would have struck Moab, but restrained himself when he saw the others watching him intently.

"In the sight of the Lord, this here's my son the day I married her. Me and him gonna be free with or without his mama."

One of the women stepped between them. "Moab Jackson, you got no call talking to him like that. If his wife don't want to be free, then she don't want it. As for this po' child, I'm taking care of him on this journey. You men folk best be getting us moving. We don't need no fighting out here."

"You need to take that chile back to his mama," Moab shouted.

"Too late for that. Ain't no sense crying over spilt milk. We gotta get on the road right now," Joe said.

"Problem is, the milk ain't just spilt. It done turned sour and we ain't even started yet. Before this over we all could be in a heap of trouble," Moab grumbled, picking up his knapsack. He pulled his pistol from his belt and held it up. "Ya'll see this here gun. I ain't never kill no man in my life, but as the Lord is my witness, I ain't never gonna be a slave no more. Now, we gonna move fast as we can. Come morning, we be at the first station. Hale, you know these trails really good. I'm trusting you to get us out of these parts. Bess, you put a rag around any of those chillen's mouths if they start yelling. Can't have no noise when we get on the road."

The group left the barn and marched single file down the dirt road a short distance. Hale led them onto a little used trail into the deep woods. The men used machetes to cut through the thick undergrowth. At first light they rested near a shallow stream. Moab placed his hand up to his ear when he heard the sounds of dogs barking in the distance. He motioned for everyone to crouch down and remained quiet. When the barking ceased, they moved out. Suddenly a woman screamed when a deer darted across their path.

"Woman, hush yo' mouth. Ain't nothing but a deer. Folks listen up. If you keep yelling like that, they will hear it clean over in the next county," Moab said.

"I's truly sorry," the woman whimpered. "That thing nearly scared me to death."

"How much further we got to go?" Hale asked.

"Can't tell for sho'. The fog slowing us down. It's beginning to lift, so we best find a place to hide."

Moab led them through a thicket of trees to a nearby brook. "Guess you better eat what little you brung." The women opened their knapsacks and distributed dried apples, dark bread and slices of cured fat back. Hale sat beside his son who began whining.

"I want my mama."

Bess took the child from Hale's lap and rocked him until he stopped crying. As darkness descended on the area, the group packed up their knapsacks and walked single file by the light of a thin, crescent moon. Several of the children began crying as swarms of mosquitoes descended on them. The men removed their shirts and covered the two smallest children. When they arrived at a plowed field, they could see a dim light from a distant window.

"This the place, but ya'll stay put while I go see if the way be clear," Moab whispered. Taking Hale with him, they made their way toward the light. When they reached a farmhouse, they saw a lantern in the window.

"The curtains in that window is white. That means its safe for us to bring the folks in. If them curtains be red that means we stay put 'cause there be danger. These here folks call themselves Quakers. Ain't no better Christians in all this world. You go get the folks while I let farmer Anderson know we here."

Hale darted from tree to tree as he made his way back to the group. He could barely contain his excitement, realizing they had reached the first station on freedom's road.

When Moab knocked on the back door, a heavy-set white-haired man welcomed him. His flowing beard reached down to his belt. Moab guessed him to be in his fifties.

"Thou art welcome, Moab. We prayed for thy safe journey," the man said, shaking Moab's hand.

"Mr. Anderson, it's sho' good to see you," Moab said.

A stout woman, wearing a black dress, a white cap and apron, entered the kitchen. Standing behind her was a tall, lanky youth who looked to be about seventeen.

"Mr. Jackson, our special room has been prepared," the wife said.

"Thank you kindly, Mrs. Anderson. Our folks be coming along 'bout now."

Moab went to the back door and motioned for Hale to bring the party into the house. As they filed through the door, Mrs. Anderson escorted them into the living room. The bearded farmer raised his hand.

"My name is Walter Anderson. This is my wife, Rebekah, and our son, John. Thou art welcome in our humble home. Wilt thou bow thy heads and each, in thine own way, give thanks to the All Mighty."

The fugitives watched as the Anderson family folded their hands and bowed their heads in silent prayer. After placing their belongings on the floor, all stood with their heads bowed. Several dropped to their knees and whispered prayers. One man prayed aloud.

"Thank you Lord, for these good folks who open they home to us. Please stay with us as we journey to freedom land."

Anderson motioned to Moab to help him remove the hand-carved oak table that sat in the middle of the living room. With the table set to one side, they rolled up the shag rug that covered the floor. Anderson reached down and opened a well-concealed trap door, then motioned for his guests to climb down the ladder. At the bottom of the steps, they groped in the dark. Moab was the last to come down the ladder, carrying two oil lamps. As he held them up, they found themselves in a room furnished with seven handcrafted bunk beds, all prepared with white cotton sheets and blankets. The women marveled as they felt the bedding, as none had ever slept on sheets before. Three basins of water and towels sat on the table in the center of the room. There were twelve chairs around a large oak table. A dozen tin plates were stacked on the table beside a bowl of apples. In the far corner sat five chamber pots half filled with water. No one dared eat or sit until Walter came and told them to wash up before eating. They took turns washing the grime from their hand and faces. After eating the fruit, they stretched out on the bunks. Most were too excited to sleep. They whispered among themselves until Moab reminded them that they needed their rest for the coming journey.

At seven the next morning, Rebekah opened the trap door and handed Moab a steaming pot of beef stew, rich with rice and vegetables and three loaves of homemade bread, hot from the oven. He thanked her and placed the pot in the center of the table. Walter and Rebekah came down and sat at the table with their guests. They watched silently as the women served the stew. Rebekah passed out soupspoons from a wooden box. For most, it was their first time using metal utensils of any kind.

"My friends, before we partake of this food, wilt thou join us in a moment of silent prayer." Everyone bowed their heads for one minute. Anderson cleared his throat and prayed aloud, "We come to thee, Lord, thankful that thou has seen thy people safe to this station. Thou hast provided us with substance to nourish our bodies. Give us faith to nourish our souls. Amen."

"These sho' are some sweet praying folk," Bess whispered to her husband. "He say short prayers, too."

"We needs all the praying we can get," Joe replied, reaching for a slice of bread.

The fugitives were amazed that Walter and Rebekah shared the meal with them. Moab knew this simple act of breaking bread together was their first experience of being considered fully human.

Moab's relationship with Walter Anderson began five years earlier at a market in Washington City. Anderson's wagon had broken down one block from the market. When Moab saw his predicament, he left his carriage and helped him make the needed repairs. Moab refused to accept any offer of payment. As they rested in the shade together, Anderson asked if Moab had been born free. Moab told him the story of his fifteen-year struggle for freedom. On Walter's second trip to Washington City, he contacted Moab at the carriage house and invited him to a meeting of Quakers. It was there that Moab first learned of the religious society whose members treated all persons as equals. As he got to know the men and women who made up the Society of Friends, he became convinced they were the only true Christians he had ever met. A year later, Moab learned that several in the group were connected with a movement to free slaves. Months later he received an invitation to join their movement. Five months later he slipped into Alexandria, Virginia and helped the first group of slaves escape. From then on he was one of the emerging Underground Railroad's most successful agents, making forays into Maryland and Virginia.

The next evening, the rested travelers prepared to leave on the second leg of the trip, but when Rebekah lifted Henry to kiss him goodbye, she discovered he was running a high fever. She placed him in a tub of cool water, and then informed Moab that the child was too sick to travel.

"You must remain here another day. You will endanger the child's life if you leave now," Rebekah said.

Walter sent his son ahead to alert the next station that the travelers would be delayed a day, possibly longer. Moab's disgust with Hale grew with each passing hour. He assigned Joe and Hale to serve as lookouts while he sat with farmer Anderson mapping plans for the coming journey.

"Thou wilt take care on tomorrow night. We have reports that bounty hunters have been searching this area," Walter said.

"I know, 'cause they been on my trail for two days, but I out foxed them and their dogs," Moab said.

"Moab, thou art a brave man."

"Not half as brave as you is, Mr. Anderson. White folks won't take kind if they knows this be one of them station's that hides runaways. I be fearing for you and your family."

"Thou shalt not fear for us. We do the Lord's work, Moab," Walter said somberly. As the shadows of the setting sun cast its red glow in the living room, they descended to the basement for evening prayers.

Dr. Steven stood at the infirmary sink and washed his hands. He took Mary Alice into the adjoining room. "I fear Ruth has a serious heart problem." Mary Alice placed her hands over her face and began to cry. The door from the infirmary opened as Ruth entered.

"You crying for me? Don't you be crying. I knows my Lord be looking over me in times of trouble," Ruth said. Mary Alice wiped her eyes as she reached to embrace Ruth.

"Doctor, I want to thank you for coming to see me this evening. Just you being here makes me feel better already," Ruth said quietly.

Dr. Steven pulled his chair closer to Ruth. "We have faced sickness and death together, Ruth. I will always remember the way you worked beside me when that fever took so many lives. I must be honest. You are very sick. I want you to know I will do all in my power to help you in the months ahead."

Ruth went over to the window and looked up at the stars. She whispered, "Lord, are you gonna make me walk through that lonely valley of death before my son is free?" She walked outside and went to her cabin. Taking a seat, she lowered her head on the table and wept, but was determined not to fall asleep until Anthony came home. When the door opened at two in the morning, Ruth rose from her rocking chair and hugged Anthony.

"Mama, what're you doing up so late?" he asked with concern.

"I been wanting to talk with you son. I'm so glad you are home safe."

"You want to talk with me about Catharine, don't you? Mama, I don't want you to be worrying about us."

Ruth placed her finger to his lips. "That's not why I waited up, son"

"Mama, what's wrong? You're not sick, are you?"

"Yes, Anthony. Dr. Steven say I've got a weak heart."

Anthony shook his head. Her words did not register with him at first. He moved his stool beside her and held her hand. "You and me, we're gonna be free one day. You'll get well, Mama. You just gotta get well." The pain in his voice rose. He was a man now and had to be strong for her. Grown men don't cry, although it seemed he had been doing his share of crying lately. "Mama, I know you've been worried about me. Please understand, I love Catharine. We've made a pledge, Mama. We placed our hands on a Bible and told the Lord that we will wait for each other no matter how long it takes. But I've got to find a way to get her away from the Bakers. She might die if she stays there." It terrified him to think that because of his weakness, she might end up pregnant.

Ruth rested her head on Anthony's broad shoulder. She marveled at how he had grown in the past six months. "I sure wish I could meet this girl that has turned your head. She must be truly special," Ruth said.

"She's really special, Mama. Just like you." Anthony sat beside her bed until she finally slept. Knowing that Reverend Harris often worked late on his sermons during weekends, he quietly left the cabin and walked over to the stable. Reverend Harris was just leaving for the night.

"Anthony, what you doing out here this late. You should be getting your rest," Reverend Harris said.

"I promised the Lord I would come see you as soon as I got home. I need to tell you something and it can't wait."

"Well now, you come right on in and tell me all about it." Anthony followed Reverend Harris to the back of the stable and into the small room that he used for his study. "Now what's troubling you, son."

For the next half-hour, Reverend Harris listened quietly as Anthony spoke of his love for Catharine, the abuse she experienced at the hands of John Baker, and the threats of the bounty hunters. Finally, he lowered his head and confessed he had 'sinned' with Catharine and had thoughts of killing John Baker. Quite certain he had provoked the wrath of God, Anthony bowed his head and prepared to hear the punishment. When Reverend Harris remained silent, Anthony looked up and saw him smiling. The preacher reached over and patted his hand.

"Anthony, I've lived a long time and had many talks with the Lord about all the sinning that folk be doing in this world," Reverend Harris said, opening his Bible. "Now you know what you done was wrong. But in this here Bible, folks done lots of worse things. In the Book of Genesis, even the sons of God slipped down from heaven and started messing with all the pretty women they could get their hands on. Lots of them women got in family way. After their children were born, some grew up to be giants and others became wise men. And there was King David who took a fancy to a married woman named Bathsheba. After she told him she gonna have his baby, King David had her husband, Uriah, killed. Ain't no worse sin than that. One of their babies grew up to be King Solomon, one of the wisest men that ever lived. But even Solomon, wise as he was, let women go to his head. And you know what happened to Samson after he got to messing with that woman, Delilah. I don't always understand the ways of the Lord. Sometime he punishes sinners, other times he don't. The Lord knows your burden got so heavy it made you weak. Now I figger, on one side of his heavenly scale he gonna weigh what them bounty hunters done to both of you, and on the other side, what you two done. I feel his wrath gonna come down on the heads of those bounty hunters. I'm gonna stay here and have a talk with him about you and that girl. Like his son, Jesus, say, 'your sin is forgiven,' but try not to do it next time you with her. That is, until you find a way to marry her. Now go to your mama, because she needs you."

*   *   *

Henry sat beside Abigail in the parlor, looking forlorn. She was leaving and no date had been set for their wedding. Hale's departure with the child had cast a pall over the visit.

"I will write you when I get home. I need time to reflect on all that I have seen and on this tragic situation that just happened," Abigail said.

"It saddens me that you had to witness it. My parents take such pride in the way we treat our people."

"Your people!" Abigail said, reflectively. "They are your people, aren't they? Henry, have you ever had a real conversation with Anthony or Ruth, or any of your people?" Her words cut deep as she held his hand.

"Am I losing you?"

"Write and tell me how all these crises are finally resolved," Abigail said. "Please do what you can for Anthony and that poor girl he loves. And tell me the truth about Cathy. Did she abandon her husband and child and remain here because she loves you?"

Henry knew these questions would decide the fate of their marriage. "She remained because she loves her home and family."

Jim came to the doorway and cleared his throat, "Miss Abigail, your carriage is ready."

Henry held her hand while they walked to the carriage. Mary Alice, Elizabeth and Louise stood waiting for them.

"Don't we get a chance to say goodbye to your father?" Abigail said, looking back at the Manor house.

"Papa sends his regrets. He left last night and was not certain if he would return before your departure."

"He's gone to bring them back, hasn't he," she said, biting her lower lip.

Henry took her hand and led her to a bench under a nearby pear tree. "Abigail, one of my favorite passages in the Bible reads, 'Prove all things, hold fast to that which is good.' I will prove to you what is good in my world," he said earnestly.

Moab awoke from a light sleep when he heard the Anderson's dogs barking. Sitting up in the darkened cellar, he reached over and shook Hale.

"You hear them dogs?" he whispered.

"Yea, I hears them. You think bounty hunters out there?"

"Might be. Don't wake the folks yet. The chillen might start crying."

They heard loud pounding on the front door and then footsteps above them. Moab groped in the dark for his trousers and picked up his pistol. There were muffled voices shouting above them. Moab's heart pounded as he felt his way to the ladder. His mouth felt dry and his hand shook momentarily. He knew their hiding place had been discovered. The muffled voices continued but the shouting ceased. They listened, but could not make out the words being spoken.

"They bounty hunters done found us," Hale whispered, his voice quivering.

"That's what I be thinking. Hale, when that trap door opens I ain't gonna let them take me. Can't be no slave. Can't let them burn me no more. If I die, I's gonna take some of them with me."

Moab heard a rapping sound on the upper floor. Three distinct raps of a cane on the pine boards. He remembered the sound, and recalled William's warning. "Hale, that's your master up there. He done found us," Moab whispered.

"How you know that?"

"I just knows. It's him for sho'."

They stood at the bottom of the ladder and waited for the trap door to open. The muffled voices grew quiet. Then there was silence. They could hear the table being dragged across the floor, the rug being removed, and the trap door slowly opening. Moab pointed his gun toward the light that flooded the entrance. His hand shook, knowing he was about to kill the man who saved his life. He wondered if he could pull the trigger. Just as he readied his weapon, he saw the face of Walter Anderson.

"Would thou harm thy fellow man, Moab?" Walter asked, his soft voice was calm. Moab lowered his pistol and placed it in his belt.

"Thou may come up, for thou hath nothing to fear. But first, hand me thy weapon. Such things hath no place in our home." Moab climbed up the ladder and handed the gun to Walter. The noise from the table being moved had awakened the adults who rushed to the foot of the ladder.

"This is the day the Lord hath made," Rebekah said, appearing at the open door.

Moab extended his hand to Hale. As both men emerged from the cellar, they blinked and rubbed their eyes to adjust to the light. To their astonishment, they saw Cathy sitting in a chair by the fireplace, with a satchel at her side. Moab felt certain that William Bradley was somewhere in the room or waiting outside. It had to be a trap.

Cathy rose from the chair and ran into Hale's arms. "Master Bradley brought me here. He say we free. Hale, we're free," Cathy cried, hugging and kissing his lips and cheek. "He give me freedom papers for you, me and little Henry." Hale sank to his knees, unable to comprehend what she had just said. She knelt beside him and whispered, "Hale, it's true. We're all free."

Moab snatched the papers and read it before handing the documents to farmer Anderson and starting for the door. Walter blocked his path.

"Have no fear, Moab. William Bradley is not waiting for thee," Walter said, placing his hands on his friend's shoulder. "You and your fellow travelers have nothing to fear from him."

Upon William's return at six-thirty the next the morning, he went to the parlor and collapsed into one of his favorite chairs. Jim assisted him by removing his boots. He placed the boots in the closet and returned with a pair of slippers.

Jim was puzzled by William's contentment. Although curious to know what had happened, he knew his brother would speak when ready. "May I fix you a drink?"

William nodded, closed his eyes with his head resting on the chair's cushion. Henry rushed into the room and sat beside him.

"Papa, we were worried when you didn't return last night. Did you find them?"

"You shouldn't have worried. My night vision is not as good as it used to be, so I stayed at an inn. As for Hale, Cathy and the child, they will not be returning. I set them free."

Thunderstruck, Henry gazed at William with total disbelief. He suddenly felt relieved, knowing Abigail would be pleased. He looked at Jim who remained as stoic as ever. Then his thoughts turned to Anthony and the plight of his beloved Catharine. As he sat pondering his options, he decided their fate would be his highest priority.

CHAPTER 26

William and Henry walked out to the barnyard to meet Abel Baker. Abel had arrived early to pay the stud fee for having his cow impregnated. He stood with one foot on the fence, gazing admiringly at William's prize Holstein bull.

"You folks sure got some fine beef over yonder. I'd give my right arm to own two or three heifers by that bull. One of my cows done gone dry on me. She ain't give us no calves, going on two years now."

"Didn't she have a calf two years ago? What did you do with it?" Henry asked.

"We had to sell it. Just seems like every other year or so, along comes one of them hot spells that sets us back."

"Abel, how many slaves do you own?" William inquired.

"Three all together. Shucks, Mr. Bradley, two of them too feeble to work the fields. I bought them ten years back, but they got so many ailments, they ain't much use to me now. That don't stopped 'em from eating, though. The old wench so useless, it crossed my mind to put her in a sack and drop her in the river," Baker said, chuckling. His laughter ceased when he saw the disgust on William's face. "The only one worth anything is my nigger gal. She's a mighty good worker, but like my old cow, she's close to fifteen and ain't had no darky babies."

"You say she's not given birth? Have you made an effort to mate her?" William asked, trying to keep a straight face.

Abel looked at William then at Henry, knowing it was useless to lie. "Lookie here, that boy of yours been coming over our place for months now. I knowed he be liking her and she be liking him. Shucks, we figger he might like a little twat now and then. We don't do nothing to stop them, but her belly just as flat as it was the day I bought her."

"You used our boy for stud service?" William asked, attempting to be serious.

"Well sir, I don't look at it quite like that," Abel stammered, wondering where the conversation was headed. "Niggers work harder if they know they can get a little twat after sundown."

"Well now, if she were a breeder she would be worth a lot more to you, wouldn't she?" William replied.

"You might say that. Would you like to buy her? She's in good health and got all her teeth," Baker asked, certain William would not be interested in a barren female slave. After all, he owned more than a hundred darkies.

"What would you say if I offered you three of my cows for her?" William asked, finding it hard to keep a straight face.

Abel's mouth dropped open. "What you say, Mr. Bradley? Did I hear you right?"

"Papa said that we might offer you three of our cows for your girl if she's in good health," Henry said, slapping Abel's back.

Abel was certain no one in his right mind would make such an offer without inspecting the property first, but it was too good an offer for him to question their motives. He extended his hand to William.

"I take it we have a deal?" William asked.

"We sure as hell do," Abel shouted, glancing at the cows then at William.

"Well, come with me to the library."

Abel followed William into the library and signed the bill of sale, conditional on Catharine being in good health. With the bill clutched in his hand, Abel mounted his horse, waved his hat in the air and rode off in a cloud of dust.

"Henry, do you think I'm getting soft in my old age?"

"You are not soft and certainly not old. It was an act of kindness I'll never forget. I don't remember the last time I said it, but, Papa, I love you," Henry said, throwing his arms around William and hugging his tightly.

"Why don't you take Anthony and go fetch that girl?" William said. "We don't want John Baker tampering with her for the last time."

"It would be a pleasure," Henry said, already formulating in his mind what he would write to Abigail. He ordered Big George to hitch up the carriage then returned to the Manor house to find Anthony. When he entered the kitchen, Betty and Hattie greeted him with smiles.

"Have you seen Anthony?"

"He and Joe working down at the front gate. That gate needed to be fixed for a long time now," Hattie replied, wondering why Henry seemed so excited. Out of curiosity, she followed him to the front door and watched as he boarded the carriage and drove away.

"Something going on and I sho' wish I know what it is?" Hattie grumbled.

When the carriage rolled to a stop at the gate, Henry called out, "Anthony, I'm going over to the Baker farm on business. I want you to drive the carriage."

Anthony's face lit up as he threw down his hammer and climbed on the seat beside Henry. "Sorry Joe. If you don't finish, we'll do it this afternoon, if I get back in time," Anthony shouted.

Thomas B. Hargrave, Jr.

Henry handed Anthony the reins. "Take your time. I don't want you to turn this buggy over. I know you are anxious to see that girl your mother's all worried about."

Anthony stared at Henry. "Mama's been talking to you about Catharine again?"

When they pulled onto the dusty road, Henry reached over and slapped Anthony's back. "Who else would she be talking about. You have broken the hearts of all the girls around here. From all I've heard, she's quite exceptional."

"She sure is. Every night I pray she will be free of that terrible place," Anthony said. He had not seen Catharine for more than two weeks. The Bakers had not requested his services and he feared they no longer needed him. Did the bounty hunters return? Was Catharine pregnant? The questions plagued his day and night. He had made up his mind to slip away one night and go see her. As he steered the carriage, he glanced several times at Henry, not daring to inquire about the reason for the trip. Would there be time for him to see her, no matter how briefly?

As they rode in silence, Henry reflected on a letter he received that morning from Cathy Sanders, post marked 'Stone Hill, Canada.' A Quaker mother had written the words down for her. His hands had shook when he opened and read it. 'Dear Henry, Hale and me and little Henry in Stone Hill, Canada. The people here are kind to us. Our son will go to school with white and Indian children when he is six years old. Hale got a job working as a carpenter. I soon will be learning to read and write and I hope one day I will be able to write by my own hand. A nice lady is putting these words on paper for me. I hope you and Miss Abigail get married real soon and that you and her will have children some day. It gets real cold some nights, but everybody is so nice to us that we feel warm all the time. Hale happy now that I'm going to have his baby. Tell Miss Abigail I hope she is happy like I am. Very truly," The bold block letters read, Mrs. Cathy Sanders.

Henry was also aware that William had also received a letter from Hale, but had refused to discuss its contents. Cathy's letter had given him a new perspective on his feeling for her. He finally admitted to himself that he had loved her, but until that moment could not bring himself to admit it.

When the carriage rolled to a stop the front of the Baker's house, John and Abel came out to greet them. John yelled, "Anthony, you sly nigger, it was you talked Mr. Bradley into this swap, didn't you?" Anthony looked puzzled.

"John, shut your mouth. The deal ain't done yet," Abel said, punching him in his side with his elbow. "Welcome Henry. Come on in, sit for a spell and have a taste of our corn."

216

"I would like that. Papa says you folks make the best corn liquor in the county," Henry said, climbing from the carriage,

"Anthony, go fetch Cat. Tell her to get her little butt back here real quick, you hear?" Abel shouted.

"Yes sir," Anthony said, barely able to restrain himself. Why did Abel Baker ask him to bring Catharine to his house? It's possible he just wanted her to serve food. Or did it have something to do with Henry's visit? He refused to allow himself to entertain any hopeful thoughts while running and shouting her name at the top of his lungs. Bewildered by all that was happening, he ran to the barn but did not find her. Rushing to her cabin, he burst through the door. Aunt May was sitting by the fireplace smoking her corn cob pipe.

"Where's Catharine?"

"Howdy Anthony. Sho' good to see you again. Last time I seed her, she was headed for the creek to catch a mess of frogs fo' supper. My spirits told me you be coming back."

"Thank you." Anthony ran across the field shouting her name. When he approached the stream, she rose up among the tall weeds along the bank, waving her straw hat.

"Anthony!" Catharine screamed, tossing her hat into the air. She raced barefooted through the cornrows into his arms. Both collapsed on the ground as she smothered him with kisses.

"What you doing back here?" she cried breathlessly. "John say they done with you fo' now. I be wondering if I ever see you again. I's so glad you back." He tried to loosen her vice-like grip, but she clung to him.

"Are you all right? Did those bounty hunters come back?"

"I's just fine, now that you here. Them men never come back," she said, touching his cheek.

"I got something to tell you," he said, trying to catch his breath. "Your master told me to fetch you." He felt her body grow rigid. "We gotta hurry. Don't be scared." He took her hand and led her into the farmhouse. When they entered through the kitchen door, Catharine lowered her head and held tightly to Anthony's arm. Abel's wife shoved her into the front room.

"It's about time you got here," Abel said.

Henry placed his glass of corn whiskey aside and rose from the chair. The exquisite beauty of her dark features struck him as he approached her. Catharine cringed when he placed his hand on her shoulder and made her turn around. He instructed her to open her mouth, and was amazed that she had all her teeth which were free of decay.

Anthony could not believe what he was seeing. He felt certain he would wake and it would be a dream. After all, many nights he had dreams of the day she would be free from the Baker's cruelty, only to wake to the harsh reality of another long day of anxiety.

Henry shook Abel Baker's hand then turned to Catharine. "Young woman, you are now the property of my father, William Bradley."

Catharine placed her hands to her mouth to stifle her cry. Wild-eyed, she turned to Anthony, seeking assurance that what she had heard was true.

"Master Bradley has bought Catharine?" Anthony asked, his voice quivering. "She's gonna live at Bradley Manor?" He heard the words that Henry spoke, but fearing some hideous trick, he dared not allow himself to believe them.

"You heard him right. Your master traded three of his fine cows for her," Abel yelled. "Cat, go get your dugs and be gone. We sure gonna miss you, gal."

Only when Anthony heard Abel's words did he turn and face Catharine. "I told you the days of glory would come," he whispered while hugging her.

"She won't be needing any clothes," Henry said. "Anthony, take her to the carriage and wait inside. I'll be there as soon as I finish this drink. I'll do the driving this time."

John sat at the table nursing his glass of whiskey. The throbbing in the nub of his little finger grew in intensity. It always throbbed painfully when Catharine was in his presence.

Catharine felt faint and leaned on Anthony's arm. She wept while leaving the room. Even when Anthony opened the door to the carriage, she could not believe what was happening. "I gotta go say goodbye to the old folks," she said. She took Anthony's hand as they ran to the cabin. To their surprise, Aunt May was standing in the doorway as though she expected them.

"I knowed you coming to say you leaving us. My spirits told me that you two was going to be together."

As Anthony watched, Catharine hugged her then went to Uncle Joe and sat beside him on the edge of his bed. She held his hand and kissed his cheek. "I's gonna miss you, Uncle Joe. Sorry I won't be around to fix you your frog soup." He stared at her but made no reply as tears filled his eyes.

After Anthony hugged both of them, he took Catharine's hand and hurried to the carriage. Once seated, she threw her arms around his neck and clung to him, fearing that John would come and drag her away.

"They will never hurt you again," Anthony whispered, kissing the tears from her face.

Henry finally walked to the carriage and looked into the window. Seeing them together, he knew how pleased Abigail would be when she learned what had happened.

"You sure you don't want me to drive back? Catharine can sit beside me," Anthony said.

"No, Anthony, stay where you are. Just behave yourselves," Henry said, winking at them.

When the carriage began to roll, only then did Anthony allow himself to believe she was beyond the Baker's reach forever. For Anthony, it was the supreme moment in his young life.

While resting on her bed, Ruth tossed and turned, unable to sleep. With a sigh, she got up and sat in her rocking chair. It was a warm night and the humidity in the cabin left her gown soaked as sweat poured down her face and chest. Another of her short breathing spells had bothered her. Earlier, Hattie had told her that there were some strange goings on.

"Sister, Master Henry went driving out of here like he be going to a house fire."

Later, Big George came to the kitchen and told her that Henry had business at the Baker farm. "I heard Massa William say Henry going over to the Baker's farm, but they be talking so quiet I don't hear all they say. Massa Henry took Anthony with him. Now Ruth, ain't nothing to worry about, 'cause Anthony's done working at that place fo' this year."

"He's done working all right, but he ain't done with that girl. I sure hope she's not in family way," Ruth replied.

"Anthony's a man now. You gonna worry yourself into an early grave 'bout that boy," Big George said. "I be looking in on you a bit later."

Ruth sat in her rocker, singing softly, *'Nobody knows the trouble I've seen. Nobody knows, but Jesus.'* She stopped singing and sat up when she heard faint voices in the distance. As the voices grew louder, she could hear Big George's booming voice. The cabin door burst open, but she could only see the shadows of figures rushing into the room. The floorboards shook from the weight of them. After someone lit a candle, she saw Anthony standing beside her. Big George, Hattie, Jim, Betty and Sarah were all there, smiling at her. But who was this strange girl holding Anthony's hand?

"Why all ya'll coming busting in here this time of the night?" Ruth shouted. She sat back when Anthony knelt beside her and kissed her cheek.

"Mama, this here is Catharine," Anthony said, his voice quivering with excitement. "Master Bradley bought her from the Bakers, and she's gonna live here at Bradley Manor."

Ruth blinked, staring first at Catharine then at Anthony. Could she believe what she just heard? Everything was a blur as her heart raced. Anthony placed Catharine's hand in hers.

Ruth threw up her hands, "Lord, sweet Jesus, please tell me this is not a dream." Heads nodded as everyone began speaking at once, assuring her it was true.

"Catharine belongs here now. Master Bradley has done the Lord's work," Anthony shouted triumphantly. Ruth rose from the rocker, held out her arms and hugged Catharine. Pandemonium broke loose as everyone began hugging and kissing each other. Betty threw her arms around Jim and kissed his lips, causing him to completely lose his composure.

"Will all of you please hush up," Ruth cried. "Let Mama Ruth take a good look at you, child." Catharine smiled apprehensively, stepping back from Ruth's embrace.

"I's pleased to meet you, Miss Ruth. Anthony done told me about all of you. I feels like I knows ya' already."

Ruth held her at arms length. "My, my, I see why Anthony's so crazy about you. You mighty pretty, but we got to get you out of those rags and fatten you up. Hattie, take this child over to your place, feed her. See that she gets a good scrubbing and find her some decent clothes to put on."

Bubba peeped in the open door. "I woke up when I hear all the ruckus. What's happening?"

Anthony motioned for Bubba to come in. "Bubba, I want you to meet Catharine." When Bubba stared at Catharine, his eyes bulged and his mouth dropped open. Everyone but Big George laughed.

Big George tapped Bubba's head. "Son, you get your yourself back to yo' house. You gonna need all yo' rest, 'cause you got lots of plowing to do in the morning." Everyone knew that Big George harbored no great love for Bubba, despite the fact he had proven to be a loving husband and devoted father to his child.

Ruth waved for them to leave. "All this excitement too much for me. I need my rest. Anthony, go with them but behave yourself."

"I see he behaves himself, Miss Ruth," Catharine said.

"Don't be too long, son. I want to have prayer with you before I sleep," Ruth said. Alone in the quiet of her cabin, Ruth blew out the candle and went to bed. She lay awake, watching the rays of moonlight shining through the window.

"That old moon is sure shining bright tonight," Ruth said. "Zach, our son's a man now." As sleep pressed down upon her weary eyes, she whispered, "Thank you, thank you, Lord Jesus for opening Master William and Henry's hearts."

William sat at his desk well past midnight reflecting on the events that had transpired that day. Henry had spoken of Anthony's happiness and had shared the contents of the letter he received from Cathy. Now he fingered the letter addressed to him from Hale Sanders. On impulse, he started to throw it into the fireplace, then hesitated. For a few seconds he reflected on his reasons for not wanting to read it. Was he afraid that a letter from his former slave might undermine his assumptions about this race of people? Taking a letter opener, he cut open the envelope and held the letter up to the light of his lamp. From the style of writing, he knew someone had written the words for Hale.

"Mr. William Bradley:

I am taking the liberty to address you on this fourth month of our emancipation, for I know of no better way to celebrate these days. A kind Quaker lady is writing these words down for me and my wife. I want to thank you for letting me and my family leave your place of bondage and come to a land truly crowned by the sweet blessings of liberty. I know that your reason for letting us go was not based on Christian charity alone. Here in this town of Stone Hill we were welcomed by white folks who judge us not by the color of our skin, but how we treat our neighbors. When they see folks hungry, they give them food. When a man's barn burns down, all gather together and rebuild it. When folks get sick, they all come together and pray for healing and give help when it is needed. When we first came here, they gave me work on one of their farms. Here I earned my first dollar as a free man. I am not a man of many words, but I wish I could tell you how happy I was when I bought my first loaf of warm bread right out of the oven. When I put my own butter on that bread and me, Cathy and our son blessed it and ate it all. Then I bought us some ham. Not the chittlings from the hog's guts, not the feet of the hog, not its ears, tails, skin or head. All them parts you gave us slaves at hog killing time. I ate me some sweet smoked ham. Now I got me three little pigs and we raising them. Cathy and me now learning to read, write and count. I was thinking how I use to hate all white folks. I don't hate like that no more because I have found in this town a people who truly love the Lord. We are living our life, just like them.

Your obedient servant, but your slave no longer, Hale Sanders"

CHAPTER 27

June 1826

The wedding of Henry and Abigail Schroeder was considered to be the social event of the decade by leading families in Prince Georges County and Washington City. Those who did not receive invitations, made it their business to pay a social call.

The evening before the wedding, twenty-three guests arrived. While the women socialized in the living room, William's male guests gathered in the library and ribbed Henry over drinks. William raised his glass.

"Gentlemen, I have an announcement to make. Beginning next month I am relinquishing the affairs of Bradley Manor to my son. No, I am not retiring. I have been asked by General Andrew Jackson to support him in his bid for the presidency and I have accepted."

The smiles on several planter's faces faded. "Damn Bill, how can you support a populist like Jackson. During the last war he had six Tennessee militiamen shot during the battle of New Orleans. He will ruin the government with his fool ideas about doing away with the Federal bank," planter Jack Anderson shouted.

"Jack, we will speak of it after the wedding. For now, raise your glasses to my son and his intended bride."

After three hours of socializing, extra cots were placed in the parlor and library to accommodate the men, while the six guestrooms on the second floor were reserved for women and children.

The morning of the wedding dawned clear and cool. Reverend Wigfall arrived and went to the parlor for a meeting with the male members of the wedding party. Henry introduced him to his best man, David Cohen, and Reverend Robert Little, pastor of the First Unitarian Church of Washington City. When told that Reverend Little, a close friend of the bride's family, would give the closing prayer, Reverend Wigfall became visibly upset.

Taking Henry aside he whispered. "Henry, this is a Christian wedding. For a Jew and a Unitarian to participate in any part of it would be an affront to our Lord, Jesus Christ. As your pastor, I insist these non-believers be excluded."

Henry excused himself, took his pastor by the arm and escorted him outside to the vestibule. "Now listen carefully. Go to your carriage and drive back to your church office. There you will take pen and paper and write a letter to the bishop. You will inform him that your usefulness to our beloved church is over and you wish to be transferred. If you refuse to do as I instruct you, it will be the last Methodist church you will ever serve. As for my wedding, your assistant pastor will officiate. Have I made myself clear?"

Reverend Wigfall wiped the sweat from his face while being escorted to his carriage. "By what authority-,"

"I am my own authority. Excuse my language, but you are one bigoted son-of-a-bitch."

At eleven in the morning, the wedding began under ideal conditions, with the temperature in the low eighties. To the music of Pachelbel's Canon played by a ten-piece string orchestra, Abigail emerged from the rose garden onto the west lawn on the arm of her father. Whispers of admiration sounded as they passed. The wedding ceremony lasted twenty minutes, ending with a short prayer by Reverend Little.

"Bless this union, O Lord. Now may you always remember that Christianity calls us to be advocates for the general welfare. Be aware of your obligations, not just each other, but for the good of the general society. Our religion requires us to love one another, to protest against national vices and to change those mistaken polices of our ancestors in introducing and accumulating an evil destined to bring grief upon our country. Amen."

After the ceremony, several planters voiced their objections to Reverend Little's anti-slavery prayer but were ignored by William. The wedding party stood in the shade of an oak tree as guests filed past. After an hour of hand shaking and kisses, the white guests moved into the picnic area, as William's workers came forward to greet the bride and groom. Anthony approached, holding Catharine's hand.

"So this is Catharine," Abigail said, taking her hand. "You are quite lovely, my dear."

"I want to thank you and Master Henry for bringing me here," Catharine said shyly.

"When we return from our trip abroad, I will see to your training and teach you to read and write."

"I sure would like that. Anthony's already teaching me my letters and how to talk proper."

When Ruth stepped forward, Henry embraced her and kissed her cheek. Several white women watching from the distance, turned up their noses and sneered. William came and escorted Henry and Abigail to the head table. Seated next to him was Frances Scott Key whom William had met during the War of 1812. Key stood and shook Henry's hand.

"It is an honor to be at the head table of a fellow St. John's alumnus and his beautiful bride," Frances said, taking Abigail's hand and kissing it.

"Are you the Frances Scott Key who wrote the Star Spangled Banner?" Abigail asked.

"Yes I am."

"Henry and I have been reading how you defended the Africans taken from the slave ship, Antelope. Your concern for the downtrodden has been an inspiration to us. We recently read that some of the Africans were released to the American Colonization Society after the Supreme Court ruled in your favor. We would like to know more about it."

"I'm delighted to know you are pleased. But on such a festive occasion are you sure you want to hear about so unpleasant an affair?"

"We would like to hear it, but after I take this first dance with my wife," Henry said, taking Abigail's hand and escorting to the platform that had been constructed for the occasion. As the orchestra played a waltz, they danced to the applause of the crowd.

When the second waltz began, William walked over and tapped Henry's shoulder. "Dance with your mother while I waltz with my new daughter." Abigail was pleasantly surprised at the grace and skill William exhibited as they waltzed around the dance floor.

Following the dinner and the cutting of the cake, Abigail turned to Frances. "I would like to finish our conversation. We read that the Supreme Court did not free all the Africans that were taken from that slave ship. Why were some made slaves and others freed?"

"I'm ashamed to say that thirty-seven were sold to help settle the seven-year court cost. We were able to free one hundred and thirty-four Africans who were settled in the newly created West African State of Liberia."

"How did the Chief Justice decide who would go free and who would be sold?" Henry asked.

"It was Chief Justice Marshall's decision that it be done by lottery."

"By Lottery! How cruel," Abigail said, her face flushed with anger.

"Now you know why I did not want to spoil such a beautiful occasion."

"You have not spoiled it. On the contrary, just hearing of your seven-year struggle for justice is more precious to us than all the gifts we have received on this blessed day," Abigail said, leaning over and kissing Frances Scott Key on his cheek.

On a mild November afternoon, Anthony, with picnic basket in hand, led Catharine and Betty to the brook that ran through the north pasture. When they reached the bank where the leaning Sycamore stood, he pointed to the exposed roots where he had hid from Joseph Hanks and his bounty hunters.

"That's where I hid until I was sure Joseph Hanks and his men were gone. I come here to pray sometimes because I'm sure I heard the voice of God speaking to me while I was hiding under those roots."

"What did you hear?" Betty asked as Catharine spread a tablecloth on a thick canopy of fallen leaves.

"I've never told anyone about this. When I felt I was drowning, I heard a voice say, 'Be still, for I am with you.' After that, I felt calm and remained there until I was sure they were gone."

Anthony opened the basket and removed the fried chicken, hard-boiled eggs, three baked potatoes and rolls. Betty had come at the insistence of Ruth who felt girls Catharine's age should be chaperoned. It was not that she didn't trust Anthony, it was just the proper thing to do.

"Listen, you two. I know you want to be alone, so ya'll have a nice time," Betty said. "Don't be doing nothing naughty." She hugged Catharine and kissed Anthony's cheek, then left after taking a roll and a fried chicken thigh with her.

While sitting together, Anthony marveled as the sunlight on Catharine's face highlighted the contours of her features. Her complexion glowed and the worry lines that once etched her face had vanished. Ruth boasted that it was her good cooking that put some 'meat' on Catharine's bones, but Anthony was sure it was the absence of stress that did wonders for her. During her first months at Bradley Manor, Catharine had awakened in the middle of the night screaming. In her nightmares, it was always the same. John Baker and the bounty hunters were pursuing her. During each episode, Hattie held her in her arms saying, "Wake up chile, you safe here with us. Ain't nobody ever gonna hurt you no more." After six months the nightmares ceased and she slept peacefully.

Catharine touched Anthony's hand. As they looked into each other's eyes, both recalled the night spent together in the loft. "Mrs. Abigail and I been talking about you."

"About me? What did you talk about?"

"Just women talk. She's real happy being married to Master Henry and living here."

"But what did she say about me?"

"She said you gonna be a leader of our people when you become a free man, and she thinks that's gonna happen by the time you twenty-one"

"By my twenty-first birthday? That's four years from now," Anthony said, barely able to contain himself, pounding his fist in the palm of his hand.

"Remember what she told me at her wedding about my learning to read and write? Well, she gave me a book and *said* that we could read it together.

And *I'm* gonna learn to cook as good as Mama Ruth." Catharine said slowly, proud that her grammar was already improving, thanks to Anthony. She opened the picnic basket. "*I'll* tell you more after we eat. *I'm* hungry."

Anthony rose, reached for her hand and pulled her to her feet. "I need to hear more about what Mrs. Abigail said about us."

"She wants us to wait a few years before we get married and start having babies. What do you think?"

"I know she's right, but it's sure gonna be hard. Almost every night I dream about us in that loft. There is something I should have told you. I told Reverend Harris that happened between us."

"You did?" Catharine asked, embarrassed. "He never put on like he knew it. He was real friendly when he took me down to the river and baptized me. When I come up out of the water, all he said was, 'Sister, now you are a child of the Lord.' Come to think about it, he sure smiles a lot when he sees us together."

"He is a wonderful preacher. He's sure the Lord understood what happened that night. But he told me I should wait until we are married. That's what I promised to do."

"Then, I'll just have to give you lots and lots of kisses," Catharine said, leaning over and kissing his cheek. A cloud formation caught Catharine's eye. "Look, Anthony. Them clouds looks just like the ones in the poem you wrote for me." They watched two clouds merge and drift toward the western horizon.

"When we get married, we will be one, floating free," Anthony said.

The cloud left Anthony with an uneasy feeling, however. It reminded him of a time when he saw the cloud shaped like a fish bone. Ruth had been complaining about shortness of breath again. She told him not to worry because the Lord wanted her to be there when he received his freedom papers. His thoughts were interrupted when seven children spied them, and came running in their direction. All giggled and laughed as they gathered around them.

"Anthony, this your girl, ain't she?" Scott, a ten-year-old asked.

"Yes she is, Scott."

The children giggled. "Ya'll gonna get married?" Sue, a seven-year-old asked.

"Yes, but not right now," Catharine replied, reaching out and pulling the girl's plat. "Tell me, what you like to do for fun?"

"We play tag," Sue shouted. "We like to play hide and seek and kick the can. We like to fish," the others shouted, their voices overlapping.

"Any of you ever catch bullfrogs?" Catharine asked.

Anthony laughed. "You are looking at the best bullfrog catcher in the world," Anthony bragged.

"Will you teach us?" Scott asked, his head bobbed up and down.

Catharine turned to Anthony. "Are there any frogs in this here creek?"

"Yeah, but I've never been able to catch them the way you do."

"Well, we'll take ya'll frog hunting, but not today. Go on home now and leave us be," Catharine said. Whooping and yelling, the children scattered across the field toward the compound.

"I'm glad we've had this time together," Anthony said, feeling concerned about Ruth.

"You think Master Bradley will free me, if we married and I have your baby?"

"You will be free, even if I have to stay here and work another seven years. But I can't wait seven year to marry you."

Catharine stood on tiptoes and kissed Anthony on his lips. "I love you so much," she whispered.

After folding the tablecloth and placing it in the basket, they walked slowly, hand in hand, to Hattie's cabin. Hattie called out, "Cat, you come on in and eat some more vittles. I know Anthony and Betty gobbled up most of what you took out of here. Anthony, yo' mama's feeling poorly. You best go see how she doing."

"I'm leaving now," Anthony said, taking Catharine in his arms. "This has been a happy day. Sometimes I wake up at night, scared that your being here was all a dream."

"It's no dream, Anthony" she said, pointing him toward his cabin. "Kiss Mama Ruth for me."

Anthony trotted back to his cabin leaping into the air and clicking his feet. With Catharine's kisses still warming his lips, he opened the cabin door slowly. He paused as he heard Ruth's labored breathing. He hurried to her bed and knelt beside her.

"Mama, you all right?" he whispered, lifting Ruth's head and adjusting her pillow. She opened her eyes and stared toward the window.

"Anthony, the moonlight's been shining green for the last couple of nights. Pea green. Did you see it?" she whispered softly.

"Mama, what are you talking about? What's wrong? You are not getting sick again are you?" He tried to calm the panic in his voice.

"Don't fret, son. Go fetch Hattie, Sarah, Jim and Catharine for me. Hurry along now." Anthony stood rubbing his hands frantically. He bolted out the door and raced to Hattie's cottage.

"Hattie, Mama's real sick," Anthony cried. Hattie rushed past him toward their cabin.

Catharine had just settled on her cot when she heard him calling. He dropped to his knees beside her. "Mama's awful sick."

"Don't you be worrying none. She'll be alright. Now you turn your head while I dress." Anthony paced back and forth as she slipped on her work dress. Taking his hand, they raced across the path to Ruth's bedside. Big George and Hattie were already there. They stepped back as Anthony and Catharine knelt beside Ruth's bed.

Ruth looked into their weeping faces. "I don't want nobody being sad around my sick bed," she said, smiling faintly. Catharine soaked a towel in a bucket of water and wiped the sweat from Ruth's face.

"I been dreaming, Anthony. In my dream you was our Moses, helping to set our people free," Ruth whispered through swollen lips. She reached over and took Anthony's hand and placed it into Catharine's palm, then turned her head toward the window. "Moonlight the color of the grass in spring. Can you see it? Looks to me like a green path leading up to heaven."

"Mama, you can't leave us. We're all gonna be free together," Anthony pleaded. He did not notice that Jim, Abigail and Henry had entered and now stood at the foot of the bed.

"It will be all right, son. I'll be with my Zach soon. He's waiting for me right over there," she whispered, pointing at dark shadows in the corner of the cabin. "We going home to see my Jesus together. Right up that long green path."

Abigail moved beside her and took Ruth's hand. "We love you. Mary Alice wanted to come, but she is not well."

"Thank you for what you done for my Anthony and Catharine. I can rest now, knowing he's gonna be free. Tell William that I forgave him long time ago," Ruth whispered. "But I think he knows that already."

Abigail kissed her cheek, then took Henry's hand and left the cabin, knowing Ruth needed only her family of close friends in her final hours.

Ruth closed her eyes and slept for several hours. When she awoke at midnight, she motioned for Anthony to come closer. When he bent down, she whispered, "Tomorrow needs doing. I know you gonna make it a good day, Anthony." She closed her eyes and slept. Her labored breathing continued until almost dawn. At four-thirty she whispered, "Zach, that you?" When the first rays of light filled the cabin, Ruth took her final breath, slipped into the green shadows of morning and was free.

CHAPTER 28

September 1830

Catharine Miles Bowen rose from her rocking chair after nursing her seven-month-old son. She placed the child in his crib and kissed his forehead, then tiptoed quietly beside Anthony. Seeing that he was sleeping soundly, she decided to let him rest a little longer. Today was his twenty-first birthday and their second wedding anniversary. Both knew the Bradley family had held discussions concerning Anthony's future the preceding evening. William had instructed Anthony to bring her and the child to the parlor at 10:00 a.m. He had been so excited, they talked well past midnight, certain the timetable for his freedom had been decided.

Uppermost in their minds were the question of Catharine's future and that of their son, Jacob. In seven years Anthony had managed to save four hundred and twenty-five dollars, not counting the 10 percent he had donated to their church. Those funds had been used to purchase a new Bible for Reverend Harris. Anthony had also contributed funds for his minister's new reading glasses and a black suit. For every dollar he had donated, William had added five.

Catharine reflected on the frightening night she and Anthony remained together in the loft of the Baker's barn. She smiled, remembering Anthony saying to her, *'You will know glory, and it's not going take seven years.'* On a rainy September morning in April 1828, they stood before Reverend Harris and took their vows in the Bradley Manor living room. Two wedding receptions followed. At Abigail's suggestion, a smaller one began immediately after the ceremony. It was held in the parlor and restricted to the Bradley family, house servants and Big George and his wife. An hour later, the larger reception was held in the barn and was open to all. The cottage that once was used by Hale and Cathy became their home. When they finally slipped away, Anthony took her in his arms and the *glory* he had spoken off had lasted until daybreak. She took a book Abigail had given her, sat beside the crib and read for the next hour.

After Catharine dressed the child, she kissed Anthony's cheek. "Time to wake up, Anthony. This is the day the Lord has made special for you. Like Mama Ruth use to say, 'The day needs doing, and we know you gonna make it a good day.'"

Three hours later, Anthony held Catharine's hand and led her into the parlor. William, Mary Alice, Henry, Abigail, Jim, and the family attorney, Edward Cranston, of Washington City, all smiled when they entered.

William rose from his lounge chair and motioned for Catharine to sit beside him. She hesitated, looking first at Anthony then at William to make sure she understood his gesture. When William nodded and patted the back of the leather chair, she timidly left Anthony's side and sat beside him. The act of sitting in one of her master's chairs left her feeling her extremely uncomfortable. Anthony took his seat next to Henry.

"Anthony, happy birthday. I find it hard to believe seven years have passed since we made our agreement. Now that you are of age, the time has come to conclude our contract. You have been a good and faithful servant and a credit to your race. You have placed in my hand the sum of four hundred and twenty-five dollars, which was the purchase price we agreed upon. I have asked Attorney Cranston here today for the express purpose of drawing up the manumission documents that will free both you and your family."

"You mean that Catharine and Jacob will be free also," Anthony asked, glancing at everyone in the room.

"Yes. You can thank Henry and Abigail. They convinced us to free all of you now."

Anthony gripped the armrest of his chair, feeling totally overwhelmed. "Thank you, Master Bradley." Catharine rose and rushed into his arms, hugging and kissing both his cheeks. The tender scene caused Abigail and Mary Alice to reach for their handkerchiefs.

Cranston sat at the desk writing as everyone chatted quietly. After William reviewed the document, he handed it to Anthony.

Anthony placed one arm around Catharine, kissed her cheek and read aloud his personal 'Declaration of Independence.'

> "To whom it may concern, be it known that I, William Bradley, for good causes, and also in consideration of four hundred twenty-five dollars, having released from slavery, liberated, manumitted and set free my Negro man named Anthony Bowen. I do declare him to be henceforth a free man, Forever."

William shook Anthony's hand. "A separate document will be drawn up for Catharine and your son, Jacob," William said.

Overwhelmed with emotion, Anthony dropped to his knees and prayed silently for forty-five seconds. William motioned for Jim to pour glasses of wine for everyone except Anthony and Catharine, knowing neither drank alcoholic beverages.

"Where will you go now that you are free?" Abigail asked, dabbing her eyes with a lace handkerchief.

"I've always dreamed of living in Washington City, Mrs. Abigail."

William was tempted to warn Anthony to stay away from Moab Jackson, but he remained silent.

"I will write a letter of introduction to my friend, Reverend Robert Little, the pastor of the First Unitarian Church in Washington City. He has friends who will assist you in finding suitable work," Abigail said, smiling.

"That's very kind of you."

"Anthony, years ago my father purchased several lots in Washington City, one of which we would like to give you as a wedding gift. It's vacant land that you may wish to build a home on someday. I understand it is now located in an area where a number of colored families now reside," William said.

"Master Bradley, I don't know how to thank you."

"You are no longer required to address me as master."

Anthony paused, and reflected momentarily. "Thank you with all our hearts, *sir*."

With the meeting concluded, Anthony and Catharine took Jacob to their cottage and left him with Hattie. They went to the barn where they found Reverend Harris preparing his Sunday sermon. He made them sit beside him as he opened his Bible. "Anthony, Catharine, you both will be leaving us soon. Hear the word of the Lord." He thumbed through the pages and adjusted his glasses. *"'The Lord is my light and my salvation; whom shall I fear? The Lord is the strength of my life: of whom shall I be afraid? When the wicked, even mine enemies and my foes, came upon me to eat up my flesh, they stumbled and fell.'* I had a vision last night. The city you will be going to will have lots of enemies that will try to eat your flesh, but in the end, their houses will crumble upon their heads. The chains that hold our people will break and a new day will be born. Now put on the whole armor of God, Anthony, 'cause he will be marching beside you every step of the way."

"Thank you for your blessing," Anthony said. He failed to notice that Catharine was trembling.

On their last night at Bradley Manor, Anthony and Catharine found Jim in the library working on the inventory books. Jim had also been given his freedom shortly after Henry and Abigail had married. He had accepted it, but had chosen to remain on at Bradley Manor, serving as bookkeeper with a modest salary.

"Uncle Jim, we've come to say good bye," Anthony said.

"Bradley Manor will not be the same without the two of you."

"Why don't you come to Washington City and live with us?" Catharine said.

"Although William has finally acknowledged me and granted what our father wanted, I have lost the will to venture into the uncertainties of the world you face. If I went with you, I'm quite certain I would not find acceptance among white or colored peoples. I've tasted the cruelty of both. You are both young and full of spirit. Oh, I may travel one day, and even visit you. But it's here at Bradley Manor I have chosen to remain. In its own way, it has become my place. Phillis Wheatley chose to remain in the Wheatley family home for some years after they granted her freedom," Jim said.

"I could never live here, especially after being a slave all my life," Anthony said without apology.

"Before you leave, one final question. In one of our many conversations, do you remember asking me why you sometimes felt you did not deserve to feel as happy as white folks?"

"It's been so long I had almost forgot. You never answered my question."

"Did you find the answer?"

"Yes. All our lives we have been made to feel inferior to white folks. There was a small part of me that began to believe it. It was my faith in God and my studies with you that made me whole."

"That is precisely why I did not answer you back then. You had to find the answer within yourself and reclaim your manhood. Even if our people were freed tomorrow, I fear that stain of racial inferiority will infect our race for generations to come. It's what happened to the Hebrews. When the Hebrew children came out of slavery, it took forty years before they laid claim to the land that God had promised them. A whole generation had to die off because they felt inferior to the peoples of Canaan. The next generation began to believe in themselves and in their God, and they prevailed. As for my future, change is in the wind at Bradley Manor. Miss Abigail has won permission from William to start a class, teaching ten of our brightest children to read and write. She and I will be their teachers."

"That's wonderful."

"Can you imagine ten little Anthonys reading Shakespeare and Wheatley? My God, I'll never get any peace. You should know that I copied most of Phillis Wheatley's poems from your book," Jim said, smiling. "My brother would not be happy to know Abigail gave me a narrative written by Olaudah Eguiano. He was an African slave who emancipated himself in 1766 and launched his own successful business. He wrote a book that was so successful it was later translated into Dutch and German. So, Anthony, I have convinced myself that remaining at Bradley Manor is part of the Lord's plan in the scheme of things."

"Thank you for all you have done for us," Anthony said, hugging Jim.

"Be on your way now, and may God guide your path," Jim whispered after kissing Catharine's cheek. He closed the door, walked to the window and watched the evening sunset. Tears blurred his vision, forcing him to postpone all work on the inventory books for the rest of the evening.

Anthony and Catharine put on their overcoats and took their son to Ruth's grave, marked by a simple wooden cross. They stood in the blowing wind with their heads bowed. "Mama, we're free. I know you and papa looking down on us from heaven. When we got married, I feared that William Bradley might make me work many more years to pay for Catharine and Jacob, but we are all free. We're going to Washington City, and I'm going to do all I can to free our people."

After handing the baby to Anthony, Catharine knelt and placed a dried rose from her Bible on the grave. "I wonder what Washington City will be like?" Catharine said, remembering Reverend Harris's last words. She took Jacob when he held out his arms for her.

"Moab told me a little about it. Just think, we will be free to make a new life for ourselves. We will not have to obey white folks anymore. At least not every night and day."

"Anthony, I hear what you saying, but I'm scared. Preacher Harris say, *'When the wicked come upon me to eat up my flesh, they stumbled and fell,'* I came from a place where a beast ate my flesh and did worse things than that," Catharine said, gritting her teeth. "I wish we could stay here. I love everybody like they are my family, especially Mrs. Abigail."

Her words stunned Anthony. He knew what the security of Bradley Manor meant to her. She would have gone insane, and possibly died, had she remained a slave on the Baker's farm. An unknown world awaited them and, at times, he too was frightened. Suddenly, he heard Ruth whispering to him, *'I been dreaming, Anthony. In my dream you was our Moses, helping to free our people.'* How could he convince her to leave with him? Should he even try?

"The Lord has called me to another Egyptland, Catharine. I know the pain you suffered and how long it took you to heal. I will not force you and our son to go with me, but I must go. I will journey back whenever I can. And when it is safe, I'll come for you."

Catharine reflected momentarily, while shifting the child on her hip. Neither spoke as they walked slowly back to their cottage. While warming herself by the fireplace, she placed Jacob on Anthony's lap, picked up the small Bible and turned the pages to the Book of Ruth. After reading silently she smiled, signaling the return of that undaunted spirit that defined her.

"These words Ruth spoke in the Bible say it for me, Anthony. 'Whither thou goest, I will go; and where thou lodgest, I will lodge: Thy people shall be my people, and thy God my God.'"

CHAPTER 29

Epilogue (1830-1870)

Anthony Bowen relocated his family to Washington D.C. in 1836. He may have delayed his departure from the Bradley farm due to racial tensions that escalated throughout the South following the Nat Turner slave rebellion in 1831. The revolt in Southhampton County, Virginia left more than sixty whites and one hundred slaves dead. Fear of slave revolts grew in the decade that followed. Southern States passed restrictive laws controlling the movement of slaves and free blacks.

Slavery was not deeply entrenched in the western counties of Virginia. Following the rebellion, small farmers began calling for the end of the 'peculiar institution'. The powerful eastern planter class that ruled the Virginia General Assembly defeated the bill to end slavery by the thin margin of five votes. With the outbreak of the Civil War, these western counties chose to remain in the Union as the State of West Virginia.

By 1840 racial tensions eased somewhat. Anthony obtained a permit for free blacks to conduct meetings and social events at what became known as "The Colored Peoples' Meeting House," located at 7th and D Streets, NW. He conducted an evening school for free adults, offering classes in reading, writing and Bible instruction. Anthony was aware that the position of "people of color" in Washington was precarious. There were daily reminders that they could never let down their guard for one moment. The ever-present threat of being kidnapped and sold back into slavery were fears they constantly endured. Despite rigid laws restricting the movement of blacks, hard working families made significant economic gains. Free blacks were regarded as Washington's finest bricklayers, cooks, watermen and domestic workers.

A few years after their arrival in Washington, Anthony's beloved Catharine died following the birth of their third child, a daughter. Brokenhearted, Anthony occasionally visited the Bradley family and old friends. In 1839, he met Mary Collins, a house slave who was owned by Mrs. Elizabeth Daniels, of Prince Georges County. Mrs. Collins, a widow, had brought Mary with her during a visit with the Bradley family. Faced with the prospect of raising three small children alone, Anthony sought Mary's permission to purchase her from Mrs. Collins. The widow agreed to a purchase price of $630. Following their marriage, seven children were born, of which four survived. Shortly after his marriage to Mary, Anthony secured a job at the U.S. Patent Office and later rose to the rank of clerk.

Although Anthony became an ordained minister, he never accepted a full-time position as minister. In his spare time, he devoted his energies to his night school and secretly supporting the growing Underground Railroad. In 1852, he became friends with William Chauncy Langdon, a young Assistant Examiner in the Patent Office. Langdon told Anthony how he and two other young white government workers had formed the Young Men's Christian Association in the City of Washington to address the growing problems of vice, alcoholism, delinquency and crime. He gave Anthony a copy of the Washington YMCA's constitution and urged him to form a chapter for free black men. In June 1853, Anthony gathered together a group of young men and formed the first YMCA for African Americans in America. Although he was then forty-four years of age, the young men elected Anthony as their first president. Their activities were restricted to meetings in their homes for Bible study and discussing the nation's growing debate over slavery. With the outbreak of Civil War, the members gave aid to the thousands of refugees fleeing into Washington from slavery.

In 1856, Anthony founded the St. Paul African Methodist Episcopal Church with the support of eight free men. They purchased a site at on 8th street, southwest, in the neighborhood where the Department of Housing and Urban Development now stands. Today the St. Paul A.M.E church is located at 4901 14th, NW.

When the Civil War began, Anthony stood in the window of the Patent Office and cheered as the first Union troops arrived to defend the capital. A southern sympathizer reported the incident to Bowen's superior who dismissed him from his position. Shortly thereafter, he was rehired, undoubtedly due to pressure from his white friends. Joining forces with Republicans, he pushed for national legislation in 1862 that provided education for the thousands of black refugees escaping into the city.

On January 1, 1863, President Lincoln issued the Emancipation Proclamation that legally freed all slaves in southern states that were in rebellion. When the U.S. Armed Forces began accepting blacks, Anthony Bowen, Reverend John E. Cook, Pastor of the Fifteenth Street Presbyterian Church, and Reverend Henry McNeal Turner, Pastor of the Israel African Methodist Church, recruited three regiments of black troops for the Union Army. Reverend Turner served as regimental chaplain. By the end of the Civil War, more than 180,000 blacks throughout the nation had served in the Union Army and Navy. More than fifty-two thousand died in the service of their country. Twenty-one African Americans were awarded the Congressional Medal of Honor.

Following the war, Anthony donated land to the District of Columbia for a school. Today the historic Anthony Bowen elementary school is located at 101 M Street, SW., Washington DC 20024.

On December 26, 1866, the Constitution of the Colored YMCA was printed and distributed to African American Churches throughout Washington. An excerpt from the YMCA preamble reads: *To the Young Men of Washington: We the colored young men of Washington D.C., feeling deeply interested in the mental, moral and spiritual improvement of our race, and believing it is for the young men of the nation, cordially extend an invitation to all young men of this city who think as we do, and who feel interested in the advancement of their race, to come and unite with us... Young men, will you not come to our aid in this desirable and heaven-approved work? If you give your aid in this direction, you do what you can to redeem our race from the dominion of sin and slavery and place it on the broad platform of mental, moral and Christian equality."*

In 1870, Anthony Bowen was appointed to the District of Columbia's Common Council where he served with distinction until his death in 1871 at the age of 65.

Today YMCA-Anthony Bowen is located at 1325 W Street NW, Washington DC. It houses the Thomas B. Hargrave, Jr. Children's Museum. Here the records of Anthony Bowen's Y are displayed, along with a collection of African arts and crafts donated by African YMCAs. In October 2003, YMCAs nationwide celebrated the 150th anniversary of Anthony Bowen's YMCA.

ABOUT THE AUTHOR

Thomas B. Hargrave Jr. is President Emeritus of the YMCA of Metropolitan Washington, having served 19 years as President and C.E.O. After 41 years of distinguished service with six YMCAs, he retired in 1992 and has devoted his energy to his twin passions, biblical research and writing historical novels. Tom Hargrave has received numerous awards for his work in civil rights and in 2001 was elected to the YMCA Hall of Fame. His accomplishments were highlighted by the Honorable Eleanor Holmes Norton, D.C., in the May 6, 1992 issue of the Congressional Record. He is the author of *The Rape of Midian: The Saga of Zipporah and Moses, and Private Differences-General Good: A History of the YMCA of Metropolitan Washington.* He was educated in the public schools of Knoxville Tennessee and graduated from Knoxville College in 1951. Hargrave currently lives in Silver Spring, Maryland with his wife, Meredith and youngest daughter, Anna. His current novel is based on the early life of Anthony Bowen, the former slave who founded the first YMCA for African Americans in our nation's capital in 1853.

Printed in the United States
1465100004B/271-309